Sociologies of Interaction

Sociologies of Interaction

Alex Dennis, Rob Philburn and Greg Smith

polity

The right of Alex Dennis, Rob Philburn and Greg Smith to be identified as Authors of this Work has been asserted in accordance with the UK Copyright, Designs and Patents Act 1988.

First published in 2013 by Polity Press

Polity Press
65 Bridge Street
Cambridge CB2 1UR, UK

Polity Press
350 Main Street
Malden, MA 02148, USA

ISBN-13: 978-0-7456-4606-0
ISBN-13: 978-0-7456-4607-7 (pb)

A catalogue record for this book is available from the British Library.

Typeset in 10.5 on 12 pt Plantin by
Servis Filmsetting Ltd, Stockport, Cheshire
Printed and bound by T.J. International, Padstow, Cornwall

The publisher has used its best endeavours to ensure that the URLs for external websites referred to in this book are correct and active at the time of going to press. However, the publisher has no responsibility for the websites and can make no guarantee that a site will remain live or that the content is or will remain appropriate.

Every effort has been made to trace all copyright holders, but if any have been inadvertently overlooked the publisher will be pleased to include any necessary credits in any subsequent reprint or edition.

For further information on Polity, visit our website: www.politybooks.com

Contents

Introduction   *page* 1

1   Pragmatism and Symbolic Interactionism   8

2   Phenomenology and Ethnomethodology   35

3   Conversation Analysis and the Interaction Order   63

4   Status and Power   98

5   The Body, Health and Illness   121

6   Work   142

7   Deviance   162

8   Leisure   188

    Conclusion   208

Notes   219
References   221
Index   237

Introduction

Social interaction – the actions and responses of people to each other's activities – fills our everyday lives. The phone rings and we interrupt our conversation with a family member in order to answer it; we get on the bus and quickly scan the area to choose a place to sit – but not just anywhere; we enter an elevator and find the only other occupant is a senior manager where we work and momentarily feel uncomfortable; we invite a friend to lunch and there is a hesitation before she turns us down, proffering a plausible excuse. These instances of social interaction are the stuff of our daily lives, at home and at work, with our friends and with strangers. Two points can be made straightaway. One is that such ordinary face-to-face dealings with one another make up the world of daily life, a world that is for us what Alfred Schutz called a 'paramount reality'. The world of daily life is paramount in our experience because it provides us with a sure sense of our being in the world – that 'this' really is 'it' for our own existence and that of others. The second point is that social interaction in everyday life is not haphazard but structured, patterned and orderly. That structure, pattern and orderliness indicates its socially organized character. It is thus not surprising that sociologists have paid close attention to everyday instances of social interaction in order to discover the sources and nature of that orderliness.

Over the past half-century, sociology has accumulated a significant body of knowledge about social interaction. The close sociological understanding of practices of social interaction and the forms and processes assumed by these practices was developed by three traditions of sociological work: *symbolic interactionism* (as defined by Herbert Blumer and Everett C. Hughes), *ethnomethodology* (as defined by Harold Garfinkel) and *conversation analysis* (as defined by

Harvey Sacks). We might follow what has become a convention and abbreviate these as the approaches of SI, EM and CA. The important and highly original contributions of Erving Goffman should also be considered alongside these traditions. While Goffman can be regarded as a symbolic interactionist, his ideas also go beyond that approach and impact on how we might understand both spoken interaction and the routine establishment of everyday order and in some respects act as a bridge between these perspectives, revealing their similarities and differences.

We want to alert readers of this book to the scope of these three traditions that make up the core of contemporary sociological approaches to interaction. While sociology's topics and approaches often seem unduly subject to pressing social issues and current intellectual fads and fashions, the work we have selected seems to us to form a set of robust traditions within which a modest cumulative knowledge can be traced, and upon which the myriad of contemporary interactionist empirical studies rest. In our view, the sociologies this book examines represent one of contemporary academic sociology's most understated achievements. One of our aims in writing this book is to curate these sociologies, to exhibit exactly what it is that makes them distinctive and productive as traditions of sociological work.

Our book examines, compares and evaluates these leading interactionist approaches to sociology. Each of the three traditions we consider might be regarded as alternate sociologies – that is, alternatives to mainstream, conventional sociological work, especially as it was practised in the second half of the twentieth century in the USA, the land where sociology has been most fully developed and most thoroughly professionalized. Similarly, SI, EM and CA are rooted in US sociology but have become diffused across the world, especially in places where sociology has flourished such as Europe, Australasia and Japan. Sometimes they are situated as arcane specialties. At other times they are claimed as the 'loyal opposition'. Occasionally it is maintained that the opposition has evaporated and that the interactionist sociologies now have been incorporated by mainstream sociology.

Whatever view is taken of their current status, SI, EM and CA originated as alternate sociologies that, as we shall show, were critical of the analytical and methodological practices of the established orthodoxies of academic sociology. These points of divergence are vital in placing each tradition in the context of debates about the nature of human action and the methods appropriate to its apprehension. Our book discusses these broader methodological issues and seeks to show how they are worked out in empirical studies. Our primary concern in articulating the three sociologies of interaction lies with these wider questions about method rather than with research methods as such. Certainly, we shall discuss questionnaires and interviews, observational and documentary research, but ours is not a research methods book. The interested reader is directed to texts such as ten Have (2007), Hammersley and Atkinson (2007) and Silverman (2011) for more detailed guidance about how to conduct studies in the styles outlined in our text.

We do not want to suggest that the three sociologies of interaction that we have identified are templates for doing studies. Certainly there are shared methodological and analytical precepts. However, there is also much variation and scope for innovation within each approach, as we try to convey in the discussions of specific studies.

We have organized the book into eight chapters. In the first three of these we will introduce the three key traditions outlined above – symbolic interactionism (including a discussion of pragmatism), ethnomethodology (including a discussion of phenomenology) and conversation analysis (including a discussion of the interaction order). Following this, chapters 4 to 8 will discuss specific concerns for all three of these traditions.

In chapter 1, we introduce the sociological perspective known as *symbolic interactionism*, formulated theoretically by Herbert Blumer and empirically by Everett C. Hughes (and their students). We show how it developed from studies undertaken at the University of Chicago in the 1920s and 1930s, and how it moved beyond these studies' ethnographic and biographical approaches to create a distinctively *interactionist* theoretical position and a set of research policies congruent with that theory. We also explain how the philosophical position known as pragmatism – based on the writings of, among others, Charles Sanders Peirce, William James, John Dewey and George Herbert Mead – informed these developments and provided a consistent epistemological basis for the position. The methodological implications of the symbolic interactionist perspective are outlined, in particular its emphasis on fieldwork as a research tool. Finally, some criticisms – both 'internal' ones, and those of other interactionists – of the approach are outlined.

Chapter 2 traces ethnomethodology's roots in phenomenology. Sociology's appropriation of phenomenology owes much to Alfred Schutz. He showed how the specialist philosophical approach that Husserl developed was of direct relevance to Max Weber's advocacy of a sociology that was interpretive in scope – i.e., that addressed the meaningful character of social action as its centre piece. Schutz's constructive critique showed how Weber's interpretive sociology underestimated the scope and importance of the common-sense cultural knowledge that social actors use in the course of their everyday actions. Yet it remained an essentially philosophical approach to common-sense knowledge and ordinary action. It was Garfinkel's ethnomethodology that succeeded in transforming Schutz's philosophical approach into an empirical programme for the investigation of knowledge and social action. On the way, Garfinkel showed how Schutz's ideas helped to remedy the omissions and shortcomings of the once-influential account of social action offered by his teacher, Talcott Parsons. The chapter charts this episode in the intellectual history, highlighting how these developments led to an analytical understanding of social competence and human action. Garfinkel offered a radically different account of what it meant to be a social being (a 'member' of society), and how members orientated to and recreated social rules. The chapter concludes with demonstrations of how this new understanding has been put into productive practice in studies of mental illness, rule-following and professional vision.

In chapter 3, we examine the interactionist approach to understanding everyday life known as *conversation analysis*. As in the two previous chapters, we begin this chapter with an outline of some philosophical ideas whose sociological appropriation proved highly consequential, including the ordinary language philosophy encouraged by the thought of the later Wittgenstein, which gave a new significance to the use of everyday language in the context in which it operated. We then move on to consider in some detail the work of Harvey Sacks, Emanuel Schegloff, Gail Jefferson and others who pointed to fundamental sequential and organizational features of naturally occurring conversation that both underpin interactional orderliness and invoke, imply, allow persons to infer, and impact on social and personal identities. Following this, we examine some of Erving Goffman's key comments on what he termed 'the interaction order' and show how and why he regards the ritualistic and dramatic aspects of spoken interaction as just as important as its sequential and organizational features for understanding interactional orderliness and identity concerns in spoken interaction.

In chapter 4, we discuss the ways these three approaches have been used to examine the concepts of status and power. Each, we argue, builds on a Weberian – as opposed to Marxian – analysis of social inequality and social stratification. The symbolic interactionist approach, we argue, emphasizes the ways in which status positions are conferred on social actors, and how they can be accepted, resisted or altered through interaction. We go on to examine the ways in which these positions are *institutionalized* – built into more complex and bureaucratized forms of interaction – to reduce the likelihood of open conflict, for example through the segregation of professionals along the lines of race. The ethnomethodological position, on the other hand, emphasizes the ways in which rules are used in interaction to legitimize forms of discrimination, separation and inequality. Rules are talked up or modified to *achieve* differences in status and power and – in extreme cases – to question the appropriateness of conferring social membership on particular individuals (such as the mentally ill). Finally, we examine conversation analytic approaches to status and power, starting with Sacks' early examinations of *membership categories* – ways of conferring a particular social identity on an actor or group of actors – and *category-bound activities* – things that are conventionally associated with people and groups so defined. We go on to consider how talk can be used to achieve dominance or submission, and how conversation analysts after Sacks have used his 'mature' analysis of turn-taking to examine how different categories of interlocutor may orientate differently to the distribution of talk across different parties.

Chapter 5 examines some themes in the sociology of embodiment, with particular emphasis on issues of health and illness. Bodies are commonly thought to lie outside the realm of society and culture, being matters of sometimes brutal biological fact. Yet the appearance and functioning of our bodies turns out to be socially influenced to a surprising degree. There is a substantial body of interactionally oriented studies of the healthy and ill body, some of it developed in opposition to Parsons' classic identification of the sick role. Alternative formulations, grounded in ethnographic research in medical settings, emphasize the performative and contested aspects of the sick role. Similarly, studies of illness trajectories and patient careers have shown the importance of the temporal dimension. Diagnoses and treatments take time, illnesses run their courses and the experience of the ill person is often shaped by hospital schedules and therapeutic programmes. The chapter considers why we make the decision to go to see a doctor, the nature of medical encounters, the vexed issue of how doctors exercise their authority, and how chronic illness, death and dying are managed as social processes.

In chapter 6, we examine the ways interactionists have examined the concept of work. Symbolic interactionists, we argue, have emphasized the temporal dimensions of work with the concepts of 'career' and 'turning point', focusing on how progression into, through and beyond employment are not smooth transitions but require complex negotiations. Negotiation and agreement are central to this perspective's analysis of how work identities are managed, but symbolic interactionists – particularly Hughes – repeatedly caution against taking those identities for granted. Status differentials between different occupations – prostitutes and psychiatrists, for example – should not prevent us from seeing what features those trades have in common. Ethnomethodologists, on the other hand, expand the concept of 'work' to include almost any social achievement, from Sudnow's study of glances to Garfinkel et al.'s analysis of the discovery of the first pulsar. They develop the temporal analysis of symbolic interactionists by considering how both the past and the (possible) future are invoked in making decisions, and emphasize the ways in which 'rules' for getting things done are interactional achievements rather than fixed, stable, independent features of the social world. Finally, they emphasize *process* over *outcome* in a radical manner, rejecting the mainstream notion that the products of social interaction (documents, policies, etc.) can be treated as adequate descriptions of how those artefacts are themselves generated. This distinction between process and outcome informs our discussion of conversation analysis, wherein we consider two approaches to work: the 'talk at work' programme of Drew and Heritage, and the membership categorization analysis of the early Sacks. While both legitimately claim their heritage in Sacks' own writings, we argue that the former tends to neglect the situated production of categories, while the latter tends to downplay the temporal elaboration of a setting through turns at talk. This tension, we argue, is perhaps an inevitable feature of attempts to 'apply' Sacks' insights, as exemplified in the field of computer-supported co-operative work.

In chapter 7, following a critical overview of various criminological perspectives on understanding deviance (classical, physiological, psychological, ecological, structural-functionalist), we move on to discuss interactionist perspectives to deviance, again organized around the traditions outlined in chapters 1–3. The chapter considers how bodies, biographies and behaviours are central to understanding deviance from an interactionist perspective, how information control and stigma management are often central to the negotiation of meaning in interaction and how, ultimately, various formal interventions can lead to the development of deviant careers. The chapter also considers how recognizing and theorizing about deviance involves practical applications of stocks of (professional and specialist) knowledge in a range of contexts (such as coroners' courts, jury rooms). Working alongside such specialist stocks of knowledge are common-sensical notions of what can be 'fairly' and 'by anyone' seen as deviance. Together, these two forms of knowledge can be extremely powerful in explaining phenomena as deviant. Finally, we consider how deviant identities can be inferred, invoked, ascribed and disavowed in and through some of the features of naturally occurring conversation discussed in chapter 3, including the sequential exploitation of talk, the use of membership categories, and adherence to or departure from the ritual and dramatic features of 'fresh talk' and other, more formulaic interchanges.

Chapter 8 focuses on the relationship between identities and leisure and consumption practices in contemporary everyday life. Looking at a range of consumption practices, leisure pursuits and recreational activities, the chapter examines how such things as rules, relationships and roles are transformed in and through leisure practices; how affiliations, associations and often authenticity can be a central concern as we go about such activities and engage in such practices; and how 'leisure experience' can be understood both against and in contrast to, and as part of, the backdrop of the everyday life. Again, we focus very much on identity concerns in this chapter and how they are realized in and through the symbolic, practical and spoken features of leisure interaction.

Finally, in our conclusion, we consider how the three perspectives relate to mainstream sociology, and the extent to which they differ from one another. Our central argument here is that they each offer convincing alternative approaches to the 'mainstream' analysis of key sociological concepts, but that they are sufficiently distinctive from one another to prevent any coherent attempt to join them together. Their differences mean that a choice must be made between the symbolic interactionist, ethnomethodological and conversation analytic approaches. If we have been successful, this book will have shown how, in making that choice, a sociologist wishing to engage in interactionist studies of the social world can mobilize a way of working that has philosophical, theoretical and methodological coherence.

1

Pragmatism and Symbolic Interactionism

Introduction

Symbolic interactionism and the Second Chicago School

The symbolic interactionist approach to doing sociology was developed at the University of Chicago in the decades following the Second World War, through the work of a gifted generation of graduate students supervised or influenced by Herbert Blumer and Everett C. Hughes. Blumer was at Chicago from 1925 to 1952, when he moved to the University of California at Berkeley, while Hughes returned to Chicago in 1938 (after having completed his Ph.D. there ten years before), staying until 1961, when he moved to Brandeis University. Blumer and Hughes, and their colleagues at Chicago (in particular Louis Wirth, Anselm L. Strauss and William Lloyd Warner), led what has been called the 'Second Chicago School' (Fine 1995). Through a series of remarkable empirical studies, students like Howard S. Becker, Fred Davis, Erving Goffman, Ray Gold, Julius Roth, Tamotsu Shibutani and Gregory Stone exemplified a way of doing sociology that stood in sharp contrast to the functionalism of Harvard and Columbia Universities, and which has had a deep and long-lasting impact on sociology across the world.

The term 'symbolic interactionism' was coined by Herbert Blumer (1937) to refer to a particular way of doing social psychology (then a branch of sociology), and his most explicit statement on the approach was published thirty years later (Blumer 1969). Only a small minority of the students associated with the 'Second Chicago School' adopted the term for themselves, however, and there is mounting evidence (Abbott 1999; Becker 1999) that Chicago sociology was as much about the personal and professional divisions between Blumer and

Wirth on one side, and Hughes and Lloyd Warner on the other, as about any shared vision for sociological work. As Becker (1999: 10) argues, however, the group epitomized a 'vigorous and energetic school of activity, a group of sociologists who collaborated in the day-to-day work of making sociology in an American university and did that very well'. We will use the term 'symbolic interactionism' to describe the kind of work done at Chicago, as it is the one most commonly used, while recognizing that many sociologists who do that kind of work – including some of the most famous such as Becker and Goffman – actively resisted the label's application. Symbolic interactionism draws on two earlier American intellectual traditions: the Chicago School of Sociology (Bulmer 1984) and pragmatist philosophy (Menand 2001).

The Chicago School

The (first) 'Chicago School' was a group of researchers, organized and supervised by William I. Thomas and Robert Park at the University of Chicago. Their remit was to treat the rapidly growing city as a sociological laboratory, wherein the most striking features of Chicago's development (rapid growth and industrialization, waves of migration, racial and religious conflict, and increasing levels of poverty and crime) were to be studied as sociological phenomena *in situ*. The city, it was argued, had a social ecology – just like a rainforest or an ocean have plant and animal ecologies – and by studying every part of the city it would be possible to map out how different social groups thrive, survive or decline in relation to one another.

What was most striking about the group was their emphasis on *empirical investigation*: sociological questions were to be answered by doing research, in particular *fieldwork* (ethnography), rather than through theorizing. This did not mean that their work was not theoretical, but rather that, for them, theory was something that *facilitated* investigations and allowed the findings from one study to be used to generate questions for the next. Researchers used a wide range of techniques, including demography, textual analysis, life-histories, interviews and surveys. Encouraged by Park in particular, however, some of the most famous and influential Chicago studies were those conducted using fieldwork, in which researchers would participate fully in the activities of those being investigated and use their own experiences as part of the 'data' under consideration. Studies employing this method included Anderson's (1923) study of homeless men and Cressey's (1932) study of taxi-dance halls (places where men could dance with women for money).

Pragmatism and practicality

Pragmatism is a philosophical approach developed by, among others, Charles Sanders Peirce, William James, John Dewey and George Herbert Mead in the late nineteenth and early twentieth centuries. It has had an immense influence in the fields of education policy, social studies, political science and law (Menand 2001), and on contemporary philosophers including Richard Rorty (1979), Stanley Fish (1980) and Gilles Deleuze (Deleuze and Guattari 1994). Pragmatism is based on the notion that meaning is based on practical utility.

This can mean that choices between alternative ideas can only be made if there will be practical implications to those choices:

> What difference would it practically make to any one if this notion rather than that notion were true? If no practical difference whatever can be traced, then the alternatives mean practically the same thing, and all dispute is idle. Whenever a dispute is serious, we ought to be able to show some practical difference that must follow from one side or the other's being right. (James [1907] 1977: 377)

The Copernican revolution in astronomy is an example of such a 'practical difference'. *Practically speaking* it makes little difference to most people whether the sun revolves around the Earth or the Earth revolves around the sun. Indeed, even though we now all agree that the Earth revolves around the sun, we still use expressions like 'sunrise' and 'sunset' which might seem to indicate that the Earth remains stable and objects in the sky move around it. The discovery by Copernicus that the sun is the centre of the solar system, however, made an immense practical difference to two groups: the Church and the scientific community. The Church advanced the belief that the Earth was the centre of the universe, with other celestial objects revolving around it. The fact that this could be demonstrated to be incorrect represented a grave threat to its authority. At the same time, however, the scientific community was developing increasingly sophisticated observations and theories about the nature of the cosmos. A theory (that the Earth revolves around the sun) that fitted these observations better, and allowed for alternative theories to be superseded, would be of immense use. Copernicus' ideas were not published until after his death, but for centuries after they were regarded as heretical by the Church – even though subsequent scientists like Galileo could not have conducted their work without them. The 'practical difference' made by Copernicus was about authority over scientific findings: who should be the final judge of what is true, religious authorities or secular working scientists? This debate is still ongoing, even though now hardly anyone seriously argues against Copernicus' ideas.

More fundamentally, pragmatism can mean that what anything 'is' depends entirely on what practical effects that thing might have: 'Consider what effects, which might conceivably have practical bearings, we conceive the object of our conception to have. Then, our conception of these effects is the whole of our conception of the object' (Peirce [1878] 1992: 132). It is this more radical approach that most strongly influenced the symbolic interactionists.

The centrality of meaning

The sociology of the Chicago School, particularly in its ethnographic form, and the philosophy of pragmatism both converge on a concern with meaning. Just as behaviour in the city was found to be orderly and meaningful by the Chicago sociologists, the nature of meaning itself was found to be the product of human activities by the pragmatists. The basis of symbolic interactionism is the entwining of these two observations: activities are meaningful, and meaning derives from human activity.

Blumer's three premises

Blumer ([1963] 1969: 79) defined symbolic interaction as 'the peculiar and distinctive character of interaction as it takes place between human beings'. Humans, uniquely, use symbols to interpret and define the contents of their world, including one another's actions, and act on the world on the basis of those interpretations and definitions. Symbolic interaction*ism*, the sociological study of human activities, rests on three 'premises'.

The first premise is that human beings act towards things on the basis of the meanings that the things have for them. Such things include everything that the human being may note in his world – physical objects, such as trees or chairs; other human beings, such as a mother or a store clerk; categories of human beings, such as friends or enemies; institutions, such as a school or a government; guiding ideals, such as individual independence or honesty; activities of others, such as their commands or requests; and such situations as an individual encounters in his daily life. The second premise is that the meaning of such things is derived from, or arises out of, the social interaction that one has with one's fellows. The third premise is that these meanings are handled in, and modified through, an interpretive process used by the person in dealing with the things he encounters (Blumer 1969: 2).

These 'premises', although formulated on the basis of previously undertaken empirical studies, can be understood to underpin the symbolic interactionist approach to research. They will be addressed in turn.

Things are acted upon according to their meanings

The meaning of objects

When Blumer says that things are acted upon according to their meanings, he is arguing against the idea that any one 'thing' has one fixed meaning. The meaning of an object depends on the uses to which it can be put. A brick can be part of a built structure, a weight to hold something down, a means of roughly measuring length, or even a weapon, depending on the intentions and needs of the person coming across it. When the brick ceases to be part of an ongoing action, it is not acted upon and ceases to be relevant: it has no meaning. If you are reading this inside a building made of bricks, what meaning does any one currently have to you? This approach to meaning derives from John Dewey's arguments about the nature of human action, in which the notion that 'meaning' derives from use first appeared.

Stimulus–response and individualism

Dewey's analysis of meaning was influenced by, and was a rejection of, early psychological notions of human behaviour. Early 'scientific' psychologists construed human behaviour, alongside that of other organisms, as a series of 'reflex arcs'. A reflex arc is a semi-automatic response to an external stimulus, forming the basic building block of more complex activities. James (1890) illustrated this with a psychological redescription of a child's encounter with a candle. Seeing the candle's light, the child reaches out to touch the flame, is burnt, and withdraws his hand in pain. A stimulus (seeing the light) elicits a response (extension of the hand to touch), which in turn leads to another stimulus (feeling the candle's heat), and another response (withdrawing of the hand). Such activities leave traces in the child's brain, so the next time he sees a candle the initial reflex arc (seeing the light and reaching for it) is interrupted by the response part of the second (withdrawing of the hand). The child has 'learnt' not to try to touch the flame, and this can be explained solely with reference to stimulus–response arcs and the residues they leave in the brain's hemispheres.

Dewey and the reflex arc

Dewey ([1896] 1981), in one of the most important papers in the history of psychology, questioned the usefulness of this way of looking at human behaviour. He made three criticisms of the stimulus–response arc. Firstly, it is based on an unresolved dualism: rather than looking at behaviour in a consistent manner it shifts from one to another, and then back again, without explaining why. Every stimulus could also be described as a response, and every response as a stimulus. The child's seeing the light is not merely a response to a stimulus, but is also an active, instrumental, process in its own right. To see the light, the child must move his eyes to face it, focus his vision, perhaps even turn his head, stop looking at other things in his visual field, and so on. All of these are clearly active, responsive, processes. Equally the 'response' of extending the hand to touch the flame could be described as a series of stimuli. To reach out and touch something accurately does not just entail the firing of motor neurons to activate muscle movements. It also requires the operation of sensory neurons to allow balance and accuracy of movement (to allow you to 'feel' that you have made the correct movement). The 'response', then, could also be described as a stimulus. It makes no sense, according to Dewey, to distinguish between stimuli and responses, as all human perception and movement can be described as *either*.

Secondly, according to proponents of the stimulus–response approach to behaviour, brain functions are divided between the peripheral and the central. Peripheral activities are those concerned with movement and perception (experiencing and responding to stimuli), while central activities are those concerned with cognitive processes (such as attention and memory). As with the distinction between stimuli and responses, it is unclear how this distinction can be justified conceptually. The nervous system is an organic unity, made up of largely identical brain cells firing at, and being excited to fire by, one another. Distinguishing between different parts of it on the basis of their apparent function – so some parts are responsible for 'thinking', and others for 'perceiving' or 'moving' – has no good analytical justification. Indeed, the unified nature of the nervous system's physiology might indicate that such distinctions actually misrepresent what is really going on.

Finally, Dewey pointed out that activities are always essentially meaningful, and the stimulus–response arc relies upon this meaningful nature without acknowledging it. Dewey argues that one can usefully distinguish between stimuli and responses, but this distinction is not a physiological one, but rather a semantic one: human behaviour can reasonably be described as being stimulated by, or responsive to, external phenomena on the basis of *what that behaviour is an attempt to do*. 'Getting burnt' and 'avoiding getting burnt again' are both *acts*, which depend on complex sensory-motor *co-ordination*, and the sense of those acts allows one to determine which elements are stimuli and which are responses. The overall sense of what someone is doing determines which parts of it are stimuli and which are responses, even in James' example of the child being burnt, but this sense does not appear in the final description: instead, the meaning of an action appears as if it is made up of those stimuli and responses, organized into ongoing (peripheral) and stored (central) sets of brain function. We are prepared to accept that some things are 'obviously' stimuli (seeing the candle's light) and others 'obviously' responses (reaching out to touch the candle), some 'obviously' sensory or motor (the firings of sensory neurons in the optical nerve or the firing of motor neurons in the radial nerve) and others 'obviously' cognitive (the firings of neurons in the brain itself). The reason we are prepared to make those distinctions, and treat them as self-evident, is that, *when viewed from the point of view of the co-ordinated act*, that is how they appear. Stimuli and responses, and central and peripheral nervous functions, do not make up a meaningful act; a meaningful act allows us to categorize nervous activity into stimulus and response, and central and peripheral function.

The meaning, therefore, of all the components in this act, are derived from the act itself. The flame can be a source of light or a source of pain, something to explore or something to avoid, depending on the intentions and understandings of the child. The flame has no 'single' or 'objective' meaning, but its sense is derived from the uses to which it can be put.

Meaning is derived from social interaction

Gestures and symbols

Meaning is not an individual matter, however. Most of our under-standings are shared, capable of being communicated to one another, and are modified by our interactions with other people. We have more complex means of understanding the world around us than other animals, because of our capacity to use *symbols* – in particu-lar language – to make sense of, classify, modify and communicate about our environment. What distinguishes us from other animals is the capacity to take one another's points of view, to see things as someone else might see them. George Herbert Mead provided the clearest pragmatist account of this distinction, and was the key influ-ence on the later symbolic interactionists, particularly Blumer.

Mead (1934: 63) argues that, for animals, action is largely *gestural*. A snarling dog will elicit a response of submission or challenge from another dog. This is not 'interpreted' or 'considered', but is directly caused by the stimulus: the snarl elicits either submission or chal-lenge as an exchange of *gestures*. The dog does not try to work out what the other intends, but simply acts on the basis of the other's behaviour. Some human activities, according to Mead, are gestural in this sense. A baby will startle at a loud noise as a reflex – without that noise having any particular 'meaning'.

Usually, however, human understandings are *symbolic* rather than gestural. We work out what is meant by someone else's words or actions, and act on them accordingly. In a negotiation, for example, neither side takes the other's opening position as a matter of fact, but rather each takes it as an opening bid to be negotiated upon. An employer calling for a pay freeze may really only want to give a pay rise of 1 per cent, while a union representative negotiating with that employer might call for a pay rise of 5 per cent when they would really be satisfied with 3. The *real* negotiation is between 1 and 3 per cent, but if the employer were to start with an offer of 1, or the union representative with an offer of 3, they would have nowhere to go in the course of the negotiations: they would not be able to move and so would appear intransigent and unreasonable. 'A pay freeze' and '5 per cent' are symbols for – as yet undisclosed – amounts which will emerge over the course of the negotiations – and both parties know this from the start. Although the employer will not know how low the union will settle, and the union will not know how high the employer will raise his or her offer, they each know that the other's starting bid is just that, a bid, and not a 'real' offer. Furthermore, each side will insist more and more strongly that their opening offer cannot be changed in the course of the negotiations, to make any concessions seem more valuable than they may be. An employer who insists for hours that there can be no pay raise will be able to make any change to that position seem to be harder-won, although the union nego-tiator will know that the employer could use that tactic, and so will attempt to work out the extent to which there 'really' can be no raise as opposed to the extent to which there may be room for manoeuvre.

The point about symbolic communication is that it requires inter-actants to elicit the 'meaning' of a behaviour by taking the point of view of the other: one must try to work out *why* someone is doing what they are doing, and determine how to respond on the basis of the attribution. This can be cynical (a union representative's attitude towards an employer's pay offer), naive (a child believing in Santa Claus because her parents tell her he exists), everyday (assuming that the person behind the wheel of a bus is the bus driver and so is the person to whom one should pay a fare) or unusual (discovering that a long-held prejudice just doesn't fit the nature of the group one is prejudiced against). In each case, however, *interpretation* is required, based on treating others' behaviour as *symbolic* and taking their point of view to work out what it is symbolic of: what its 'real' meaning is.

Interaction and meaning

Sensory stimuli are thus designated as objects on each occasion of their appearance, to ascertain their usefulness, suitability, poten-tial for resistance, and so on. This means nothing has a 'meaning' fixed outside use: the same length of copper wire can be a logistical problem for the person trying to deliver it, an engineering problem for the people installing it, or a financial advantage for the person subsequently stealing it. Its salient features (weight and volume when delivering it, length and flexibility when installing it, potential market value and ease of discreet access when stealing it) are not intrinsic features, but are the designations particular human beings make to themselves in the course of their wire-related actions and interac-tions. Although these definitions are not intrinsic features of the thing being designed, they are equally not individualistic or arbitrary: one cannot decide what something is without reference to how that thing will be used in interaction. How something is defined is a function of how it is to be *used*: how it is to be incorporated into social inter-action. What something 'means' depends on how it can be brought into a line of action, which typically involves considerations of other people. Taking the example of the wire again, the delivery person has to orientate to the capacity of the vehicle he or she has been allocated, what other deliveries have to be made, what delivery time has been requested, and so on: all these factors provide further nuance and depth to what 'the wire' is, and, crucially, all involve an orientation to other people: managers who allocate vehicles and delivery jobs, other customers whose different requirements have to be reconciled, and the wire's particular recipient. All human action, then, is mediated by interpretation and definition, and that mediation involves a complex orientation both to the purpose of the action and to any other people who might be relevant to the action's development over time. The purpose, the other people, and the purposes of other people can change over the course of the action, thus changing its meaning and organization.

On cooling the mark out

A good empirical example of how these issues map out can be found in Goffman's (1952) analysis of giving bad news. Goffman uses the organization of a confidence trick as an exemplar of how this works. If someone is conned in public, he argues, she does not just lose money. More importantly, she loses her sense of being a shrewd operator – after all, she would not have taken part in the con if she had not thought she could win (and thereby demonstrate her superiority over the people organizing the trick). It is here that the con artists' assistant comes into play. This assistant 'cools the mark [the person being conned] out' by shoring up their sense of self, making them accept the situation they are in and, most importantly, preventing them from making life difficult for the people organizing the con.

Goffman describes a number of techniques that can be used to cool out marks, which have in common an attempt to ameliorate real practical damage by saving the victim's face, sense of self. Breaking up with a partner, being made redundant, realizing that one has been treated shabbily and has no recourse, being turned down for a date, and so on, are all events that are typically handled by making the person who is being disappointed feel that this is not their fault. It is rare that someone is given bad news without some kind of sugar-coating, as in the British situation comedy *The Thick of It*, in which the Prime Minister's 'enforcer' Malcolm Tucker tries to persuade a Minister that his sacking might actually have a positive spin:

Look, people really like it when you go just a bit early! You know, steely
jawed, faraway look in your eyes! Before they get to the point when
they are sitting round in pubs and say 'Oh, that fucker's got to go!', you
surprise them! 'Blimey, he's gone! I didn't expect that! Resigned! You
don't see *that* much anymore! Old school! Respect! I rather liked the
guy! He was hounded out by the fucking press!' How about that, ah?
What a way to go! Yeah!

This, like Goffman's use of a confidence trick as an example, is funny
because we recognize it as a ubiquitous feature of letting people
down: it has been done to us and we have to do it to others, and,
indeed, some people are employed specifically to do it. These forms
of interaction are symbolic because they require one to take the point
of view of the other into account – successfully cooling someone
out means working out what is valuable to them, and demonstrating that, although they are right to be disappointed in *some* ways,
they have other grounds to feel that their sense of self is undamaged.
Information is not simply given to the 'mark': it is tailored to what
they believe and feel, and the risk of them taking things further –
making trouble – is reduced.

Meaning is thus symbolic rather than gestural, and social interaction depends on it having this status: any one social activity is social
to the extent it relies on the actor taking into account the likely
beliefs, values and actions of others.

Meanings are interpreted

Against causality and structural determinism

Blumer's third premise, that meanings are interpreted, is a radical
rejection of the notion of cause and effect being appropriate concepts to use in sociological investigation. Much sociology (and other
branches of the social studies such as psychology, human geography,
history, demographics and so on) accounts for human behaviour by
looking at what precedes it, and by considering the structural context
in which events take place. Blumer argues that such 'causal' and
'structural' explanations cannot possibly account for human behaviour in any meaningful sense.

'Causal' explanations are those which seek to account for human
phenomena in the same way as 'hard' sciences like physics, chemistry
and biology. Human actions are to be accounted for on the basis of
their 'causes', which must be both *necessary* and *sufficient*. To take an

example from physics, water boils at 100 °C. Applying heat of more than 100 °C to water will therefore make it boil: its state changes from being a liquid (water) to a gas (steam). The heat *causes* the water to boil because it is *necessary* (without heat the water would not boil) and *sufficient* (the heat is enough on its own to effect the state change: nothing else is required).

Symbolic interactionists reject the application of such causal models in sociology for two reasons. Firstly, they simply do not reflect how human behaviour works. The most important feature of sciences, according to Blumer, is that they are *empirical*: they seek to explain how things work with reference to the real world, rather than with reference to theories (as in philosophy) or beliefs (as in religion). Any cursory investigation into the workings of the social world will reveal that it does not operate in a cause–effect manner. The 'same' phenomenon will make different people respond in radically different ways (and so that phenomenon cannot be sufficient to cause a particular effect), and the 'same' behaviour can be elicited by all manner of different influences (so no one influence can be necessary to cause that behaviour).

A decrease in interest rates, for example, might encourage people to spend their savings and take out loans, for example, thus stimulating the economy. It could also, however, have the opposite effect: if people take the decrease to indicate that they are in troubled economic times, it could signal to them that shoring up their finances by spending less and paying off more would be more sensible. This brings us on to SI's second critique of causal models: that human behaviour is *always* interpretive. Apart from a very small number of purely biological reflexes, we can give reasons, justifications, for the things we do. These reasons are based, in turn, on how we interpret the conditions of our acting: if we believe that the economy is in trouble we may act more cautiously, while if we believe that we can get a bargain we may take a risk. The two behaviours make some sense, but can be 'caused' by the same set of circumstances. Without reference to the meaningful nature of human behaviour, it appears chaotic and uncertain: any 'cause' can make people do radically different things, and the 'same' effect (behaviour) can be caused by a very wide range of different 'causes' (circumstances).

'Structural' explanations are those which seek to explain individual human behaviour with reference to 'macro' social-structural changes. A classic example of such an account is Durkheim's ([1897] 2006) analysis of suicide. Durkheim pointed out that, far from being a purely psychologically determined phenomenon, people typically commit suicide when there have been major changes in their life circumstances. Sudden changes in one's personal arrangements, like losing a job or breaking up with a partner, seem to increase the likelihood of committing suicide but, strangely, so do other, more positive, life changes. Some people commit suicide after coming into large amounts of money, or after achieving a life-long ambition. These are strange findings, quite at odds with what we would expect: surely people should be more likely to commit suicide when they are suddenly unhappy, when their lives change for the worse, rather than when good things suddenly come right? Durkheim goes on to point out that all such changes have one thing in common: they tend to weaken the bonds between an individual and those close to him or her. Just as a divorce breaks an individual's ties to those he or she knew in common with his or her spouse, a sudden and unexpected increase in income or status makes relationships with former peers more difficult to maintain. Durkheim went on to argue that contemporary societies are increasingly *anomic* – characterized by individualism and moral deregulation – and it is this structural characteristic of such societies that makes suicide more likely. Without adequate moral regulation, individuals feel cut off from the community as a whole, and tend towards the enactment of less well-controlled urges. Suicide, then, although it may be 'set off' by personal changes, is actually caused by the moral order of society as a whole.

Symbolic interactionists reject such explanations for two reasons. Firstly, they obscure individual differences: there are lots of reasons why people might kill themselves (indeed, Durkheim lists four kinds of suicide: altruistic, anomic, egoistic and fatalistic), and different people kill themselves for different reasons. Even if society is more anomic in its moral order, that does not mean that all the suicides in that society will be anomic ones: some people may still commit suicide for altruistic reasons (for instance, so their family members may gain an insurance payment). Social-structural factors cannot, therefore, explain all individual actions.

Secondly, structural explanations are problematic as they implicitly rely on individuals' interpretive activities. For someone to commit suicide they have to weigh up the pros and cons of the action, and make an active decision to carry it out. Even if societies are becoming more individualistic and alienating, and even if those social changes push people into committing suicide, the people who do commit suicide still have to make a decision to do so. Society does not 'cause' them to do anything without their having any say in the matter. Rather than causing behaviour, then, social-structural changes seem to make it more likely that larger numbers of people will make similar choices, and that those choices will then form a pattern that, in turn, changes the social structure. A perception that a tax is unfair, as with the 1990s Community Charge in the UK, may lead to individuals choosing not to pay that tax and thereby risking prosecution. Should enough people make that choice, the tax will become impossible to collect and administer, and will have to be changed or abolished as a result. The tax system, even though it appears to be 'structural', in fact depends on the consent and acquiescence of those charged with paying, collecting and administering it. If they fail to engage in these activities in the ways expected, they will change their structural conditions – from ones of being subject to an unfair tax to ones of being in rebellion against it.

Marijuana use

Becker's (1953) account of marijuana use provides a good example of the way meaning is derived from interaction. The first times someone uses marijuana, they typically do not know how to smoke the drug, and as a consequence it has no real physiological effect. Even once they have mastered a technique of successfully smoking, however, marijuana users do not get high: they are unable to recognize the physiological effects. Becker discusses how novice users have to have the 'symptoms' of marijuana intoxication pointed out to them by others to understand that they constitute being high. Thus, eating, giggling, feeling numb or cold, having rubbery legs and so on all have to be *pointed out* to the novice user as 'symptoms' before he or she can recognize them as 'being high'. Even 'internal' states – feelings – derive their sense from others' interpretations of one's behaviour, and can be classified and corrected by any competent other person who can 'take one's point of view'.

Structure, contingency and regularity

Methodological individualism

These premises seem to point away from sociology and towards some form of psychology. It might appear as if the world is made up of individuals defining situations, rendering meanings, and working out what is going on, in quite individual and arbitrary ways. Blumer's early definition of his enterprise as 'social psychology' (after W. I. Thomas and the Chicago School's use of this term, not its contemporary meaning) seems to give further weight to this suspicion. As any sociologist knows, however, the world is not so arbitrary or individualistic: regular patterns of activity and understanding persist across large groups of people, and are resilient over time. Furthermore, society is not just made up of interacting individuals, but is also a collection of institutions, from kinship organization (the ways families are structured and organized) to national and international bodies (armies, the United Nations), from faith groups (the Catholic Church) to instrumental and practical enterprises (people who sweep the streets). How can a sociology that does not recognize these institutions, enterprises and organizations claim to be sociology at all?

Blumer and the symbolic interactionists do not reject or ignore social structure, but construe it in a very different way from other sociological perspectives. As mentioned above, symbolic interactionists reject the notion of structural *determinism* (the idea that social structures shape and determine human behaviour), but that does not mean that they reject the notion of social *structure*. Structures exist, but – for the symbolic interactionists – they are the *product* of human behaviour, and have no existence separate from that behaviour.

In this sense the symbolic interactionists share Weber's notion of methodological individualism. Methodological individualism is the idea that any collective description – an army, a church, the family, the nation state – is a shorthand term for the activities, understandings and orientations of the people who make it up. In principle, something as complicated as Islam should be capable of being described in terms of the activities of all those who subscribe to, disagree with, join or leave the faith – because it is through their actions (or non-actions) that the religion is constituted. Weber's point is not that this is always possible or desirable (why would such a description, even if it were logistically possible to put one together, assist in proselytizing for or condemning Islam?) but rather that it should *in principle* be something which could be done. This means that – unlike other intellectuals and commentators – sociologists should always keep in mind that collective terms and descriptions are shorthand descriptions of complex and integrated activities. What constitutes 'Islam' today is very different from what constituted it twenty, fifty or a hundred years ago – and the disputes and debates (internal and external) concerning what 'it' might 'really' be are a *part* of its nature.

The difference, then, between symbolic interactionist notions of structure and those of other sociological perspectives, is that the former do not *essentialize* structures and organizations. There is no attempt to determine what any structure 'really' is, because its contradictions and ambiguities are as much a part of it as those things that maintain its unity. The question for symbolic interactionists, therefore, is not how structures are organized, but how they are *maintained* over time: how, despite changes in personnel, attitudes and beliefs, language and so on, institutions carry on across generations.

Language is always social

The basic building blocks of social organizations are, for symbolic interactionists, people working in collaboration with a shared, often collective, orientation. This is built upon a shared language. As Mead argues, what distinguishes humans from other animals is their capacity to use symbols: to allow the same sentiment or understanding to appear to all parties to communication. This could be as simple as seeing someone fall and injure herself eliciting feelings of shock and pain in an observer, or the shared understanding of a teacher realizing why a pupil cannot understand a mathematical transformation and explaining it again to get past the blockage. The point of symbolic interaction is that it generates the same feelings or understandings across interactants, thus allowing them to organize themselves through interaction (rather than as individuals operating separately in a shared space).

For people to do this, they require a shared symbolic system: a language. Language is always social, taught to each and every member of a culture and passed on, generation after generation. It changes over time, and there may be differences between how older and younger people speak, but the capacity to share experiences, information and understanding through language defines a culture. Language is the basis of social symbols, and it is our capacity to understand one another through language that allows us to take one another's points of view. Equally, however, our capacity to work together requires us to use language to picture and describe *collective* activities and endeavours, not just those of particular other individuals. Again, Mead describes how this capacity might develop.

Play, game and the generalized other

Mead (1934: 152–64) describes how, as children develop, their capacity to see things from others' points of view develops in turn. Initially, he argues, children *play* with their parents and with one another. Play is a simple, fun, form of interaction often based on repetition. A baby will happily gurgle at her father hiding his face behind his hands and then revealing it again – now you see it, now you don't – for long periods of time. This play enacts disappearance and reappearance, but does not have a 'start' or a 'finish', it does not develop over time, and it does not require either competition or co-operation to occur. It stops when one or both parties to the play becomes bored, falls asleep or is distracted by other tasks and responsibilities. The parties to the play are 'self' (the baby) and 'other' (the father), and each orientates to the other directly without reference to anyone or anything else. Children playing, therefore, have to learn to take the other's point of view – to see things from the point of view of the specific other person they are playing with – to have fun. Play is interesting to the extent that each participant can imagine what the others are doing and seeing.

As children grow, however, they start to learn more complex forms of play that involve rules and regulations. *Games*, these more structured forms of play, typically require an orientation to external sets of rules (such as the rules of Snakes and Ladders or Snap) to make sense and be fun. They may have winners and losers. Furthermore, some games (like football or rounders) require participants to orientate to co-operation as part of a team as well as competition with others. In these more complex games, children do not just have to orientate to specific others: they also have to orientate to the *generalized other*. As well as taking the role of the specific other person (as in play), they have to take the role of the generalized other, a collection of other people viewed as a unit or a normative orientation to the game as a whole.

By 'generalized other', Mead means two kinds of things. Firstly, he argues, the generalized other can relate to the general expectations and requirements that any participants in a particular game need to have. The rules of Snakes and Ladders, for example, are generalized because they apply on each occasion the game is played. They cannot be varied, even if varying them would make the game more fun (i.e., one cannot decide not to go down a snake one has landed on just because that would make it easier to win). Rather than the specific, *ad hoc*, improvised nature of play, games require their players to show a held-in-common orientation to a situationally independent set of rules. The 'generalized other' in this sense is the shared values of a community of players, as codified in a rulebook. Secondly, however, the 'generalized other' can be a group or team understood as a collection of co-operating participants. In playing football, for example, one must orientate to the opposing team as a group of people joined together with shared strategies and tactics. One cannot orientate simply to a particular player, but must intuit how that player's strategies might link in to those of his team-mates. In this second sense, taking the role of the generalized other can ultimately require one to take the perspective of 'society at large', reflecting the views, ideals and norms shared by all members of a community.

Self and other

The 'self', then, for Mead, is made up of how a person views his or her actions with respect to others' orientations. The manner in which one behaves – the ways a situation is defined – depends crucially on which roles are taken by, and attributed to, parties to the situation. In an interview, for example, a candidate might orientate to the interests and opinions of particular members of the interview panel, but also to the aims and objectives of the organization they represent. By taking the role of particular others, the candidate can try to present him/ herself as 'likeable', 'reliable', 'smart' and so on; by taking the role of the organization as a prospective employer, he/she might also seek to demonstrate how his/her particular skills and abilities will be of use. The 'other' one takes the role of may be inconsistent (if you realize in the course of an interaction that what you thought was a friendly drink is actually a date, you will have to review and revise your previous assumptions and conduct in the light of the new information). It may also be 'wrong', for instance, if you take the role of the other as a representative of a particular generalized other and then find out that this is not the case. By and large, however, role-taking is an unproblematic and automatic process, requiring little or no conscious deliberation: paying a bus driver, having a conversation with a friend, etc. This allows routine social interaction to be conducted unproblematically.

Definition of the situation

When roles are aligned correctly – where parties to an interaction make compatible attributions about one another – the situation is mutually defined in a coherent manner. What this means is that, by reciprocally taking 'correct' roles, parties to the situation generate a particular kind of encounter based on shared values, commitments, aims and goals. An interview situation, for example, is generated and maintained by virtue of the interviewers and interviewee taking these roles, rather than alternative ones (mother, daughter, friend, political activist, etc.), and correctly taking the role of each other in accordance with that role-taking.

As W. I. Thomas (Thomas and Thomas 1928: 572) famously stated, 'If men define situations as real, they are real in their consequences'. If I behave as a lecturer, stand in front of a class, and talk about a particular topic for two hours, and parties to that class take notes, ask questions and leave feeling that they have grasped the topics under discussion, the situation is a lecture. It does not matter if I am underprepared or unqualified, or if members of the class have come to the wrong room and are too embarrassed to admit this and leave: the mutual role-taking and situation-defining generate the situation as a 'lecture' and allow it to proceed as a routine matter. By orientating to shared understandings and roles, social stability is produced.

Self and self: I and me

Crucially, for Mead, we do not just take the roles of particular others and generalized others. We can also take ourselves – our own actions – as an object for reflection and definition. Mead distinguishes between the 'I' and the 'me'. The 'I' is the acting, unreflective individual, going about his or her everyday business without difficulties. Although you might be able to say what you have done so far today, much of the detail of this is lost as it was not being attended to. You might remember having breakfast or travelling into work, but the details of eating the food (manipulating a knife and fork, chewing, swallowing, etc.) or of your commute (indicating to turn left or right if driving, waiting for a bus or train) are probably sketchy or forgotten altogether. There is no need to deliberately think through what one is doing much of the time – one acts 'on automatic pilot'.

Particularly when interacting with others, however, people are much more concerned about their own activities. You might monitor your own talk to make sure you are not being offensive or boring, or try to control your appearance and manner to seem sincere or playful. To do this, one must make *oneself* the object of role-taking – thereby transcending the unreflective 'I'. Mead used the term 'me' to refer to this: the 'me' is the self made an object for its own contemplation, thus allowing self-monitoring, self-criticism and self-correction. Taking the role of oneself – making oneself an object of the 'I' – is an almost automatic process, but it is tremendously powerful. When you realize you are not alone (although thought you were) and 'jump', its power is revealed.

Self and society

For symbolic interactionists, 'social structure' is the stable production and reproduction of situations through parties to those situations accurately taking the roles of one another, orientating to compatible generalized others, and maintaining socially acceptable behaviour by monitoring their own behaviour by making themselves objects of their own perception. By orientating to different *reference groups* – collections of people one can compare oneself to, feel a part of, oppose – individuals are able to fulfil complex and varied social roles, and manage and maintain the complexity of social structures in all their detail.

The temporal dimension

Institutions and going concerns

Social structures – organizations, institutions and so on – tend to be consistent over quite long periods of time. The fact that they are built up from individuals sharing orientations over the course of interactions might make them appear somewhat fragile, however. Common criticisms of symbolic interactionism are that it is 'individualistic', it does not acknowledge the reality of complex social phenomena, and it fails to move beyond small-scale 'microsociology'. This is not the case, however. As Weber pointed out, methodological individualism does not require one to deny the existence of social structures, merely to recognize their status as being the produced outcome of complex behaviour and activities.

Everett Hughes ([1957] 1971) recognized this in his references to social institutions and other stable social forms as 'going concerns', things which are produced and reproduced with strong stability over a long period of time and independently of the particular individuals comprising them at any one time. Social order, social stability, then, is, for the symbolic interactionists, a *temporal* achievement – something requiring people to keep doing the same things, to orientate to the same stable features, over a protracted period of time. This contrasts again with the more Durkheimian approaches to sociology which posit social order as being something dependent on shared 'things' – values, norms, rules and so on.

Regularity, habit and stability

William James ([1892] 1977) argued that, in order to attend to the most important things in one's life, one must make less important things *habitual* – i.e., do them in regular ways, at the same time, without much thought – so as to keep one's attention free for things that really matter. In Meadian terms, unless something requires attention, it should be undertaken by the unreflective 'I' rather than troubling the self by requiring monitoring or correction. Habit and unreflective activities are the basis of many features of social stability: we are able to do a huge amount by virtue of the fact that we do not need to look beyond the grossest and most instrumental roles others fulfil.

When shopping, for example, while one might have to work out where particular products are available in a supermarket, one does not need to attend much to either other shoppers or supermarket staff. The store is organized in such a way as to make it easy to find things (aisles typically labelled) and go through paying and bagging with minimal effort. One does not need to work out who it is that can scan groceries and process payment: the store is laid out in such a way that those people are waiting for customers between the goods and the exit. Goods are placed on a conveyer belt to be scanned, and delivered back to the customer on another conveyer belt after being processed. The person one needs to deal with is already present, and their role and function is clearly marked by the fact that they are sitting behind the checkout counter – indeed, if someone is sitting in this position and they are *not* dealing with customers this will typically be indicated with a sign to prevent the 'natural' assumption from being made.

The point of this is that the organization of a supermarket allows the relevant roles – customer and checkout operator – of parties to the encounter to be structured by the physical layout of the store and by the way customers naturally move through it. The design of the store allows relevant activities – gathering shopping together, having it processed, paying for it – to be undertaken with minimal thought or effort, and with minimal human interaction. For the person operating the checkout, nearly all customers' personal characteristics are irrelevant (except in particular cases, such as for young-looking customers attempting to buy certain prohibited products such as alcohol), and for customers it does not matter who is operating the checkout: they simply go to whichever one is nearby and looks likely to have a shorter waiting time.

These interactions are structured to allow almost entirely habitual, anonymous and instrumental role-attributions to be made, providing for the smooth operation of a complex social organization. The efficient running of the supermarket depends on all parties to its organization each having one clearly defined instrumental role, and orientating to one another solely on the basis of these roles. Stability over time is ensured by simplifying role-taking and making, and restricting the range of possible uses people can make of one another and of their environment.

Negotiated order

Very often, however, such routine and habitual role-taking and making is impossible. In many areas of social life, for example, complex decisions have to be made, with a conclusion being arrived at by evaluating the pros and cons of lots of different possible lines of action. Little consideration is required to buy a train ticket, as one's encounter with the person selling the ticket is very simple, as role-taking is simple and reciprocal: customer and ticket agent are the only roles parties to the encounter need to orientate to. In more complex situations, such as making decisions about the best course of treatment for psychiatric patients (Strauss et al. 1964), however, the situation is necessarily more involved. Different professional groups may well have different ideologies, and the facts of any particular case are capable of being interpreted in lots of different ways. A social worker seeing signs of improvement, for instance, may believe that a patient is ready for a graduated release from hospital, while a doctor – who is legally responsible for the patient's case – could argue that a more cautious approach is warranted. The doctor might even want to try a different and more invasive treatment regime, requiring further inpatient care, to see whether it would have a more beneficial effect on the patient's symptoms.

In cases such as this, role-taking might prove to be a divisive rather than constructive matter. The social worker could become entrenched in his position – identify with his role too strongly – or the doctor could dismiss the social worker's opinions as merely ideological – taking an inaccurate view of the other. In such complex cases, however, role-taking is undertaken in a more nuanced, negotiated, manner. This means participants are more tentative in their role-taking and attribution, details of the case at hand are talked about at length, relevant rules and precedents are invoked and considered, previous similar cases are weighed up and re-examined, and action is only undertaken once a consensus has emerged. As practical, pragmatic, social actors, parties to a situation in which disagreement is occurring orientate to overcoming the disagreement and making sure that an appropriate line of action can be followed. Stability is thus maintained, even if it contains and embraces disagreement and dispute, over time and on a case-by-case basis.

Careers and turning points

In the longer term, stability may come under threat. Actors (and, indeed, institutions) have to adapt, often quite rapidly, either to changing circumstances or to developing tensions. Hughes ([1952] 1971) argued that these larger changes over time can best be understood through the concepts of 'careers' and 'turning points'. One's autobiography – the story of your life – is not a seamless list of events following one after another, but is characterized by long periods of relative stability (being at high school, being in a particular relationship) punctuated by sudden changes and upheavals (leaving home, deciding to get married). These latter Hughes calls 'turning points', occasions in which, either by choice or as a result of changing circumstances, a period of stability has to end and a new one commence. At an institutional level, these turning points allow for change to occur as required against a background of relative stability. Their implications, and the ways they manifest themselves in practice, will be taken up in the subsequent chapter on work.

Method and methodology
Radical empiricism

The pragmatists, following James ([1909] 1977), adopted a policy of radical empiricism. As argued above, this represents a suspicion of abstract and premature theorizing, and a privileging of investigations of the real world as the best means of answering philosophical and sociological questions. Theory is a tool to allow these investigations to take place, and is to be generated through investigations: in contrast to other philosophical and sociological approaches, theory is at the service of research rather than the other way round. This manifests itself in symbolic interactionism methodologically and at the level of methods of investigation.

Comparative analysis

At the level of methodology, symbolic interactionism pursues its empiricist remit by rejecting variable analysis and instead conducting comparative analyses of the formal features of social organization and activity. Blumer ([1956] 1969) pointed out, in a similar manner to Dewey's ([1896] 1981) earlier criticism of the reflex arc concept in psychology, that *variable analytic* sociology is incoherent.

Variable analysis is the, usually statistical, attempt to explain social organization by demonstrating relationships between different abstract concepts. These might be, for example, levels of unemployment and the rates of crime. Measuring the two, and correlating the results, might provide for an argument that increases in one 'go with' increases in the other. By focusing public policy on reducing unemployment, it could be argued, levels of crime could be reduced.[1] Blumer points out that such analyses are incoherent in a number of ways. Firstly, there are no clear guidelines on what does or does not count as a variable: one can make *anything* a variable and then conduct studies accordingly. This means that often variables are simply imported into studies as matters of theoretical interest: one can study, for example, relationships between gender and any aspect of social organization, regardless of whether or not gender is a relevant category for the actual activities being investigated. Variables, in short, do not emerge from settings but are imposed upon them. Secondly, many 'generic' variables are ill defined and unclear. What counts as 'community cohesion', for instance, depends on the methods of study and topic of enquiry of particular pieces of research: cohesion in a family unit, for instance, could be measured by the family members' levels of agreement on certain important issues, while cohesion in a neighbourhood could be measured by how many of his or her neighbours' names each person living in the neighbourhood knows. Both measure *something*, but exactly how agreement on matters of fact and knowledge of names *both* measure *the same thing* is unclear. Thirdly, by investigating 'variables', sociologists necessarily have to shear away unnecessary and irrelevant data – even though those data might be informative and relevant in their own right. In Durkheim's *On Suicide* ([1897] 2006), for instance, suicide rates are shown to relate to the degree to which cultures are more or less anomic, fatalistic, egoistic or altruistic. This is fine, but it does not tell us anything about the specific reasons particular people commit suicide in those cultures: their personal motivation, social and financial circumstances, and so on. The most general features of a phenomenon are shown to relate to one another, and then used to account for the detailed specifics of *each instance* of that phenomenon.

Symbolic interactionists, in contrast, seek to undertake comparative analyses of social activities to determine what formal similarities and differences they might have. As Everett Hughes ([1951] 1971: 316) argued:

> The comparative student of man's work learns about doctors by studying plumbers; and about prostitutes by studying psychiatrists. This is not to suggest any degree of similarity greater than chance expectation between the members of these pairs, but simply to indicate that the student starts with the assumption that all kinds of work belong in the same series, regardless of their places in prestige or ethical ratings. In order to learn, however, one must find a frame of reference applicable to all cases without regard to such ratings.... Both the physician and the plumber do practice esoteric techniques for the benefit of people in distress. The psychiatrist and the prostitute must both take care not to become too personally involved with clients who come to them with rather intimate problems.

In Goffman's ([1961] 1991) classic account of 'total institutions', *Asylums*, he points out that the study of the workings of psychiatric hospitals could be used as a leaping-off point for the study of other similar institutions, such as ships, prisons, the military and so on. By undertaking detailed studies of particular settings, symbolic interactionists seek to generate relevant concepts and theoretical frameworks (Glaser and Strauss 1967) that will allow for comparison with other forms of social organization.

Interviews versus fieldwork

Although symbolic interactionists use a variety of investigative techniques (indeed, one group, the Iowa School, used primarily quantitative, questionnaire-based methods), there is a tendency for qualitative data to be gathered and examined. This preference derives from the earlier investigations of the 'first' Chicago School, dominated by Robert Park's (Bulmer 1984: 97) injunction to: 'Go and sit in the lounges of luxury hotels and on the doorsteps of flophouses; sit on the Gold Coast settees and on the slum shakedowns; sit in the Orchestra Hall and in the Star and Garter Burlesque. In short go and get the seat of your pants dirty in real research.'

Becker and Geer (1958) argued further that the best way to 'get the seat of your pants dirty' in this way was to undertake fieldwork, sometimes called participant observation, or the ethnographic study of real-world settings. In contrast to interviews, the other dominant method of qualitative data collection, they argued, fieldwork allows researchers to immerse themselves more fully in the situations they are investigating, and thus to understand the meanings and roles of participants more completely. Furthermore, because it typically takes place over a longer period of time (interviews being, by contrast, 'snapshots' of a particular moment), fieldwork allows researchers to follow meanings as they change and develop in the course of their use.

Criticisms

A number of criticisms have been made of symbolic interactionism, not least from ethnomethodologists and conversation analysts. The perspective, it is argued, is 'loose, impressionistic and personal' (Bittner [1973] 2003: 100), allowing for different researchers to interpret and account for social activities in different ways. Symbolic interactionism is incapable of addressing the fine detail of mundane activities in the ways ethnomethodology and conversation analysis do, and its reliance on 'the point of view of the actor' means that things which members of society take for granted (and therefore do not see) cannot be made visible to sociological analysis.

Blumer, in particular, has been criticized for introducing unachievably high standards of rigour and methodological purity into sociology (Becker 1998: 10–11), and so simultaneously emphasizing the importance of empirical investigations while making their conduct – according to his study policies and recommendations – almost impossible. Indeed, the personal divisions within the approach (in particular between Blumer and Hughes) has meant that there has been little integration of Blumer's 'theoretical' and 'methodological' concerns with Hughes' programmes of fieldwork and sociological investigation in which theory is implied rather than explicitly formulated. Although Blumer and Hughes are compatible with one another, their relationship manifests itself most strongly in their students' work rather than in any coherent programmatic statement both could adhere to.

Developing this theme somewhat, some (e.g. Becker 1999) have argued that 'symbolic interactionism' or the 'Second Chicago School' never really existed: there is a body of great sociological work, but it does not represent a coherent related set of studies, underpinned by a shared theory or methods used in common. The same criticism has been made of the pragmatists, many of whose most important works were written as criticisms of one another, such as Dewey's ([1896] 1981) critique of James on the reflex arc, or Peirce's ([1905] 1998) criticisms of James' understanding of the concept of pragmatism itself.

It has also been argued that the pragmatists, and later the symbolic interactionists, tended to psychologize features of the social world. In Mead's account of the development of the self, for instance, there is a tendency to see the 'inner' world as reflecting the features of the 'outer' one: internal, psychological, processes have to be brought into alignment with external, social, ones. The ethnomethodologists, whose work we will consider next, have a radically different way of formulating these kinds of relationships.

2

Phenomenology and Ethnomethodology

All social life is essentially practical. All mysteries which lead theory to mysticism find their rational solution in human practice and in the comprehension of this practice. (Marx [1845] 1975: 423)

Origins of the term, roots of the concept

Ethnomethodology (EM) has proved to be one of contemporary sociology's more unusual and controversial approaches, as well as one of its most productive. It represents the major attempt to adapt for sociological inquiry the principles of the philosophical approach of phenomenology. Central to phenomenology is the attempt to take seriously the distinctive characteristics of diverse types of human experience. Analysing the distinguishing features of any experience – be it interacting face-to-face with other people, or playing a musical instrument, or watching a play in a theatre – is a leading objective of phenomenological investigations. In this chapter, we describe the development of ethnomethodology and trace its indebtedness to phenomenology.

Perhaps the first thing that needs to be noted is that, regardless of the '-methodology' element of its name, EM is not a research method comparable with methods such as structured interviewing, content analysis, participant observation or photo elicitation. Rather, it is a sociological approach or perspective. It sets out a novel agenda for sociological inquiry, informed by theoretical and methodological premises not commonly entertained in mainstream sociological research. The purpose of this chapter is to outline this agenda, and to introduce those premises, in order to indicate the scope of ethnomethodological work. This discussion will provide a basis for understanding the ethnomethodological studies considered in later chapters of the book.

The term 'ethnomethodology', and the approach to sociological inquiry it signifies, were devised by Harold Garfinkel (1917–2011) in the mid-1950s. Garfinkel (1974) recalled that around 1954 he was working on a study of decision making by jurors in Wichita, Kansas, and was looking for a general term to characterize what he had observed. Analysing tape-recordings and interviews, Garfinkel noticed how jurors went about the business of their jury-room discussions in an organized, methodical manner. They were concerned with matters such as the credibility of witnesses, the adequacy of testimonies heard in court, the plausibility and relevance of the evidence provided, the likely motives of persons providing courtroom testimony, the standards of proof that the law insisted upon, and so forth. In other words, they were concerned with *the grounds of inference and action* of the events set out in courtroom questions and testimony. It was on this basis that jurors attempted to ascertain matters of responsibility, liability, guilt and innocence. Garfinkel characterized the jurors' concerns as 'methodological' because they were manifestly reasoned, methodical and patterned in character. Although not 'methodological' in the professional sociological sense, the jurors assessed 'matters of fact, fancy, hypothesis, conjecture, evidence, demonstration, inquiry' (Garfinkel 1974: 12) about the case that they were called to consider. Garfinkel went on to suggest that it is not only jurors who engage in such practical reasoning about the matters that concern them. People in many other organizational and everyday contexts also engage in practical reasoning about the situations in which they find themselves. What Garfinkel became sensitized to was how their reasoning was socially organized and shared, not haphazard, idiosyncratic or individual.

The 'ethno' element in 'ethnomethodology' refers to the understandings that people have about their own actions. It explicitly draws upon a standard anthropological analogue. The prefix, 'ethno', refers to people's understandings of whatever it is they are doing. Garfinkel had already established an interest in the actor's point of view in his doctoral dissertation at Harvard (Garfinkel 1952). However, while 'ethnobotany' studied people's understandings of plant life and ethnophysics their understandings of matter and energy, Garfinkel wanted EM to point to a more general field of study, the methods or practices that people employ in constructing and making sense of their own, and others', actions.

Thus EM studies how social actions are produced and recognized by members of society. Just what makes EM's interest in ordinary social actions – such everyday practices as answering the phone, greeting a friend, giving way to oncoming traffic, approaching a stranger for directions or answering a stranger's queries – so novel and distinctive within the established analytical frameworks of sociology and the social sciences requires some explanation. EM is often assumed, not entirely incorrectly, to be a 'micro-sociology' or a 'sociology of everyday life'. Like symbolic interactionism, EM addresses those minutiae of ordinary action first brought to attention by Simmel's sociological microscopy. But it draws upon some influential European philosophical approaches, most notably the social phenomenology of Alfred Schutz and also the later philosophical thinking of Ludwig Wittgenstein, to forge an approach to the study of the everyday practices of members of society that is quite different from anything that has gone before.

Ethnomethodology has several features that distinguish it from other sociological approaches. These include:

- people's experiences of everyday life are not random or chaotic but ordered – their experiences are organized so as to be intelligible to themselves and others;
- that orderliness is 'achieved', that is to say it derives from members of society using certain practices or methods appropriate to the situation and context;
- that orderliness can be investigated by close attention to concrete and actual records and reports of social life – thus the concern with the 'average', 'typical' or 'hypothetical' that satisfies the analytic purposes of much sociological inquiry is considered inadequate for EM's studies;
- EM is 'incommensurable' with orthodox sociologies (including SI) because it addresses foundational concerns that orthodox sociologies overlook, about how sense is made and ordinary actions constructed in everyday situations.

These characteristic features were gradually developed by Garfinkel from the 1940s onwards. Thus they can best be brought into relief through a review of the evolution of his sociological thought.

Garfinkel before ethnomethodology

Leaving his New Jersey birthplace in 1939, Garfinkel began graduate studies in sociology at the University of North Carolina. There
he found a lively interest in the development of a sociology that took
seriously the actor's point of view. There was also a strong interest in
social problems. Garfinkel undertook a study of interracial homicide
for his Master's thesis at North Carolina (later published as Garfinkel
1949). Garfinkel's awareness of the issues produced by prejudice and
segregation found early expression in a short story he wrote: 'Color
trouble' (Doubt 1989). It presents a sympathetic portrayal of an
'incident' on a bus when an African-American woman fails to observe
the 'correct' seating arrangements. The story was first published in
1940 and subsequently reprinted twice. There are striking affinities
between Garfinkel's story and the noted 1955 event in US civil rights
history when Rosa Parks refused to move from her seat on a bus.
Although presented as a short story, it seems that Garfinkel witnessed
the events it describes, making it a kind of literary ethnography.

Garfinkel completed his MA degree then undertook war service
in the military. In 1946 he enrolled for graduate work at Harvard
University, where he studied with Talcott Parsons (1902–79), who
was becoming the dominant figure in American sociology. Garfinkel's
1952 Ph.D. thesis, 'The perception of the other', played a pivotal role
in the development of his thinking. In it, he accepted the centrality of
the problem of order that Parsons had proposed as sociology's central
theoretical problem. But Garfinkel offered a very different solution
from that of his eminent teacher and, by extension, from many of the
prevailing assumptions of established sociological thought.

The problem of social order, for Parsons, was about explaining
how social life could be patterned and predictable. How can a collection of individuals, all pursuing what they feel are their own best
interests, ever produce anything that is orderly? How is co-operation
possible? Thomas Hobbes first posed the question in the seven-
teenth century, suggesting that if individuals simply followed their
own interests there would be a war of all against all. To avoid this
unhappy state, Hobbes argued, individuals cede some of their rights
to a sovereign authority, which in turn offers certain protections
to those individuals. Parsons took up Hobbes' question as a useful
formulation of the problem of social order but suggested a different
solution. In its basics, Parsons proposed that the key to orderly social
life was the individual personality's internalization of the customary
norms and values of the society. This occurred through the process

of socialization, which instilled norms and values into individuals, who thereby learned what kinds of conduct were acceptable and valued. Socialization was a process promoted and supported by the major institutions of society and their constituent roles. Incumbents of the 'parent' role within the institution of the family, for example, were charged with the tasks of primary socialization (acquisition of language, control of elimination, regulation of the emotions). Other institutions, such as those making up the polity and the economy, socialized new members into the relevant norms and values – the society's acceptable ways of making political decisions, of producing and consuming goods and services, and so on.

This was the broad shape taken by Parsons' reasoning about the problem of social order by the late 1940s. For Garfinkel it must have been a disappointment. The theoretical significance that Parsons (1937) had earlier accorded the actor's point of view in his theoretical schema seemed to have disappeared. By the late 1940s and early 1950s, Parsons saw action as the simple absorption ('internalization') and application by the actor of norms and values grounded in the society's institutions and culture. Parsons' earlier voluntaristic conception, in which the actor made choices between alternative courses of action, was replaced by a much more deterministic version that saw action as conduct in accordance with internalized norms and values. Garfinkel would later suggest that Parsons – like so much sociology of the 1950s and 1960s – turned the actor into a 'judgemental dope', devoid of the capacity to figure out features of social settings. More specifically, the actor became a 'cultural dope', defined as 'the man-in-the-sociologist's-society who produces the stable features of society by acting in compliance' with that which 'the common culture provides' (Garfinkel [1967] 1984: 67–8). Any serious analytic formulation of the actor's point of view, Garfinkel suggested, had to do much better than this. It needed to take account of the everyday reasoning of the actor who routinely chose between alternative courses of action, for only in this way could the logic of the actor's knowledge be accommodated (Heritage 1984: 29).

Garfinkel proposed a very different and contrasting solution to the problem of social order. It rested on the idea that the actor's lived experience is thoroughly orderly in character. In this view, the root of the social orderliness of society lay in the organized properties of people's experience. Garfinkel's solution to the problem of order was a bottom-up solution, in contrast to Parsons' top-down view that sourced orderliness in institutions and culture. In order to articulate this view, Garfinkel drew upon the

phenomenological writings of Alfred Schutz (1899–1959). In the
1940s Garfinkel became personally acquainted with Schutz and
his colleague Aron Gurwitsch (1901–73). Together they furnished
Garfinkel with fresh resources for the exploration of the actor's point
of view in addition to those American sociological points of reference with which Garfinkel was already familiar. Specifically, Schutz
and Gurwitsch showed Garfinkel the potential of the European phenomenological tradition, initiated in its modern form by Edmund
Husserl.

Phenomenology as a resource for ethnomethodology

Modern phenomenology is a branch of philosophy developed by
Edmund Husserl (1859–1938), who presented it as the study of
human consciousness from a first-person point of view. Its aim was to
provide *rigorous descriptions* of consciousness. Husserl greatly admired
the achievements of the modern natural sciences but felt that they
promoted 'perspectival' thinking. They only produced knowledge
of the world from a particular point of view: chemistry, physics,
biology and psychology, for example, isolated the chemical, physical, biological and psychological properties of objects respectively.
What was missing was knowledge of things as they are apprehended
by humans in their ordinary experience. Husserl's response to the
'crisis' in the sciences was to propose a complementary, philosophi-
cally rigorous approach to human experience that sought to establish
the most general features ('essences') of human consciousness. From
the outset Husserl conceived of phenomenology as an attempt to
overcome the fragmentation of our knowledge of the world presented
in the contemporary European sciences.

Phenomenology was thus designed by Husserl to concentrate on
the phenomena of human experience. For Husserl, humans are self-
aware beings whose consciousness is the central focus of concern for
phenomenological investigations. The basic feature of consciousness is 'intentionality'. Consciousness never just *is*, it never merely
subsists in itself. It is always directed towards something – towards
that to which we give attention. Our consciousness is always directed
towards reading a book, preparing a meal, listening to a radio programme, finding a phone number in the telephone book or whatever
else we are attending to. A major concern of phenomenology was to
articulate the *particularity* of such experiences, to show how they are
constituted as the distinctive activities that they are. This could be

done by carefully inspecting the experiences in order to determine their essential features.

Husserl's aim, then, was to develop a systematic knowledge of human experience that would run alongside the knowledge developed by the modern sciences, and which would complement it by focusing on the unity and intelligibility of human experience. Husserl did not, however, show how the phenomenological approach could inform the problems of the social sciences. Instead, that task fell to Alfred Schutz, who used Husserlian insights in order to deepen the project of interpretive sociology begun by Max Weber (1864–1920). Schutz argued that Weber's project could be improved by application of phenomenological insights to some of its basic concepts.

In Weber's famed definition, interpretive sociology was the 'science concerning itself with the interpretive understanding of social action and thereby with a causal explanation of its course and effects' (Weber 1968: 4). Schutz argued that certain of Weber's terms of reference, such as 'action' and 'understanding', required the kind of clarification that phenomenology provided. For example, according to Schutz, Weber did not distinguish between action in progress and the completed act, or between the actor's and the observer's point of view, often treating them as overlapping or identical.

Schutz (1972) also highlighted a number of difficulties with Weber's account of understanding. He argued that Weber's distinction between the direct, instant understanding of action ('she is directing the traffic') and understanding that explains actions in terms of a wider context of meaning ('she is a police officer who is empowered to act in this manner') is a matter of degree, not of different kinds of understanding. Motives were embedded in even the most straightforward descriptions of actions. Schutz (1962) also suggested that discussions of understanding in the social science literature often mix up three issues that are quite different in character:

1 Understanding as a philosophical problem. As members of society we all believe that other people have minds similar to our own and that we can obtain a reasonably accurate knowledge of, for example, 'what is on your mind' right now. The question that has exercised philosophers is, how is this certainty possible? How can we 'know' other minds, given that minds are private and hidden from view? What is the *general* basis that allows humans confidently to assume that they know and understand how others are thinking and feeling?

2 This philosophical problem can be distinguished from a problem

specific to the social sciences: to what extent is social scientific knowledge of society concerned with the understandings held by members of society? How far is social science dependent upon observing regularities separate from the understandings held by members of society? This question has long vexed those concerned with the methodology of the social sciences. The issues overlap with questions about the extent to which the social sciences can be like the natural sciences in their scope, methods and ambitions.
3 For Schutz this second problem, a methodological problem, can be distinguished from a third issue – namely, how understanding works as part of the fabric of social life. In an important sense social life is 'constituted' by – made up out of – people's understandings of it. Their concepts and beliefs shape or frame what they see and understand. These concepts and beliefs provided by the culture allow us to identify the kinds of conduct that make up everyday actions such as 'giving a friendly wave', 'making an insulting remark' or 'taking part in an act of shoplifting'. Without the concepts and beliefs surrounding 'friendliness', 'insults' and 'shoplifting', we would not find these notions intelligible whenever we encounter them in our daily lives.

Schutz maintained that phenomenology could most effectively contribute to interpretive sociology's advance in this third aspect of understanding. He sought to use phenomenology to elucidate people's lived experience. Describing this project as a 'constitutive phenomenology of the natural attitude', Schutz (1972) began with the person acting in the world ('actor'), occupying what he called the 'natural attitude' where the wide-awake person treats everything in their world just as it appears to be. In the natural attitude the actor's reasoning is overwhelmingly guided by practical concerns: what to do now, what to do next? The everyday world was, Schutz insisted, from the outset a shared, 'intersubjective' world. The actor's experience of everyday life was not wholly idiosyncratic or peculiar to them. Actors share 'common-sense knowledge' with others when they stand in a queue or when they give directions to others trying to find, say, the nearest cashpoint. Of course, not all the actor's knowledge is completely shared with others. In addition to common-sense knowledge, actors possess bodies of specialist knowledge particular to, for example, an occupation or a gender category. As well as the shared knowledge that provides the basis of intersubjectivity, Schutz noted that there is a 'social distribution of knowledge'. The knowledge an actor has of her or his society is akin to the knowledge a person has of a city: everyone has some parts they know well and others with which they are less familiar. This social distribution of knowledge is something the actor orients to in, for example, seeking the advice of a 'professional' about an educational or legal or medical matter. Thus Schutz allowed both for the sharing of common-sense knowledge and for differences in the 'stock of knowledge at hand' held by any actor in his or her unique 'biographically determined situation'.

The social world was stratified, and known to be stratified, by people acting in accordance with their common-sense knowledge. Schutz identified two principal bases of this stratification:

1 *Worlds of face-to-face relations, contemporaries, predecessors, successors.* Schutz suggests that there is a special immediacy to the face-to-face relations we have with others because in the face-to-face situation we share both space and time with those others. But we also live in a world full of people not directly known to us ('contemporaries'). This world of contemporaries is not entirely of their own making. We know that it has been shaped by the actions of our 'predecessors'. Similarly, we also know that there will be generations who follow us –'successors' – and our actions are shaped in part by this knowledge, as for example when we write a will.

2 *Multiple realities.* The actor's everyday world is, Schutz maintained, a 'paramount reality'. It is the foundation of the actor's experience. Schutz also suggests that actors can occupy other 'finite provinces of meaning' such as the worlds of science or of dreams. Each of these finite provinces of meaning makes sense in its own terms. Our occupancy of these other worlds is always temporary: in the end we always return to the world of daily life with its pre-eminently practical concerns ('What shall I do now? What shall I do next?'). Sometimes we experience a sense of shock as we move from one reality to another, as when we wake from a vivid dream or when the curtain comes down and the lights come on at the end of a theatrical performance. We are pitched back into the world of daily life ('What time is it?' or 'Where did I leave the car?').

Schutz was especially interested in the world of science, a finite province of meaning governed by scientific rationality and scepticism. Schutz highlighted a problem for sociology, which aspires to be a science of persons whose conduct is governed primarily by the natural attitude of daily life. There is a risk of scientific logics imposing a 'grid' that sifts and sorts only some of the relevant features of daily life. How can this issue be resolved? Schutz's solution was to propose a 'postulate of adequacy': 'Each term in a scientific model of human action must be constructed in such a way that a human act performed within the life world by an individual actor in the way indicated by the typical construct would be understandable for the actor himself as well as for his fellow-men' (Schutz 1953: 34). There ought to be a 'consistency' between social scientific constructs and those employed in common-sense experience.

A common difficulty for sociologists coming to phenomenology is that it sees human experience in egological terms, that is, from the point of view of the experiencing individual. While Schutz retains this broad frame of reference, his constitutive phenomenology of the natural attitude has two distinctive features that make it especially amenable to sociological concerns. One is the central role given to *common-sense knowledge of the social world*. Many ordinary actions are only possible because, as members of a culture, we use this recipe book-like knowledge in all our daily activities. The second is the notion of *intersubjectivity*. Much of human experience is not subjective and private but shared between people and groups. The shared character of common-sense knowledge and the intersubjective character of experience made Schutz's ideas congenial to sociological interests.

Schutz's ideas have been taken up in sociology in two main ways. One has been to incorporate Schutz into extant sociological theorizing in order to deepen its 'interpretive' aspect. This was achieved primarily through Peter Berger and Thomas Luckmann's (1966) influential book, *The Social Construction of Reality*, which demonstrates how a Schutzian account of the world of everyday life was compatible with interactionist sociologies as well as key elements of the classical sociological tradition of Marx, Durkheim and Weber.

The other, in many ways more radical, response was Garfinkel's attempt to work through the implications of Schutz for sociological theorizing and research.[1] From the mid-1950s Garfinkel began to examine the ramifications of a Schutzian position for the practice of sociological inquiry. Around this time he worked for a year with Aaron Cicourel (b. 1928), who was especially interested in problems of measurement in sociological research. Jointly and separately, Garfinkel and Cicourel developed a critique of conventional assumptions about the conduct of sociological research. At its core was the idea that the pervasiveness of the common-sense rationalities of the world of daily life significantly compromised the ambitions of sociological methods to scientific standing.

Ethnomethodology and research methods

From the first, EM was critical of many of the standard methods employed in conventional sociological research such as interviews, fixed-choice questionnaires, experimental designs and demographic methods (Filmer et al. 1972). Such methods were seen as problematic devices for accessing the point of view of the member of society. They embodied the sociologist's theoretical preconceptions, which might not match the attitudes, beliefs and cultural understandings of the persons whose social conduct he or she sought to investigate and understand. For example, a questionnaire may use terms such as 'childcare' that are understood differently by the researcher than the respondent, or it may ask a question – about, say, who is responsible for an aspect of childcare in a household – that obliges the respondent to answer in ways that he had not considered hitherto. In this way researchers can impose their own meanings on the activities whose features they are seeking to discover.

EM criticized sociology's claim to be at its most scientific when adopting quantitative methods. The general argument extends Schutz's contrast between the world of daily life and the world of science, and in particular his claims about the *postulate of adequacy*. This postulate maintained that the sociologist's constructs should be understandable to the social actors whose conduct they describe and explain. In other words, the sociologist's analytic constructs should be consistent with the constructs making up common-sense experience of actors. The EM critique of conventional social survey techniques, content analyses, demographic investigations and the like holds that use of these methods renders problematic any consonance between sociologists' and the members' constructs. Their use makes it difficult to provide any assurance that the postulate of adequacy has been met.

These arguments were first presented systematically in Aaron Cicourel's (1964) landmark book, *Method and Measurement in Sociology*. As a graduate student and beginning researcher, Cicourel developed an advanced knowledge of the mathematical bases of statistics (Witzel and Mey 2004: 10–16) and, from that vantage-point, his critique centres on the difficulties of establishing 'equivalence classes' in sociology (e.g. classifying people as 'Republicans' without knowing in detail the degree of their commitment to Republican beliefs). Cicourel (1964: 12, 28) claims that 'measurement by fiat' is occurring whenever sociologists determine that a given observational measure will act as an indicator of a theoretical concept. In other words, sociologists simply *presume* that, say, attendance at local party meetings or a donation to party funds can be used as an indicator of the concept 'political commitment'. Cicourel's point is that the connection may be quite arbitrary. It requires further investigation of the everyday life experiences of the people under study. Using a fixed-choice questionnaire, for example, demands determining the relationship of the questions to the kinds of common-sense cultural knowledge that respondents use. The upshot is that the empirical indicators of many sociological concepts may not measure what they claim to measure.

The central issue Cicourel raised concerned the validity of socio-logical concepts, given conventional sociology's accepted ways of working. The researcher's own common-sense knowledge and inter-actional skills derive not from professional sociological training but from the researcher's wider cultural competence as a member of society. This knowledge and these skills play an important if unac-knowledged role in sociological inquiry. Cicourel gives substance to Garfinkel's idea that 'professional sociological reasoning' is parasitic upon 'lay sociological reasoning' – that what the researcher 'knows' culturally and how this is manifested in their practical reasoning, conversational abilities, capacity to 'get on' with people, etc., play a vital but often overlooked role in empirical sociological research.

Cicourel (1964) can be thought of as a kind of 'proto-ethnometh-odology' (Lynch 1991), clearing the way for EM studies proper. It left an ambiguous legacy. Some of Cicourel's arguments seemed couched in a 'remedial register' while others adopted a more 'subver-sive register' (Lynch 1991: 84–6). At times Cicourel seems to write in a remedial voice, implying that attention to practical reasoning, common-sense knowledge and language use in everyday life would help to fix the problems identified with conventional sociological methods. At other times the tone was more subversive. Cicourel could be read as using a methodological critique to present a new *topic* for sociological investigation, the methods used to produce and recognize ordinary social actions. Conventional sociology conducted its investigations using this set of phenomena as an unacknowledged *resource*. EM would make the production and recognition of ordinary action its *topic* for investigation. Cicourel's own subsequent work pursued a course of research that he dubbed 'cognitive sociology' (Cicourel 1973), a development neighbouring EM but departing from it.

In many respects Cicourel's critique displayed a concern with issues of validity – the extent that sociological measures give a truth-

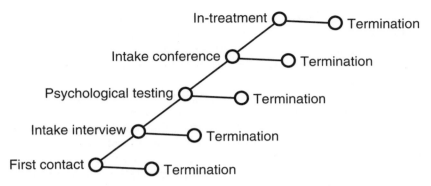

Figure 1   Career paths of patients of a psychiatric clinic
Source: Garfinkel ([1967] 1984: 19)

ful picture of reality or are commensurate with the research phenomena addressed (Witzel and Mey 2004) Garfinkel shared some
of Cicourel's general misgivings but extended his concerns into
questions usually linked to sociological interests in reliability – the
degree to which a method can generate the same results when the
same procedures are followed. This is evident in Garfinkel's ([1967]
1984: 18–24) study of how researchers follow coding instructions.
Garfinkel was involved in a research project that aimed to establish
the criteria by which people were selected for treatment at a psychiatric outpatient clinic. Patients could follow a variety of possible paths
following their first contact with the clinic. These 'careers' could be
schematically outlined in figure 1.

The project sought to discover the characteristics of patients, staff
and their interactions linked to each of the possible careers. Patient
files – some 1,582 folders completed by staff of the clinic – were
obtained as data. Two graduate students were asked to code the
information in the folders onto a coding sheet. The coders were
trained and given elaborate instructions about how to assign folder
information to a coding sheet entry in order to ensure that they were
proceeding in accord with accepted social scientific standards of reliability. Garfinkel found that, no matter how much explicit instruction the coders were given, they unavoidably used a variety of 'ad hoc
considerations' in order to secure a match between the contents of
the folder and an item on the coding sheet. These ad hoc considerations included notions of '*et cetera*', 'unless', 'let it pass' and '*factum
valet*' (where an action forbidden by a rule is allowed once it has been
done). Only by using such considerations could the coders make a

fit between the information in the folders and the headings on the coding sheet. What the coders were doing was using their 'common sense' to figure out the details of what was in the folder, how the clinic must operate and what necessarily follows, given what is stated in the folder.

Note that Garfinkel is not proposing that the coders were somehow being defective in carrying out the task of coding by using ad hoc considerations to do their work. Rather, Garfinkel emphasizes that the use of ad hoc considerations is *inevitable*, no matter how explicit the instructions given the coders. Following coding rules, indeed following any social rules, requires an interpretation of the immediate circumstances to ascertain the rule's relevance. Nor is Garfinkel suggesting that staff do not competently supply the 'right' kind of information in the folder. As he suggests elsewhere (Garfinkel [1967] 1984: 186–207), there are 'good organizational reasons' for clinic records that are, from a sociological research point of view, 'bad' – clinic folders are put together to contain information primarily relevant to the purposes of clinical work, not sociological research, and assemble that information in the practical circumstances of working with patients in the clinic. Still less is Garfinkel arguing that ad hoc considerations apply only to ambiguous cases. Rather, generic to the practice of coding is the use by the coder of their 'common-sense knowledge of social structures'. Coding practices are not simple objective exercises in matching folder information to a coding scheme's item but involve the coder in 'practical sociological reasoning' about both folder information and the rules of the coding scheme.

From Cicourel's early work, EM developed a suspicion of the many ways in which orthodox sociological techniques codified or classified ordinary actions in line with the second-order constructs of sociological theorizing. What emerged was a preference for observational research techniques and methods that represented ordinary action *in vivo*, notably documentary sources and audio and video recordings of everyday social actions. The methodological rationale for this research strategy was that there was no escape from mundane cultural competence and common-sense reasoning in inquiry, EM's included: 'We can recognize their effects but we cannot avoid their influence' (Cicourel [1968] 1976: xx). In seeking to make a topic out of the common-sense knowledge and capacities that other sociologies take for granted as a resource, ethnomethodologists typically reproduce portions of the data (transcripts of interviews, courtroom transactions, sketch maps and diagrams, photographs and the like) under analysis. The rationale for the display of data is transparency. By displaying the data on which EM analysis was founded, any questionable inferences can be challenged because the reader enjoys the same access to the data that the analyst has.

Exhibiting common-sense knowledge

Garfinkel enlisted the help of his students to carry out 'experiments' that would exhibit the existence of taken-for-granted aspects of everyday life. Some of these experiments involved disrupting everyday routines followed by students, their friends and families. In one experiment, students were asked to act as lodgers in their own homes. They behaved in a very circumspect and polite manner with their parents and siblings, only speaking when spoken to, using formal terms of address and courteously requesting if they could fix themselves a snack. The experiment proved very hard to sustain for any length of time. Very quickly other family members responded with 'astonishment, bewilderment, shock, anxiety, embarrassment, and anger, and with charges . . . that the student was mean, inconsiderate, selfish, nasty, or impolite' (Garfinkel [1967] 1984: 47). The taken-for-granted assumptions informing how the students should conduct themselves as family members were breached.

In another experiment, students were asked to demand literal interpretations of remarks occurring in casual conversation. This resulted in exchanges like the following:

Subject (S):   I had a flat tire
Experimenter (E): What do you mean, you had a flat tire?
She appeared momentarily stunned. Then she asked in a hostile way, 'What do you mean, "What do you mean?" A flat tire is a flat tire. That is what I meant. Nothing special. What a crazy question!'
(Garfinkel [1967] 1984: 42)

In another case the conversation unfolded as follows:

S: How are you?
E: How am I in regard to what? My health, my finance, my school work, my peace of mind, my . . .?
S: (red in the face and suddenly out of control) Look! I was just trying to be polite! Frankly I don't give a damn how you are.
(Garfinkel [1967] 1984: 42)

From these and other experiments Garfinkel concluded that the sanctions invoked against the experimenters indicated the profoundly moral character of common-sense knowledge and practical reasoning. Breaching these common understandings violates the trust that provides the deep-seated moral order underpinning everyday actions. More, the experiments suggested that understanding was not just a matching of the knowledge in people's heads but was a process, a procedure that depended on shared methods of making sense. 'I had a flat tire' and 'How are you?' did not simply prompt a meaning in E's head but were interpreted. What S said did not simply translate into what was meant. Instead it became a basis for questions that come to be inferred as 'puzzling', 'annoying' and the like. The disruption experiments point to a domain of members' methods for making activities intelligible. Understanding involves the mobilization of methods of sense-making. Members of society, Garfinkel suggests, are not to be characterized (as in so many social scientific models) as 'judgemental dopes'.[2] This can be seen also in the minority of cases of students acting as lodgers in their own homes, when the response from a family member was to answer ironically or in a jokey manner. And this is another lesson Garfinkel (1988) offers: there is no 'time out' from making sense.

The theme of no time out from making sense is a prominent feature of Garfinkel's case study of Agnes, a male-to-female transsexual. Agnes was brought up as a boy but when she met Garfinkel as a nineteen-year-old she bore the outward appearance of a young woman. Garfinkel's attention focuses on how Agnes succeeds in 'passing' as a woman. For Agnes her status as a woman is problematic – her gender identity is an 'enduring practical task', an 'achievement' (Garfinkel [1967] 1984: 118). 'Passing' refers to the 'socially structured conditions' within which 'the work of achieving and making secure her rights to live as a normal, natural female' occurs. The work of passing was a serious business for Agnes who needed to be constantly vigilant about 'the possibility of detection and ruin' (Garfinkel [1967] 1984: 118, 137). So, how did she manage to pass?

Garfinkel shows how Agnes was especially sensitive to all the 'normal appearances' associated with being a 'normal, natural female'. She engaged in a 'secret apprenticeship'. When her boyfriend's mother offered to show her how to cook Dutch food, Agnes was not simply learning about cooking Dutch food (or indeed cooking in general) but was also learning how to do small talk with another woman and how to express her feelings in typically feminine ways. Agnes was a 'practical methodologist' who learned the talk and conduct appropriate to her new gender within the occasions when she was expected to act in gender-specific ways. Garfinkel claimed that Agnes learnt to do gender identity 'on the job' as it were. She was skilled at withholding information and had a detailed awareness of what was expected in a wide range of everyday situations. She was also alert to the various contingencies to which these situations were vulnerable.

Garfinkel maintained that Agnes' passing practices could not be properly understood as if she was playing a 'game' or engaging in Goffmanesque 'impression management'. Both games theory and impression management interpretations of Agnes' passing practices assume a time-out period when Agnes can plan her strategies for an upcoming situation. This was a luxury Agnes did not have. Her passing was embedded in the practical circumstances that she had to deal with, moment by moment. Agnes' passing practices were improvized on the spot – but not out of nothing – with no time out. She was neither a strategist nor a cultural dope but a *practical methodologist* dealing with the practical circumstances she encountered in order to secure her gender identity.

The disruption experiments, as well as the natural disruption experiment represented by the case of Agnes, cleared a space for ethnomethodological investigations of situated practices – the ordinary activities people carried out in actual social settings. Garfinkel's project sought to develop a programme of investigations of situated conduct. He conceived of EM as an empirical not a theoretical enterprise, dedicated to observation and analysis. But this research programme required some general theoretical ideas, 'study recommendations', to guide analyses of situated practices. To this end Garfinkel ([1967] 1984) introduced the notions of members' methods, indexicality, accountability and reflexivity. These general notions built upon Schutz's work but went beyond it to open up the detailed empirical analysis of situated conduct.

Members' methods: the procedures and practices that people employ in order to recognize and produce ordinary social actions. Making sense is a process that involves the artful application of culturally appropriate members' methods.

Indexicality: for Garfinkel the meaning of everyday talk is thoroughly indexical, that is, dependent upon context. Who the speakers are, their relationship at this point in time, the knowledge they hold about the matter in hand, the unfolding interaction between the speakers, the tone in which the utterance is delivered, all shape the *actual* meaning of the words as understood by the speakers. The meaning of utterances cannot be established simply by consulting the standard or typical meanings contained in a dictionary. Members of society are not interested in such typical meanings. When asked 'do you have the time?' they do not engage in a philosophical inquiry about the range of potential meanings attached to these words. They simply inspect the details ('indexical particulars') of the situation and make appropriate sense of the remark as a request to be answered by looking at your watch or a request to be turned down when you look at your diary. (See Goffman 1981: 68–70 for an attempt to organize the possibilities of response to this question.) Members 'repair' or 'remedy' indexicality by application of practical reasoning about the indexical particulars observable in their immediate situation.

Accountability: how any action is recognized as the action it is – an insult as an insult and not a tease, for example. This very much depends upon the special sense that Garfinkel gives to the concept of *reflexivity*. Here Garfinkel suggests that contexts and their constituent actions are mutually constitutive. 'Here he is' can be heard as a 'sarcastic remark' when said by a member of a committee greeting its chair who arrives ten minutes late for the meeting he is chairing. The circumstance of the late arrival provides the context for greeting the chair sarcastically while the utterance, 'Here he is', is only understood as sarcasm because of the circumstance of late arrival. More simply, actions do not merely communicate information to others. In being enacted, they always accomplish something socially.

The concepts of members' methods, indexicality, accountability and reflexivity are designed to alert the investigator to ways in which the *details* of ordinary actions are socially situated aspects of ordinary conduct. How these ideas help promote EM sensitivities to their topic matter can be seen in the three studies by Dorothy Smith, D. Lawrence Wieder and Charles Goodwin discussed below. They each use different research methods and focus on very different questions. They provide an initial sketch of the diverse ways in which Garfinkel's orienting notions have been put into practice.

'K is mentally ill': members' methods for describing actions

Dorothy Smith's (1978) breakthrough paper, 'K is mentally ill', analyses a series of events that appear to show how a young woman slides into mental illness. The origins of the article are an undergraduate assignment that Smith set for a class she taught in the sociology of deviance. Students were asked to interview someone they knew who had direct acquaintance with mental illness. One student interviewed Angela, who had lived with K and considered herself K's friend. The student gave an oral presentation of her interview with Angela in one of Smith's classes. Smith recollected that as she heard Angela's story unfold she anticipated that K would end up coming to the attention of the professional psychiatric services, which is what did transpire. It was only when she read the typed-up version handed in afterwards that Smith began to see that the events described in Angela's account could be interpreted very differently. Instead of a narrative of increasing psychological problems, Smith became aware that it could be read as a story of exclusion, of K being cut out of relationships with her friends. Reading the account of the student's interview with Angela produced a classic figure–ground effect for Smith – a kind of *Gestalt* switch encountered in the reading that was quite different from the account that Smith previously only heard. This led Smith to examine the text of the interview more closely in order to understand how she could have arrived at such a different interpretation. Interpreting K's conduct as mental illness was by no means as secure as she previously thought. How then was it possible to understand the account in the first place as describing K's developing mental illness?

This question led Smith to look more closely at how the account was constructed. In the words of the article's subtitle, Smith investigates 'the anatomy of a factual account'. The facts that the student interviewer reports are not at issue. Rather, what Smith addresses is the question of how we know from reading this account that K is becoming mentally ill. To answer this question requires a dissection of the constituent components of the account. Smith presents the full written text of the interview with Angela. The text itemizes a series of events featuring K that seem 'odd' or 'bizarre'. Each line of the interview (which runs to 138 lines) is numbered to enable precise identification of relevant text for analysis. Smith's attention is directed towards how K's conduct is reported so that it is recognized in the way that it is. In Garfinkel's terms, how is K's conduct made 'accountable', i.e. recognizable for what it is as mentally ill-type conduct?

Mental illness as a form of deviance is ambiguous. In Scheff's (1966) conceptualization, it is best regarded as a form of 'residual deviance'. The criteria for many forms of deviance (e.g. shoplifting, speeding, lying) are relatively clear-cut. For mental illness, this is not the case. When people cannot describe deviant behaviours under any of the accepted terms for deviance, they infer that a person 'must be mad'. 'Mental illness' is the term we use to understand forms of conduct that cannot be comprehended under any of our standard terms for known types of deviance. It is 'residual' in that sense.

Smith draws attention to three important features of the account that drive us towards the interpretation that K is indeed mentally ill. First of all, Angela states that K 'was becoming mentally ill' very near the start of the account (line 17) and this assertion is not challenged in the remainder of the account. In this passage (lines 15–17), Angela works to establish her credentials as a good friend and reliable witness, claiming that she was the last of her close friends to admit that anything was wrong with K. The account confirms K's mental illness at the outset and preserves that understanding throughout its course.

Second, the account 'authorizes' Angela as the teller of the tale. Her account has to be treated as authoritative in the absence of any others. Her way of collecting events in the account is treated as an authoritative interpretation of what actually happened. Smith (1978: 36) notes that additional weight is given to Angela's account by its 'additive structure'. First, Angela alone notices that something is odd about K, then Angela and Trudi (the fellow flatmate of Angela and K) notice something is up, then Angela's mother is introduced as finding K's behaviour odd, then a friend of the girls sharing the flat notices. The structure of the account resembles the children's song, 'Old MacDonald's Farm' – the increasing numbers of persons introduced who notice something odd about K's behaviour serve to corroborate Angela's judgement about K's mental state.

A major feature of the account is the way it reports many of K's doings which, when taken out of context and seen in isolation, are not that unusual. However, as presented in the account told by Angela, these are reframed to seem odd or bizarre. Smith suggests that readers of the interview text employ certain devices (Garfinkel's members' methods) to make sense of the reported conduct of K as evidence of her mental illness. The generic members' method at work here is termed a 'contrast structure' by Smith. In its simplest form, the contrast structure consists of two parts. The first part sets the scene in such a way as to provide a context for the second part of the description. In this second part, readers are told what K actually did, which is at variance with the expectations of 'normal' conduct that the first part has established. Some examples of contrast structures in two parts are:

> When asked casually to help in a friend's garden, she went at it for hours, never stopping, barely looking up (lines 34–6)

She would take baths religiously every night and pin up her hair, but she would leave the bath dirty (79–81)

When something had gone radically wrong, obviously by her doing, she would blandly deny all knowledge (87–8) (Smith 1978: 39)

Some of the contrast structures have greater complexity. For example there are three-part contrast structures:

(i)   We would go to the pool or beach on a hot day
(ii) I would sort of dip in and just lie in the sun
(iii) while K insisted she had to swim 30 lengths (lines 21–3)

On this occasion, in order for K's behaviour to be understood as 'bizarre', it is necessary to precede the description of her behaviour with both (i) and (ii) – (i) on its own will not work. In addition, the phrase 'hot day' sets up an expectation of 'lazing behaviour', confirmed by Angela's statement in (ii). The imperative form and choice of words in 'K *insisted* she *had* to swim 30 lengths' also lend 'an obsessional cast' (Smith 1978: 44) to K's swimming behaviour.

Contrast structures are examples of the members' methods that Garfinkel suggests are used to produce and recognize ordinary actions, such as finding someone's conduct 'odd', 'incongruous', and perhaps evidence of a mental illness problem. Although it might be possible to query some of the characterizations in the account (e.g., in the three-part structure described above, the inference of mental illness-type behaviour is undercut by the earlier description in line 7 of K as 'so very athletic'), overall it is impossible to construct an alternative understanding that would allow all her reported conduct to be read as normal. There is nothing beyond the text to provide a resource for any alternative reading. Although based on only a single case there is reason to believe that any description of someone's behaviour as mentally ill would involve the use of contrast structures. Smith's work has thus proved especially relevant to sociologists who work with documentary sources.

Telling the convict code: Ethnomethodology as reflexive ethnography

D. Lawrence Wieder's (1974) study of a halfway house for paroled convicts in East Los Angeles shows some of the implications of ethnomethodology for conventional ethnographic analysis in the social sciences. The formal objectives of the halfway house were to provide work and a drug-free environment to help parolees develop a sense of responsibility and control over their lives. The changes in residents' conduct and outlook developed in the halfway house's therapeutic community would allow their successful integration into the wider community at the end of the parole period. The halfway house was not a success: only about 30 per cent of parolees left in the approved manner and moved into some form of independent living. The rest deserted the programme or were returned to jail.

Wieder quickly became aware of a 'convict code' that seemed to account for the distance that residents expressed towards staff and the lack of interest of residents in the formal goals and rehabilitative activities of the halfway house. This code could be expressed as a series of maxims or rules that residents seemed to follow – 'do not snitch' (inform), 'do not cop out' (do not admit that you have done anything illegal), 'help other residents', 'do not trust staff' and so on (Wieder 1974: 115–18). The existence of the convict code was not a new discovery on Wieder's part. Earlier studies of prisons, for example, demonstrated the compelling character of the convict code as a cultural force that could explain many aspects of inmate behaviour. Under the code, staff members were treated as the 'enemy', as part of the 'system', to be distrusted by inmates. Moreover, the code was a feature already known to both staff and residents of the halfway house. It was a Durkheimian social fact for them, external to residents and staff as individuals and constraining their conduct in specifiable ways. Staff used the code as a device to explain why residents would not sustain trusting relations with staff, or become fully involved in group activities in the house. Residents claimed that group therapy programmes were based on 'snitching, snivelling, and copping out' because they involved disclosing deviant aspects of their own life or other men's lives and thus, 'in their terms, a "good grouper" was likely to be a "kiss-ass"' (Wieder 1974: 137–8).

Criminologists often invoke the convict code to explain the failure of halfway house programmes like the one Wieder studied. The rules that make up the convict code are taken as the causes for the failure of residents to follow house rules, become involved in trusting relationships with staff, and so on. Residents' conduct is explained by interpreting it as governed by or following or conforming to or guided by rules. The existence of certain cultural rules seems to cause certain kinds of problematic conduct. But Wieder suggests that, instead of simply offering the code as an explanation for problematic conduct, it may be more ethnographically accurate and productive to examine how the code is actually used by residents and staff in the actual circumstances of life in the house. This tack allows Wieder to avoid the questionable notion that actions are in some way caused by rules (the convict code) and allows him to explore a more profitable line of inquiry: how residents and staff use the rules – how the 'code' figures in dealings that residents and staff have with one another, and with Wieder as a researcher.

Wieder examines the ways the code is 'told' by residents and by staff. The code worked first as a sense-making device, rendering many everyday actions accountable by giving an answer to the question, 'what's going on here?' Early in the fieldwork, Wieder asked residents to volunteer for an interview with him. They either answered in the negative or gave equivocal replies such as 'in a couple of hours' or 'tomorrow'. Not volunteering for anything was part of the code and the equivocal and negative responses were instances of the code being 'told'. As soon as residents were directed to be interviewed by Wieder, usually upon admission to the halfway house, they readily co-operated. Staff also made sense of a large number of actions – including being late for a committee meeting, ridiculing a parole agent, never siding with staff on any issue – as instances of displaying loyalty to other residents, a feature of the code.

Wieder also shows how the code works as a persuasive device. Invocations of the code made plain the moral character of the everyday actions within the halfway house. Apparently friendly conversations between staff, residents and Wieder could be terminated by the resident saying 'you know I won't snitch'. Wieder examines the reflexive aspects of this statement, which simultaneously conveyed information and crystallized some features of the encounter. First, they characterized what had just happened ("You asked me to snitch"). Second, they formulated a response to what happened ("I'm not going to snitch"). Third, they provided an account of the resident's motives ("The reason I'm not answering is because I won't snitch"). Fourth, they pointed to the relationship between the parties to the encounter (along the lines of "You are an agent of the state and I am a resident-parolee"). Within this frame, the phrase "You know I won't snitch" was consequential for the subsequent actions in the encounter. It negatively sanctioned the staff member or researcher. It succeeded in terminating a line of talk. It left staff ignorant about what might have been learned if the request or question had generated a full response. And it signalled the resident's unco-operativeness if the questioning continued. Residents could design their conduct in accord with the code, and staff would recognize this, just as surely as they recognized residents' departures from the code.

The convict code is not a cultural feature that floats freely above the ordinary activities of the halfway house, determining the character of those activities. It is not a set of rules that cause certain forms of conduct. Rather, it is a part of those activities and helps to make features of those activities observable – to staff, residents and researchers. The code is 'reflexive' in the ethnomethodological sense that it makes observable the activities it describes. Wieder shows how sociological description requires grounding in ordinary everyday activities. Wieder also provides a strong illustration of ethnomethodological notions about rule use. The actions of residents and staff cannot be properly understood as caused by the rules of the convict code. They are not cultural dopes. The rule is interpreted on each and every occasion of its use. The model advanced by ethnomethodology is that members as *users* of rules invoke and interpret those rules in light of the practical circumstances they encounter.

Professional vision: The accountability of working knowledge

Ethnomethodology has been interested in detailed studies of working practices (Garfinkel 1986; Rouncefield and Tolmie 2011), often guided by Garfinkel's (2002) 'unique adequacy' requirement – that the investigator be proficient in the occupational practices analysed. Occupations, from bricklaying to brain surgery, tend to develop their own specialist bodies of skill and knowledge. Often, a particular way of seeing the world is associated with each body of skill and knowledge. The idea that shared specialist knowledge provides the basis for specialized ways of looking lies at the heart of Charles Goodwin's (1994) influential concept of 'professional vision'.

The notion of 'professional vision' was designed to show how all occupational specialists work within the accepted ways of seeing licensed by their professional domain (Goodwin 1994). Goodwin examined how field archaeologists and lawyers draw upon occupationally specific ways of seeing in order to accomplish their professional work. In particular, he proposed that: 'Discursive practices are used by members of a profession to shape events in the domains subject to their professional scrutiny. The shaping process creates objects of knowledge that become the insignia of a profession's craft: the theories, artifacts and bodies of expertise that distinguish it from other professions' (Goodwin 1994: 606).

Goodwin examined how a profession's craft is embodied in its routine practices with especial reference to the visual dimensions of that work. To investigate the professional vision of archaeologists and lawyers, Goodwin principally drew upon videotaped data of archaeological field schools in Argentina and the USA, and videotapes of the first Rodney King trial. Videotape preserved both participants' talk and body movements, rendering them amenable to repeated, detailed scrutiny. Recorded talk in particular was amenable to transcription (CA systems of notation – see chapter 3 of this book – have become the standard in EM). Goodwin's analysis focused upon three practices in each of his two settings: (1) the 'coding schemes' used to transform features of a setting into objects of profession-relevant discourse; (2) the 'highlighting' practices used to mark as significant certain specific phenomena in the setting; and (3) the production and articulation of graphic representations.

In the case of archaeological fieldwork, Goodwin shows how students are taught to use Munsell colour charts as coding schemes to identify systematically the colour of the dirt they are digging in to find artefacts. Munsell colour charts resemble the paint charts found in decorator's stores, except that they have a small hole next to each colour so that the chart can be laid over the dirt in order to get an accurate match of colours. Highlighting in the field is often done by the trowel work of archaeologists, who use their trowels to mark lines in the ground to identify features of interest such as moulds of posts that may once have supported a house. Archaeologists also produce sketches, maps and diagrams that are graphic representations of features of archaeological relevance. Their production is a collaborative and sometimes contested endeavour.

The element of contestation was much more pronounced in lawyers' work. The novel move Goodwin then made was to suggest that the same framework of coding, highlighting and graphic representation can be used to illuminate the trial of Rodney King, the African-American motorist filmed by an amateur photographer apparently being violently beaten by four Los Angeles police officers in 1991. But did the film depict King as a 'victim of an assault' or a 'suspect resisting apprehension by law enforcement officers'? Goodwin provided a detailed analysis of how King's conduct was coded by the officers' defence lawyers as aggressive, his body movements minutely highlighted and pointed to as indicative of incipient violence, so that the amateur video of the beating could come to be seen as a representation of 'police craftwork' in dealing with an 'aggressive offender'. This reading of the film, in which a police version of professional vision was accepted in court, allowed three of the officers to be acquitted of wrongdoing at the first trial.

At a later Federal trial, two officers were found guilty of assault. Here the prosecution succeeded in reinterpreting the film so that what were previously seen as displays of incipient aggression were now seen as the normal physical reactions of a man reacting to a beating. Both versions (police craftwork in managing an aggressor / a set of physiologically normal reactions to a beating) are made accountable by the situated actions of lawyers and their agents in court. They talk to the court, show the film, slow and stop it while they point to specific elements of what is shown in the frame, all the time giving a spoken and gestural commentary that glosses what is happening 'for all practical purposes'. As evidence, the film is mute. It needs to be interpreted through the professional knowledge and professional vision of the parties contesting the case in court.

Goodwin developed his analysis of professional vision with close attention to stills and videos of archaeological fieldwork and the trial as shown on TV. He made the now standard EM observation that the use of videotaped data rendered his analysis open to ready checking and challenge by other researchers. In conclusion, Goodwin (1994: 628) emphasized that professional vision is not merely a frame of mind or mental set. Professional vision is made manifest through people's embodied, situated practices, and it is through these practices that something as apparently subjective as ways of seeing can be accessed for analysis. The practices themselves require processes of learning, whether in archaeology field school or police and legal training. He also suggested that professional vision could be seen as part of the workings of professional power, especially if power is understood in the Foucauldian sense of discourses that articulate the conditions of rationality in a society and the kinds of talk that can and cannot be heard. In this way, Goodwin points to some ways in which EM can deepen and enrich the understandings provided by other social scientific perspectives.

Conclusion

This chapter has attempted to trace the origins of EM and set out some of its characteristic concerns as a distinctive form of sociological practice. It emerged from primarily European interests in interpretive sociology and phenomenology. In this respect, its origins are quite separate from those of symbolic interactionism, which, as the previous chapter has shown, is a sociological outworking of the US pragmatist tradition of philosophy. Ethnomethodology itself provided a major impetus for the third major sociology of interaction treated in this book, conversation analysis (CA). Sometimes the term 'speech ethnomethodology' is used to describe CA to indicate its close affinity to EM's concerns. In other respects CA departs from the basic premises of EM, especially in its attempts to generate a formal analytic sociology that presents findings that are 'context-free' yet 'context-sensitive' (Sacks et al. 1974). Garfinkel, especially in his later work (e.g. Garfinkel 2002), rejected such formalizing ambitions and reaffirmed the phenomenological roots of EM.

EM attracted much criticism from more traditional forms of sociology. EM neglects power, it is said, or it overlooks structure in its preoccupation with situated social practices. EM has its own answers to these complaints. Power can be traced through situated practices as we saw in Goodwin's work on professional vision (see chapter 5). Power's workings are often only one of many things that are taking place when ordinary actions are studied up close. It cannot be given any special analytic privilege. Similarly, social structure need not be accepted in the conventional way as an institutional framework somehow divorced from the situated sense-making work of society's members, but can be construed as 'what happened previously'. In this model, any situation's 'context' is primarily determined by what preceded it – a previous turn at talk, noticing something novel, etc. – rather than by anything 'external'. How the connection is forged between the micro and macro levels of analysis and how the relationship between agency and structure is best conceptualized have animated much theoretical and methodological debate (e.g., Giddens 1979; Knorr-Cetina and Cicourel 1981) in part stimulated by EM studies.

For some critics, EM is somehow misguided because it fails to challenge and correct the beliefs embedded in common sense. Much traditional sociology sees common-sense beliefs as sources of prejudice and ideology that need to be challenged and corrected by the findings of a more objective social science. EM sees common sense and practical reasoning as something to be understood and their workings analysed in order to show how they are used to bring out the orderliness of people's activities. EM, to borrow from Wittgenstein, leaves everything just as it is. It does not propose solutions or remedies, for good reason. The precept of 'ethnomethodological indifference' demands the analysis of situated actions be conducted 'while abstaining from all judgements of their adequacy, value, importance, necessity, practicality, success, or consequentiality' (Garfinkel and Sacks 1970: 345). It is a form of methodological bracketing designed to focus analytic attention on the operative structures of practical reasoning. That is not to say that EM studies are irrelevant to problem solving. It is to recognize, as Weber did long ago, that the application of research findings to practical problems involves drawing on values that are not themselves part of the research process and which belong to the wider world, not just the researcher.

As subsequent chapters of this book will indicate, EM has become an influential perspective within contemporary sociology that has spawned many innovative empirical studies. Its distinctiveness derived from Garfinkel's resolute faith in Durkheim's injunction to explain the social socially by attempting 'to pursue communicative actions all the way down to their constitutive details' (Lynch 2011).

3

Conversation Analysis and the Interaction Order

Introduction

Innovators in the analysis of everyday spoken interaction: Sacks and Goffman

Harvey Sacks and Erving Goffman are two (perhaps *the* two) iconic figures in the sociological study of spoken interaction. Both focused on the systematic analysis of face-to-face interaction, and spoken interaction lay at the heart of their concerns. Harvey Sacks was the founder of what is commonly termed conversation analysis (often abbreviated as CA). Famously, in one of his lectures he told his students 'I invented it' (Sacks 1992b: 549). Such a grand claim was not without foundation as, before Sacks' lectures and early publications, naturally occurring conversation was, in effect, unexplored and unanalysed by sociologists. Equally unique was what Goffman (1983b) – in a posthumously delivered overview – referred to as the Interaction Order. Over the course of his short career (he died at the age of forty), Sacks published relatively little. Indeed, Sacks' greatest body of 'published' work today is his posthumously published lectures, edited and introduced in two substantial volumes by his close co-workers Gail Jefferson and Emanuel Schegloff (Sacks 1992a, b). Goffman left a more diverse and readily-accessible body of work. Although differing in their approaches and methodology (see the end of this chapter), both shared some key concerns and based their work on key propositions about ordinary, everyday, spoken interaction and, to varying degrees, identities in talk. This chapter will examine some of these issues.

Both Sacks and Goffman saw language as a central system of communication, and of culture: communication in that speakers communicate ideas and meaning and achieve shared understanding and intersubjectivity through spoken interaction, and culture in that particular types of activities (e.g. greeting, teasing, telling stories, giving accounts) can get recognizably and normatively done this way. Although considering talk in a range of settings and contexts, naturally occurring, ordinary, everyday conversation was regarded by both as the primordial means in and through which members of society communicate and engage in a range of routine, mundane everyday activities.

Rather than seeing ordinary, everyday conversation as 'messy' and chaotic, both Goffman and Sacks saw it as fundamentally 'orderly' – it demonstrated, for Sacks (1984a: 22), 'order at all points'. If and when 'disorderliness' does arise in spoken interaction (as we shall see below, Sacks and Goffman had different interpretations of this) this is routinely repaired or remedied in and through ordinary everyday spoken interaction. This everyday orderliness does not just 'happen', but relies on persons' collaborative actions and practical skills. First and foremost, Sacks and Goffman saw the maintenance of orderliness as being based in reciprocal collaboration and close co-ordination of activities – it was an interactional accomplishment. However, this was shown to require a high level of competence on the part of persons involved in interactional encounters. Indeed, for both Sacks and Goffman, competence meant being able not just to construct meaningful utterances, but to take account of co-participants in conversation in doing so, to monitor closely co-participants' actions, to reply to them quickly at appropriate points in the talk, to respond in appropriately expressive ways as spoken interaction unfolded and even to use such competences to exploit spoken interaction. Indeed, as we shall see below, such competences can be shown to operate from a very young age and are a key part of becoming a 'useable' member of society.

Finally, both Sacks and Goffman demonstrated how identities were played out in and through, and impacted on, spoken interaction. As we shall see below, this can be illustrated in many ways from how conversational expectations underpin inferences about identities, how persons are invariably 'accountable' for their spoken actions, through the explicit use of identity typification and categorization in and through talk, to how situated or occasioned identities can be seen to apply.

The tenets of conversation analysis were not just plucked out of the air, but were heavily influenced by and rooted in the intellectual contexts in which Sacks (and Goffman) worked. Whilst the two learned much from each other, concerns with practical competence, the achievement of intersubjectivity, expressive moves and ritual can be traced to scholars such as Schutz (1962, 1964), Garfinkel ([1967] 1984), Wittgenstein ([1958] 1968) and Durkheim (1915). For conversation analysis, the influences of ethnomethodology, Schutz and Wittgenstein have been fundamental.

Ethnomethodology and conversational orderliness

You will recall that a central idea put forward by ethnomethodologists was that social actions are mostly not explicit, but 'glossed'. The vast majority of the time we don't 'say' (in so many words) what we are doing, or even engage in unnecessarily elaborate actions. Rather, we tend to gloss over sets of actions and expect others to 'figure out' what it is we are doing. To this extent, intention and meaning are routinely implicitly encoded rather than explicitly revealed.

We noted earlier that Garfinkel ([1967] 1984) identified three key features of social action. First was the notion of *indexicality* – that is, the meaning of any action can only be derived from the context of its use. For this reason, actions are usually designed, in some way, to 'point to' – and make available for other persons – those particular aspects of context that are needed to correctly interpret and understand any given action. In that sense, social actions contain the 'contextual DNA', so to speak, that is necessary for their meaningful interpretation. In this way, social actions are designed to be interpretable by those to whom they are directed, or by those who may witness them. Second, not only are social actions indexical, but they possess the quality of *reflexivity* – that is, they not only encode context, but have the capacity to change it. In this way, social actions can bring into being context, and, context can be 'done' and re-done. Doing this allows participants in social interaction to continually change or update the context in and through their ongoing, real-time, social actions. Finally, because social actions are taken to be intentionally motivated and designed things, they are *accountable* things – that is, not only are they 'recognisable and describable', but when they are made – or, alternatively, when they are omitted – some conclusion may be drawn about what it is the person who performed those actions, or not, is actually 'doing'. Moreover, persons can be, in effect, 'held to account' for their actions or omission thereof (see, for example, Garfinkel's ([1967] 1984) 'breaching experiments' discussed in chapter 2). These features point to what Garfinkel termed the documentary method of interpretation – that is, social action *documents* – or is read as an example of – some wider underlying, recognizable, pattern of action. Documentary interpretation underpins the practical accomplishment of mundane activity and, as we shall see over the following pages, these features of social actions can be seen to operate at the level of conversational organization, from individual turn design, through placement and timing of turns and the organization of particular types of conversational sequences, to the management of whole conversational episodes.

Schutz, intersubjectivity and conversation

As noted in chapter 2, Schutz's concern was with the nature and accomplishment of shared experience – of intersubjectivity – and how members of society could come into one another's presence and achieve (at least, for all 'practical' purposes) a 'reciprocity of perspectives'. Again, this requirement places inferential and interpretative demands on social actors and carries with it some degree of risk. As Heritage succinctly puts it:

> The task of fellow-actors . . . is necessarily one of *inferring* from a fragment of the other's conduct and its context what the other's project is, or is likely to be. Thus any fellow-actor's inferences about what some other is 'up to' are inevitably contingent and tend to be subject to revision and adjustment 'after the event' . . . [The] co-actor must thus 'take chances' in responding on the basis of an interpretation of the other's action'. (Heritage 1984: 60–1)

The successful achievement of intersubjectivity is greatly aided by what Schutz saw as '*typical* sequences and relations' of actions (Schutz 1964: 80). As part of everyday reality, social actors come into one another's presence with a shared stock of knowledge about these actions, sequences and relations. Moreover, this knowledge can be and is routinely conveyed via a shared vernacular language – what Schutz saw as 'the typifying medium par excellence' (Schutz 1962: 14). In this way, intersubjectivity is achieved in and through 'typified' and 'typifying' everyday vernacular language. Schutz's ideas influenced the development of conversation analysis in many ways, offering suggestive leads about how we achieve intersubjectivity in and through naturally occurring conversation, how we must – and do – routinely take chances in our interpretations of conversational actions (and have those interpretations revealed as accurate or not), what happens if our interpretations are revealed to be inaccurate or faulty, and, generally, how we use and recognize typical conversational categories, actions and sequences of actions.

Wittgenstein, language games, and meaning

Both Schutz and Garfinkel have been discussed in greater detail in preceding chapters. However, another figure to have a salient impact on Sacks, and to a lesser extent on Goffman, was the Austrian-born philosopher Ludwig Wittgenstein. Wittgenstein's ([1958] 1968) seminal text *Philosophical Investigations* presented a fresh and original approach to how philosophers and linguists had attempted to tackle the problem of meaning and truth in language. Linguists from de Saussure to Chomsky perceived ordinary, everyday language as, in effect, too messy to be studied for meaning or 'truth'. For Wittgenstein, the answer to understanding language lay in looking at precisely that – to ordinary language and its actual use in everyday contexts. To illustrate this Wittgenstein drew on the idea of 'language games', which constitute much of what we actually do with language in everyday life. Such games are routine ordinary collective actions achieved in part in and through spoken ordinary language and can include such things as *describing, reporting, speculating, storytelling, joking, play-acting, asking, greeting, cursing* and so on ([1958] 1968: para. 23) – in fact, all the things people do in actual, ordinary, everyday conversation (paras. 107, 108). By definition, the meaning of any utterance can only be understood in the context of the particular language game in which participants are involving themselves. The meaning is in no small part related not simply to the ideational content of the specific words uttered, but to the part any utterance is playing in any given language game – to its meaning as some kind of 'move' (para 22). Again, moves are essentially indexical in nature, i.e., don't say in as many words what they are saying, so to speak. For example, to 'assert' something (a move) is to say that such-and-such a case without actually *saying* 'such-and-such is the case' as a spoken sentence (para. 22). Although there are countless ways in which words and sentences can be used to make moves in various language games – indeed, countless language games that persons may engage in – Wittgenstein pointed to regular and routinized ways of doing talk – to *customs* (uses, institutions) (para. 199) that cultural members recognize and collaboratively orient to when engaging in the various language games that mark everyday life (as in the examples above). However, although he did recognize the existence of rules as a type of 'sign post' to guide persons in language use, Wittgenstein also pointed to the fact that not all uses of language could be explained in terms of rules, and that language could also be used in a flexible and spontaneous way. This pointed to a certain indeterminacy in ordinary language use: 'We can easily imagine people amusing themselves in a field by playing with a ball so as to start various existing games, but playing many without finishing them and in between throwing the ball aimlessly into the air, chasing one another with the ball and bombarding one another for a joke and so on' (para. 83). Thus, what might appear to be a 'ball-game' following definite rules may in fact contain much indeterminacy, aborting of particular aspects of the game, and switching between one aspect and the other (e.g. serious game and 'messing around'). Finally, in engaging in language games and doing so both in accordance with regularities recognized by others and in a way that allows for the indeterminate and essentially unfolding nature of meaning and moves, persons demonstrated some mastery of practice and technique (paras. 199, 202) – some practical competence.

The ramifications of Wittgenstein's perspective on understanding language formed part of the movement referred to as the *linguistic turn* and fed into various developing approaches to analysing everyday talk such as Speech Act theory (Austin 1962; Searle 1969) and Pragmatics (Grice 1975), both of which would later influence Politeness theory (Brown and Levinson 1987) and the examination of the concept of 'face' (Goffman 1967) as a guiding feature of spoken interaction (see below). The influence on the study of spoken interaction was significant in that it not only recognized the primacy of ordinary language, but focused on its use-in-context as being fundamental to interpreting its meaning.

Conversational systematics

Turn-taking and turn-allocation

The starting point for understanding how conversational orderliness is achieved was outlined in a seminal paper entitled 'A simplest systematics for the organization of turn-taking for conversation' (Sacks et al. 1974). In this paper, Sacks and colleagues outlined some features of conversational organization that were blatantly obvious, but until that point 'hidden due to their mundaneness'. First, *turn-taking occurs in conversation*; second, *one speaker tends to talk at a time*; and finally, *turns are taken with as little gap or overlap as possible*. These may appear to be the most mundane and 'obvious' of observations and hardly worthy of mention. However, they form the bedrock of conversational orderliness. Breaching, being ignorant of or lacking the competence to follow these basic requirements of conversational organization can cause considerable problems for the transmission of meaning, achievement of intersubjectivity and completion of a myriad of social actions and practical tasks and, as we shall discuss shortly, can carry quite serious implications for identity.

These three requirements for orderly conversation require both finely tuned and closely co-ordinated conversational actions. One of the features of and demands placed on any given conversation is that these requirements are demonstrably oriented to, and one of the hallmarks of a 'competent conversationalist' is the capacity not only to to modify his/her conversational behaviour in line with these requirements, but to work closely and collaboratively with co-conversationalists who can be expected to be conversing similarly. This co-ordinated collaborative orderliness is evident when one considers turn 'distribution' and 'allocation'. The name given by Sacks and colleagues to those points in conversation where speaker change can occur was 'transition-relevance place'. Two basic rules operate at such points in conversation:

> Rule 1:- a) If the current speaker has selected another speaker, then that speaker should take the next turn at talk; b) if no such selection has been made, then any next speaker may (but need not) self-select at that point; c) if no next speaker has been selected, then alternatively the current speaker may (but need not) continue talking with another turn-constructional unit, unless another speaker has self-selected, in which case that speaker gains the right to the turn.
> Rule 2:- Whichever option has operated, then rules 1(a)–(c) come into play again for the next transition-relevance place.
> (Derived from Hutchby and Wooffitt 2008: 51)

Of course, what Sacks and colleagues pointed out here were not invariant 'laws', but rather institutionalized rules. Orientation to these rules is a routine feature of orderly conversation and, as we shall see below, allows us to produce typical sequences of action with our co-conversationalists. Moreover, again as we shall discuss below, we often quite consciously find ourselves under normative pressure to abide by these rules not only for the sake of maintaining conversational orderliness but to, for example, avoid appearing bullish, aggressive or even rude to our fellow-conversationalists. Certainly, the 'serial interrupter' is the sort of person who might be conveniently 'overlooked' in invitation lists on many a social occasion (you may be able to think of examples from your own experience here!).

Alternatively, the conversationally inept may find themselves, more often than not, 'not getting the chance' to speak.

Conversational looseness and normative overlap

Although ordinary conversation is orderly, it is not a rigid and 'pre-fabricated' turn-taking and turn-allocation system. It is a 'machinery' used to facilitate the purposes of conversationalists. We do not find ourselves talking like robots, or as if we were reading from a script. We do find often, for example, that at transition-relevance places 'overlap' occurs. Indeed, the mere existence of such normative rules (minimizing gaps between turns and attempting to self-select) means that infraction will inevitably occur in conversations. However, whilst the frequent overlap between turns at talk may suggest the conversational propensity for disorder, the manner, timing and sequencing with which it is conversationally attended to and the length of its duration, in fact, reveal a high propensity to order.

As Hutchby and Wooffitt note: 'While it may seem that overlapping talk is disorderly . . . both the onset and termination of overlap are indeed extremely *orderly*. In fact, the occurrence of overlap is one prime way in which we can observe participants orienting to the rules of turn-taking' (Hutchby and Wooffitt 2008: 54; emphasis added).

Several studies (Jefferson 1986; Schegloff 2000) have revealed how 'tries for the floor' (attempts to get a turn at talk) are left until possible transition-relevance places, or quickly terminated if another conversationalist 'beats us to' the following turn at talk. Although we routinely display our awareness of these conversational rules, we often have somewhat competing obligations to make utterances as and when talk is underway by other persons, 'mid-turn' so to speak. Again, conversational murmurings uttered as turns are 'in progress' are not signs of disorder, but of more co-ordinated and normative conversational actions. Indeed, we often 'look to others' for such overlapping utterances. What are referred to as 'acknowledgement tokens' (Jefferson 1984a) or 'continuers' (see Schegloff 1982) are examples of this. These utterances include "hm mm", "uh huh", "yeah", "awe", "right", "really", "wow" and the like, as well as a range of 'non-lexical' utterances like intakes of breath, splutters, sniggers and titters and, of course, laughter (see also our discussion of Goffman below). Such utterances do much to show not only our interest in whatever a fellow conversationalist is saying, but also our reception of and general aliveness to it, and do much to signal positive interpersonal relations between us and the current speaker.

Turn formulation: recipient design and occasioned usage

Within this organizational framework for ordinary talk we have the job of generating – of 'constructing' – actual turns. Although there is no similarly 'formalized' set of rules for 'what' we say as there is for 'when' we say it (or at least, when we might 'utter'), there are still normative obligations and expectations guiding our turn-constructional behaviour. The point here is that turns are not randomly put-together pieces of information, but are 'designed', to quite a sophisticated level. Now a 'turn' at talk is quite a loose notion – we all know what one is in practical terms, but it is difficult to suggest that a turn should be this or that length, should contain this or that content, should include one or several propositions, etc. Indeed, as we have just seen, there are many things we 'utter' (and 'splutter') in conversation that might not be regarded as real turns at all, depending on when we utter them or what particular 'noises' we make. We may take very long or very short turns, we may utter things that can't really be described as 'words' as such (like grunts, breathy noises and other non-lexical utterances) and, of course, laughter is a frequent feature of conversation. All these things 'count' for conversation analysts though, as they feature in the way we design, respond to and co-ordinate our utterances and conversational actions.

One important feature of turns as formulated and designed units is that they are constructed for our co-conversationalists. Turns (and all conversational utterances to some extent) are 'recipient designed', that is, designed in a way that makes them appropriate, relevant, economical and intelligible for whomever we are engaged in conversation with. As with orientation to turn-taking rules, there is a normative expectation and obligation on the part of conversationalists to factor recipient design into their turns as part and parcel of doing conversational orderliness. Not only are turns designed for the ears of our recipients, but they are often 'occasioned' – that is, they are constructed out of items that are relevant to the there-and-then requirements of the conversation. One risk of looking at or listening to turns 'out of context' is that they may not only misrepresent the meaning, but also be quite unintelligible. Again, this is due to the indexical nature of turns – that is, they point to some context but often do not explicitly reveal it. Thus, in the following dialogue (Sacks 1992a: 17 April lecture), the occasioned use of information only makes sense once the context of the talk is known (see below for the answer!):

A: I have a 14 year old son
B: That's fine
A: I also have a dog
B: I'm sorry

Monitoring, projectability and anticipation

Although the content of a turn is not prescribed in advance and conversation develops in an indeterminate fashion, conversationalists
work routinely to, to some extent, try to 'predict', or at least anticipate, the future of talk, or at least the immediate future of a turn. To
achieve this end conversational turns are closely monitored by our co-
conversationalists. This combination of design and monitoring gives
conversational turns some degree of 'projectability', that is, we can
(try to) anticipate to some extent what is imminently about to happen
with them. This ability to project and anticipate – at least, take a cal-
culated conversational risk at doing so (see our earlier discussion of
Schutz in chapter 2) – allows us to, at the level of turn organization for
example, attempt to self-select in time to secure the next turn at talk
or even minimize the gap between turns in conversation if we can hear
their imminent completion 'coming up'. Projectability also allows for
conversational actions based on the content of particular turns. For
example, if we can hear some unfavourable turn being designed (e.g.
a 'criticism' of us), we may decide to conversationally act to 'stave
off' such a turn – to nip it in the conversational bud, so to speak. This
predictive reading of turns has a significant set of consequences for
how issues such as identity and 'face' (Goffman 1967) are managed
in conversation (see below). Indeed, as we shall discuss shortly, not
only those in receipt of such turns but also those producing them can
orient to this projective quality by modifying 'turns in progress'.

Of course, in conversation, what is anticipated is not always a
correct interpretation – we may grasp the wrong end of the stick
before it's even thrown, so to speak. Fortunately, whatever we have
made of (or anticipated about) any turn tends to be apparent, or
evident, in the following 'next' turn. This points to a key feature of
turns, that is, they contain within them not only a prospective dimension (i.e. what it is they are about to or intend to do), but also a retrospective one – that is, any turn contains within it the 'understanding'
and interpretation of the immediately preceding one.

These features and qualities in no small part impact on how turns
are sequentially organized.

Conversational sequence

The sequential foundation of everyday conversation: adjacency pairs

The concept of 'adjacency pair' points to 'a fundamental ordering principle of conversation' (Heritage 1984: 261). Adjacency pairs are fundamental to understanding conversational orderliness, in terms of turn design, sequential organization, intersubjectivity, normative organization, and how potential implications for identities arise and are managed in and through conversation. The term refers to normative 'paired actions' that routinely occur in conversation – that is, two conversational turn types that conventionally 'fit' together. Moreover, these are sequentially linked – that is, when one is heard, the second one is listened for. A given conversationalist will do something with his/her conversational turn, and another will do something in his/her *next turn* at talk as a result of and in normative response to this first turn. Examples are found throughout conversational encounters. For example, most encounters begin with some form of mutual greeting (Schegloff 1968), or 'access ritual' (Goffman 1981) ("hello"–"hello"). Likewise, conversations are normatively terminated with similar paired turns ("bye"–"bye") (Schegloff and Sacks 1974). Within any given conversation various adjacency pairs are found (indeed, conversations may consist wholly of such paired utterances) (Schegloff 1972). Examples might include questions and answers (from simple "How are you?" – "Fine" / "And you?" – "Fine"- type interchanges to more extended Q–A sequences); assessments of places, people, objects, experiences, etc., and 'second' assessments in response to these; invitations and subsequent acceptances/declinations; offers and acceptances/refusals; compliments and responses to them, or alternatively criticisms and their responses; accusations and admissions/denials, etc.

It is apparent from this feature of ordinary conversation that turn design and its monitoring, projectability and interpretation is as much guided by sequence as it is by recipient design and occasioned usage. Adjacency pairs can be used to sequence turns across larger stretches of talk, as they are expanded or chained, or one is inserted into another, as in the following example.

Mother: Do you know who's going to that meeting?
Russ: Who?
Mother: I don't know
Russ: Oh::h Prob'ly Mr Murphy . . .
                                      (Terasaki 1976: 45; abridged)

This short interchange exhibits what is known as an 'insertion sequence', with one Q–A inserted into another one. As might be apparent from this example, adjacency pairs are central not only to sequential organization, but to the emergent interpretation of meaning and achievement of intersubjectivity. We noted in the previous section that turns display and are monitored for the understanding a speaker has of the immediately preceding one. Here we can see that, via the use of adjacency pairs, both misunderstanding is evident and the two speakers are able to 'repair' (Schegloff 1992b) this understanding, and thereby achieve intersubjectivity (shared understanding). This is done quickly, economically and inferentially. Thus, sequence and intersubjectivity are intimately related, and adjacency pairs are crucial to their orderly achievement.

Perhaps not surprisingly, there is a powerful normative set of expectations around adjacency pairs. That is, when a person utters some 'first-pair part' (makes an invitation, for example), a relevant 'second pair part' is not simply invited but becomes 'conditionally relevant' (Schegloff 1968) in the next turn. That is, responses to questions, assessments, invitations and the like are expected (and to some extent 'waited for'). Conversationalists monitor next turns to see if they are, in the first instance, forthcoming. If they are not, a 'noticeable absence' (Schegloff 1972) can be heard to have occurred – that is, something conversationally hasn't happened, or doesn't seem to be happening, that should have/be. Sequentially, such absences can mean that unanswered greetings, questions, invitations, offers and the like are 'pursued' (repeated until the relevant second pair part is forthcoming). However, as importantly, conversationalists not only monitor such turns for the understanding they display of our preceding turns (e.g. whether our turn has been interpreted as a declaration of knowledge or a request for information; see Schegloff and Sacks 1974: 240) or their absence/presence, but for the particular conversational actions they can be heard to be performing in response to our turns. We noted above the projectability of turns. This plays no small part in the interpretation of such adjacent utterances. Thus, we often 'know' whether or not, for example, an invitation is going to be accepted or rejected before any such rejection has occurred.

Preference organization

Turns are often deliberately recipient-designed in such a way as to allow their recipients to draw such inferences from them, in terms of not only their content but also their sequential placement and timing.

This has as much to do with identity concerns as it does intersubjectivity and normative sequencing. The phenomenon of 'preference organization' nicely illustrates this. Rather than, as the term might imply, referring to personal preference for how to, for example, design or sequence one's turns (a predilection to formulate lengthy and verbose turns, or take one's time by leaving lengthy pauses), the term rather refers to the '. . . sequence and turn organizational features of conversation' (Schegloff et al. 1977: 362n4). That is, conversation as a system displays certain preferential features.

We've described conversation as 'orderly'. However, sometimes 'troubles' occur, and these require some sort of reparative work if conversation is to proceed in an orderly and meaningful fashion and intersubjectivity is to be sustained. The phenomenon of preference organization allows us to understand this. Schegloff et al. (1977) showed that, after some 'trouble' has occurred in a particular turn (e.g. some factual error has been made or there has been some articulatory problem on the part of a speaker), conversationalists work collaboratively and sequentially to attend to and correct that trouble so that meaningful conversation can continue. For example, if a speaker wants to convey some idea, relay some fact or draw on some information in his/her turn, he/she may find that he/she has some difficulty doing so (finding him-/her-self fishing for names that are 'on the tip of the tongue', getting this or that fact wrong, or simply having difficulty getting one's words 'out' are examples of this). Such troubles set a sequence of turns in place, which conversationalists use to get the necessary repair work done. What tends to happen is that, if such a troublesome turn is in the process of being formulated, recipients of this particular turn will hang back on their possible self-selection and 'allow' the owner of that turn to repair any trouble with it him/herself. Thus, speakers struggling to find names will be allowed to find them, those making factual errors allowed to recognize their error and correct it themselves, etc. If, after the completing of a turn, some trouble with it is apparent, recipients of that turn, again, rather than immediately self-selecting to correct some hearable error, tend to hold off their turn, extending the transition-relevance place (see above), thereby giving a speaker a chance to 'hear' that extension, infer that something is not quite right because of it, realize their mistake and initiate and complete the repair themselves (for example, realizing they have just said something wrong and correcting it). If an owner of such a 'trouble source turn' does not take the conversational opportunity to initiate and complete repair at these extended transition-relevance places, a recipient may take the opportunity to

point out the error in some way. However, this tends to be done indirectly and, importantly, involves the recipient of this trouble source
turn simply initiating repair (simply pointing to the trouble) rather
than completing it (actually correcting the error). The 'floor' is then
given back to the original speaker to correct the error in his/her next
turn (this being the third turn in the sequence). A remaining option is
for the recipient of a trouble source turn to both initiate and complete
the repair (both point out the error and correct it), but this tends to
be the conversationally dispreferred option.

What these observations show is that there exists in conversation
a preference for self-correction, evident in the way that recipients of
problematic turns both formulate their turns (often indirect forms
of correction) and sequentially organize them (held off and delayed)
(see also Schegloff 1992b).

The features of 'dispreferred' actions (delay, indirectness, etc.),
together with converse features of what are referred to by conversation analysts as 'preferred' actions (immediacy of response and direct-
ness of turns), are seen in a range of other actions. We mentioned
above some particular examples of first-pair part actions and the
second-pair parts they make conditionally relevant, or 'invite'. For
example, assessments invite agreement or disagreement with those
assessments, invitations invite acceptances or declinations of those
invitations, and self-deprecations invite agreement or disagreement
with those self-deprecations. In conversation, those conditionally
relevant second pair parts tend to be routinely produced in particular
ways depending on what action they are performing in relation to
whatever action invited them (e.g. agreement turns are *done* differently from disagreement turns, acceptances of invitations are done
differently from declinations, and agreements with self-deprecations
differently from disagreements with such self-deprecations). There is,
for example, a strong preference for *agreement* in conversation (Sacks
1987), with turns that disagree with some proposition or assumption in the preceding turn being produced in similar ways to 'other'
corrections noted above (held off, indirect and with any explicit
disagreement being delayed within the turn itself and often prefaced
by some other 'component' like "Well" or "I don't know" which
effectively 'signals' an imminent disagreement). Disagreements can
even be initially 'shaped' to sound like agreements. For example, if
you and I were having a conversation about this section of the book
(which, for the sake of argument, you didn't understand) and I asked
"Does that make sense?", the conversational likelihood is that you
would say something like "Yeah it does yeah, well, I mean, it's a bit

confusing so, not 100%", and so on). Conversely, agreements tend to take on features that signal their preferred status (done quickly, directly and explicitly). The same is true of *responses to assessments* (Pomerantz 1984). Turns containing an assessment of some referent ('the weather', 'food being eaten in a restaurant', 'next door's dog') in effect invite a second assessment of the same referent by the recipient of those initial assessments. Similar assessments tend to be conversationally preferred and, indeed, are often 'upgraded' (for example, I may say "It's a nice day" and you might reply with "It's absolutely gorgeous"). Differing or contradictory assessments on the other hand tend to be delayed, with less explicitness, and are often prefaced by 'weak agreements' and the like. Another frequent set of conversational actions that has been shown to be guided by preference organization is how *invitations* and *requests* are made and conversationally handled (Drew 1984). One way of 'indirectly' rejecting an invitation, for example, is by 'reporting' – "I'm washing my hair that night" being an archetypal example of rejection by use of report. Acceptances require no such elaboration or 'beating around the bush'.

The notions of monitoring and projectability discussed above also feature here. For example, when making a range of actions such as *invitations, offers, requests* or *proposals* (Davidson 1984), speakers may recognize elements of a dispreferred turn such as delay, weak agreement or other signs of rejection or refusal such as as "well", "uh", "erm" and the like as fellow-conversationalists are responding to them and, anticipating a rejection or refusal may reformulate invitations, offers, requests invitation, etc. – redesign the turn – with an orientation to obtaining agreement or compliance or, alternatively, back-tracking and discreetly retracting them (indeed, we are often given a way out of having to take rejection by co-conversationalists' willingness to 'give us a hint' as to what sort of action is coming up in the way they design their turn in a dispreferred fashion).

An interesting exception to this rule is seen in responses made by other conversationalists following instances of our *self-deprecations* (negative assessments of self). In such sequences, the preference is in effect, reversed, with conversationalists ensuring they are quick and direct to disagree with any self-depreciative remarks made by speakers. A second apparent exception (or at least one which is more conversationally difficult to handle) is responses by conversationalists to *compliments* that might have been made to them in the preceding turn (Pomerantz 1978). In such situations, conversationalists are stuck between disagreeing with such assessments and a general rule of 'self-praise avoidance'. What happens is that speakers tend to produce turns that tactfully accept the compliment but quite clearly avoid 'blowing their own trumpet' or 'milking the compliment', so to speak.

Although, then, preference organization refers to institutionalized features of turn design and sequence, an intuitive reading of these features points also to interpersonal concerns (i.e. not wanting our co-conversationalists to feel offended, embarrassed, etc.), and ultimately identity issues. As Heritage, along with several others working in the field of conversation analysis, has pointed out:

> Preference organization must be related strongly to concerns with face . . . Although preference organization resides in the conversation and not within the individuals who produce it, it seems likely that the origin of such an institutional design is the rudimentary requirement of respect (i.e. face) that must be accorded all interactants if a conversation is to occur at all . . . face-work is probably the major goal underlying preference organization. (Holtgraves 1992: 148)

We discuss this in more detail later in this chapter, when we look at ritual features of conversation orderliness.

Sequential collaboration in everyday talk: topic talk and storytelling

For conversation analysts, the sequential organization seen in adjacency pairs and preference organization can be seen to underpin all aspects of conversation, from opening moments of talk, through what might be treated as the 'main' body of the conversation, to the closing phases and ultimate termination of conversation.

For example, when involved in conversational encounters, persons orient to some common topic – something which requires their shared conversational focus and collaborative actions (Button and Casey 1984, 1985). Again, the way topics are handled reveals the features of sequential organization and turn formulation discussed above. Often (at least in Anglo-American culture) topic talk features some element of storytelling – some relaying of personal (or vicarious) experience (see the discussion of the Interaction Order below). An examination of how stories are handled reveals some interesting features about how this is achieved. Stories can be, for example, offered, invited, pursued or even refused. Routinely, persons intending to tell stories use various prefaces and pre-sequences in order to attempt to open up the conversational space to tell the story. Recipients of such turns (hearing them as such) can choose to respond favourably. Sequentially, knowing that stories need some time to get told, this involves giving the conversational floor to storytellers and bringing about what is, in effect, the temporary suspension of transition-relevance places discussed above (i.e. agreeing not to self-select for the 'hearable' duration of the story). Alternatively, of course, recipients may choose not to adopt such a receptive position towards a potential storyteller and (by, for example, themselves changing the topic), deny storytellers the space needed to tell stories. Usually, in order to be heard as such, stories are required and expected to have some aspect of 'tellability' or 'newsworthiness' to them, alongside some 'relevance' for their recipient(s). To this end, speakers work not only to carve the required extended turn, but also to 'align' their recipients as not only recipients but 'relevant' recipients – that is, recipients who have some interest or 'stake' in what they are being told. This allows us to understand how the same event can be told in different ways, according to the recipient it is aimed at.

As with many other turns at talking, stories are then 'occasioned', that is, they are formulated to fit the current context of telling (see Jefferson 1978). Once underway, recipients conventionally use utterances not to attempt to self-select, but to in effect fuel the developing story. Thus 'continuers' ("mmhm", "uh huh" and the like, mentioned above) are used, which not only encourage continuation of stories but also signal the relevance to the recipient and show his/her involvement. Studies have also revealed how even expression of amusement (endemic to Anglo-American conversation) in the form of laughter, although seemingly random and spontaneous (see our discussion of sociable conversation in chapter 8), is sequentially organized (Jefferson 1979, 1984b). Of course, stories must have some conclusion or climax, and speakers work to ensure that recipients are aware of what this climax might look like, indeed, recipients may be aligned so as to be able to, to some extent, 'project' and 'predict' the conclusion or climactic point of the story (see above). Just as speaker change occurs (see above), so storyteller may change, leading to talk characterized by second, third, etc., stories. Again, these are sequentially 'linked' together in the process of doing everyday conversation.

All this is achieved in the way that storytellers pitch for, tell and conclude stories, and the way in which recipients accept overtures for stories and are subsequently aligned to enable them to correctly interpret, appreciate and to some extent project why the stories are being told (even though they can be expected not to have heard the tale before).

Conversation and identity

'Membership': mastery and accountability

Conversational orderliness is achieved then, in and through our ability and willingness to abide by culturally recognizable sequential requirements and normative expectations. Indeed, much of how we are perceived not only as conversationalists, but as persons, relies on the collaborative part we play in the maintenance of this orderliness, and our accountability if we are demonstrably unable or unwilling to do so. In this sense, 'membership' of a group, culture or society can be equated with a demonstrable and accountable 'mastery of natural language' (Garfinkel and Sacks 1970). Indeed, although young children are given some leeway in terms of their ability to engage in 'adult' interaction and forgiven for 'cute mistakes', these conversational competences are in fact demonstrated from a young age (see Sacks 1972 b). Moreover, these assumptions of competence and accountability run throughout all conversational encounters, from their initiation (Schegloff 1968) to their termination (Schegloff and Sacks 1974), and at all points in between.

Of course, we are all susceptible to causing conversation 'troubles'. For example, as the work on repair outlined above has shown, the type of momentary conversational 'incompetence' or 'incapacity' evident in 'trouble source turns' is not usually heard as some fundamental failing or fault with the speaker, but as a routine feature of turn formulation. Indeed, attempts to, for example, construct a meaningful, factually valid, recipient designed, occasioned and coherent turn by false starting, word-searching and self-correcting is itself actually a demonstration of one's competence in formulating such turns. However, if such troubles might seem to point to more serious issues with competence, conversational resources are available for us to draw on to account for them. For example, perturbations in openings can be accounted for and legitimized by reference to, for example, having some other issue that is interfering with one's ability to reciprocate at that point in a conditionally relevant way ("sorry, what did you say, I didn't catch that?"). At the other 'end' of conversationally encounters, one cannot suddenly and abruptly end talk with a "bye"–"bye" type adjacency pair 'mid-conversation', or terminate a conversation by just stopping talking. Rather, conversationalists build up to an ending by closing down topics of talk, perhaps agreeing a plan of action such as meeting again, exchanging "OK"s and "good"s before getting to the closing of the conversation proper. In other words, such terminal exchanges must be sequentially arrived at by opening up and moving through closing phases over a series of turns (Schegloff and Sacks 1974). Failure to run through such phases can be accounted for by "Oh, sorry, is that the time, I must dash . . . bye"-type accounts, etc. Within conversation, structurally, breaches of the turn-taking system can be accounted for with "sorry, I don't mean to interrupt" when seeking to self-select away from transition-relevance places, or "sorry, I've not finished yet", etc., when not yet ready to relinquish the floor. Noticeable absences, which, as we have seen in the previous section can be extremely inferentially rich as regards identity concerns and interpersonal relations, can be similarly accounted for ("sorry, I'm not ignoring you"). As has been implied throughout the preceding discussion, as conversations are developed, in general a turn's talk will be heard as directed to a prior turn's talk '. . . unless special techniques are used to locate some other talk to which it is directed' (Sacks et al. 1974: 728). So, utterances such as "by the way", "Oh I must tell you this", "Sorry to change the topic" or even utterances such as "Oh. . .", which point to some possible 'disjunct' between the preceding talk and the turn in progress, might account for our apparent flouting of the sequential expectations regarding coherent topic talk, etc. (see Jefferson 1978). Even unexpected outbursts of laughter may require some type of explanation, not only due to their sequential placement, but for the inferences these may lead to about persons laughing – or, alternatively, being 'laughed at' or 'about' – in conversation. Many of these conversational actions and accounts allow us to answer the "Why that now?" question – or, in the case of noticeable absences, "Why not that now?" – that may arise and any implications for our competences that may arise in this.

As we shall discuss below, competence and accountability are important as they signal not only one's mastery of natural language but also one's moral integrity. This issue has perhaps wider implications for identity in conversation as morality is often drawn on during, or implied by, conversational typification of persons. Although the notions of competence and accountability may lead to implications for identity in talk, the issue of identity and typification is more explicitly examined in the study of what conversation analysts refer to as 'membership categorization'.

Typing others and self: membership categories

Membership categorization points to the fact that in conversation we are constantly 'selecting' various ways in which to describe people – ourselves, our co-conversationalists or absent third parties. Although we may be referring to particular individuals, our reference to them often involves the use of various social 'typifications'. We do this not only to provide factual classification (describing someone as belonging to this or the other category of persons), but to imply certain things about persons. The range of categories we may draw on is virtually limitless – woman, lawyer, scorpion, Christian, football fan, octogenarian, marathon runner, conservative, etc. (all of which *could* actually be used to describe one and the same person, depending on what we wanted to say about them). In order to work, such categories have to be culturally recognizable (as those listed above are to English-speaking cultures) and our fellow-conversationalists need to know something 'about' them and, quite often, the relationship between any two or more categories that might be used to refer to two or more persons (see Schutz 1962, 1964). With this shared awareness and understanding in place, membership categorization becomes an extremely economical and *inferentially rich* way to invoke identities in conversation and say many things, in not so many words. Consider the following, oft-cited example (see Sacks 1972b):

"The baby cried the mommy picked it up".

This short account makes sense for several reasons. First, it contains two recognizable *membership categories* – a baby and a mommy. Second, these two categories seem to naturally go together in some normative relationship (much like husband–wife, employer–employee, doctor–patient, lecturer–student, etc.): they form a *standard relational pair* (SRP), and there is nothing unusual to be 'read into' having them drawn upon together, in the same utterance, to describe the same scene. Next, we know what type of things each category might be expected to do. This includes, for babies, crying, and for mommies, picking babies up. In short, we know about *category-bound activities*. This not only includes normative ways of behaving, but also obligations, rights, attitudes and morals associated with each category. Thus, mommies also feed, nurture and protect babies from harm etc. and there is nothing unusual about the mommy picking the baby up in this reported scene. In fact, there is a certain expectation and moral obligation that she do this, when in the presence of a crying baby. Finally, although not drawn upon, daddies, grandmas and brothers and sisters could have also been invoked without any problem of interpretation as to *why* (these) now, each of these additional categories belonging to the wider *membership categorization device* (essentially a conversational way of clustering several categories together) of 'the family'. This is why we 'hear' the crying baby to be the baby of the mommy who picked it up.

Thus, the story makes sense – and has been designed (in this case by a small child) to make sense – because of the identities selected, the relationship between them, and their reported actions. As importantly, given the inferential richness of these (and all) membership categories, we can easily see how their selection and juxtaposition can be used to 'say' a lot about the identities of the person to whom they are applied. In the above account, for example, the mommy appears to have been a 'good', 'responsible', 'alert', etc., mommy. However, report that she *didn't* pick the baby up when it was crying, or that it cried *after* she had picked it up, and the story and its implications about her *as a mommy* (indeed also about the baby) would be quite different. Moreover, select another category for the same individual (not mommy but 'social worker', 'child abuser', 'drunk') and the implication for both identities (e.g. child abuser and abused child) and the scene as a whole could change quite dramatically.

Membership categories are not only applied to stories about absent others, but are routinely claimed, ascribed, accepted, contested, negotiated, disavowed and ignored as part of everyday face-to-face conversation. Whenever we introduce ourselves on the telephone or in face-to-face encounters, for example, we are selecting some membership category (and therefore claim some *social identity*) that we assume our fellow conversationalist will find meaningful and interpretable, and be prepared to appropriately respond to (announcing yourself as 'Dr' or 'Prof' rather than plain old 'Mr'/'Mrs' results in strikingly contrasting responses, whether in telephone calls to call centres or when buying plants at the local garden centre!). We may (in fact, in Anglo-American conversation often do) tell stories about ourselves and in doing so select various categories to describe ourselves and others. We may also have categories ascribed in the immediacy of face-to-face encounters by co-conversationalists (which we can choose to accept, contest or negotiate – "You're being too kind, I'm not really a good pianist").

As well as influencing our own and others' identities, membership categories can be used to signal solidarity with, distance from, or even power over or subservience to, others. This needn't be done explicitly, but can be achieved through more implicit reference to various membership categories.

We often tread very carefully with the membership categories we select to describe ourselves or others, because of this inferential richness and the implication they may make about a person's identity. Indeed, because of a shared awareness of various activities and the categories they might be normatively 'bound' to, in conversation we often let our fellow-conversationalists infer what categories we are indexing by simply referring to those activities (and beliefs, attitudes, morals, etc.). Thus, our fellow-conversationalists are left to figure out what we are 'getting at' based on the 'categorical' information we are giving them about ourselves, them or third parties (see, e.g., Smith 1978). Of course, the beauty of such unspoken but indexed categorization is the deniability of it if challenged – "Oh no, I wasn't saying *that*" may be an easily acceptable account, even if everyone knows that that is exactly what you were saying. The wider notion of membership categorization device mentioned above also allows such implicature and inference (sometimes unintentionally!), as, if a particular category is invoked, subsequent persons may be 'heard' as belonging to *that* device. Thus, talking about the CEO of an organization 'in the same breath' as Adolf Hitler or Pol Pot (membership categorization device of 'ruthless megalomaniac dictators') might lead fellow-conversationalists to infer the category we are assigning to the CEO, draw somewhat negative assumptions about his/her management style and impute a less than desirable identity.

Finally, although there is some argument that there are such things as 'natural' categories (which 'mean' the same thing in all contexts – a rapist is a rapist no matter when, where or how that category is used to describe a particular individual), as we have suggested throughout this chapter, many commentators agree that the implications that categories carry are heavily influenced by the conversational context. Thus, for example, a teacher might, in effect, claim the category of a *teacher* in a classroom not by repeatedly proclaiming "I am the teacher", or wearing a badge to that effect, but by her category-bound activity in that context – for example, the manner in which she exploits adjacency pairs by asking the question and giving the directives, with the children answering the questions when asked and following those directives when issued. However, the same teacher, if talking to one of the parents in a similar manner might be responded to with "Just hold on a minute, you're not talking to *a child* now you know". Likewise, when reporting some event, the utterance "He's in his *40s*" when referring to some third party may mean one thing to describe this or that person in the context of topic talk about suitable candidates for the promotion at work and quite another when describing someone riding a skateboard through a town centre; again, the meaning – and implications about identity – would seem to be best understood as lying in the occasioned usage.

This contextualized use of categories also points to the fact that, even though there are some clearly recognizable category devices (e.g. 'the family' as above), talk often places seemingly unrelated categories together, to the point that their meaning can be almost incomprehensible without having access to the context of their use. Thus, in the example we left you with earlier, although having a fourteen-year-old son and being a dog owner may appear categorically unconnected, the context of their use, however, reveals that they both belong, at that point in talk, to the device 'possible disqualifiers for renting a room'!

Although seemingly ripe for exploitation in the study of identities in interactions, conversation analysis has somewhat neglected the study of membership categorization following an early interest in the work of Sacks, although ethnomethodologists have recently taken an interest in the issue (see, e.g., Hester and Eglin 1997).

Institutional identities

We have talked in large part about how identities can be related to competence and categorization. However, since the 1990s a series of studies have looked at institutions, identities and how the latter are occasioned in interactions. Institutional identities and interactions have been examined in a range of fields, such as medicine, education, business, the media and specialized encounters such as emergency service calls (Heritage and Clayman 2010: 1). These studies have sought to understand how spoken interaction is used in the context of these organizations, to deploy institutional identities, arrive at some shared definition of institutional encounters, settings and contexts, and get organizational work done and objectives achieved (from cross-questioning in court – see chapter 7 – to doctor–patient encounters). Heritage and Clayman (2010: 34) outline some features of interaction involving institutional identities: first, the interaction normally involves participants in specific goal orientations which are tied to their institution-relevant identities; second, interaction involves special constraints on what will be treated as allowable contributions to the business at hand; and third, interaction is associated with inferential frameworks and procedures that are particular to specific institutional contexts (Heritage and Clayman 2010: 34). Some of these issues will be dealt with in subsequent chapters.

Conversational forms, frames and footing

Conversation as moves

We have so far looked at issues of the technical requirements of conversation, turn design and sequencing, and how these allow for the maintenance of intersubjectivity, demonstrable competence of natural language, the indexing of identity, and ultimately conversational orderliness. These technical systematics and institutionalized features have their expressive, dramatic, performative and ritualistic corollaries in what we termed earlier the Interaction Order. This approach to understanding spoken interaction – developed by Erving Goffman – involves a re-specification of some of the central notions underlying the conversation analytic approach, which, when read as a unified approach provide an arguably richer – and some might say more human – heuristic for the analysis of ordinary conversation.

Central to the discussion of conversation so far has been the notion of 'turn'. However, Goffman (1981) displayed a preference for the broader notion of 'move'. Echoing Wittgenstein's conceptualization discussed above, Goffman saw 'moves' as essentially expressive acts that may be part of whatever 'game' conversationalists are involved in. From this perspective, conversation progresses not in the first instance as the sequencing of conversational turns, but as the 'interplay' or 'meshing' of 'moves' (Goffman 1981).

Goffman pointed out some general features of move formulation and their interplay that raised some apparent limitations for the sequential focus of conversation analysis. For example, in terms of their relationship to turns, moves can be equivalent to turns, may stretch over several turns, or any given turn may contain several moves. In terms of their sequential relevance, although moves can in effect invite other responsive moves, this need not be in the sequential 'next' move but can reach beyond the immediacy of that point in talk, or even that particular conversation (for example, when we provide an account in response to a complaint, not at the time of the complaint, but in some subsequent talk). Indeed, some moves are made that have no 'sequential consequentiality' (e.g. momentary self-talk during a conversation), and some responses come to moves that have never actually been made conversationally (e.g. a conversational response to a 'glance'). Another observation pointed to assumptions about – and in effect problematized – the idea of recipient design. For example, although moves may be directed at addressed 'ratified' others, unaddressed others, bystanders, eavesdroppers or even the speaker him/herself can be the recipient of (and respond to) any given move. Echoing notions of indexicality and documentary methods of interpretation seen in conversation analysis work, Goffman also recognized that, rather than containing within them all available information for their interpretation and understanding, moves often operated on the basis of innuendo, tacit understanding and collusion. Thus, through the formulation, interplay and interpretation of moves, participants in spoken interaction achieve a level of shared understanding that allows them to inhabit a shared 'mental world' (see Goffman 1983a). As we shall see, this allows conversationalists to achieve understanding and intersubjectivity not only for all practical, but also for all 'dramatic' and 'ritual', purposes.

Conversational footings and participation frameworks

Goffman problematized not only the notion of turn (assumptions about formulation and sequencing), but also what he saw as the 'crude' (Goffman 1981) notions of 'speaker' and 'hearer', which had underpinned much communication theory and were implicitly foundational to conversation analysis work. In his (1981) discussion of 'footing', Goffman showed how conversation is routinely characterized by multiple roles that speakers adopt and different statuses that hearers can have in relation to any given utterance, at any given moment, in any given conversation. These roles and statuses are routinely *aligned* in the collaborative doing of ordinary conversation, or 'fresh talk' as Goffman called it, and provide the 'structural underpinnings' (Goffman 1981) of such talk.

The notion of 'footing' refers not to utterance construction per se in terms of the meaning of the turn, but rather to stances speakers take towards their utterance (the speaker's *relationship* to the words spoken). Bearing this in mind, any utterance can be analysed for its 'production format'. For example, firstly, when formulating a turn at talk, whatever is being said is inevitably attributed to some source, '. . . someone whose position is established . . . someone whose beliefs have been told, someone who is committed to what the words say' (Goffman 1981: 144–5). Goffman called such a source a 'principal'. A principal in conversation can of course be that person speaking – i.e. that person is expressing his or her own, personal views, etc. It can also of course be someone other than the speaker, as in when we are simply telling others what some other (usually absent) person (whom the others may or may not know) has said, claimed, expressed, etc. Secondly, speakers' actual words are attributed or attributable to some 'author', that is, some source of the actual words, verbatim, as they are spoken. So, for example, if we paraphrase what an absent third party has said, we are the author whilst that person remains the principal, unless of course we are also claiming those beliefs, in which case we may adopt the footing of author and principal. Drawing on these two roles in the production of utterances gives a high degree of flexibility for speakers. For example, if I say "I blame the credit crisis on the bankers", I can be assumed to be both principal (what I believe) and author (these are my words); "A friend of mine blames it all on the bankers" would make my friend principal but I would remain as author; and "A friend of mine calls this 'the banker's botch-up'" would make me neither necessarily principal nor (as I'm directly and verbatim quoting my friend's phrase) author. In conversational reality, speakers are constantly changing footing and may do so several times in the process of one conversational 'turn at bat'.

In respect of the notion of hearer, or recipient, Goffman used the concept of 'participation status' to refer to any given person's relationship to any particular production format of any given conversational move. Perhaps more accurately, 'every' person in the situation in which any given move is made enjoys some participation status in it. Indeed, moves 'project' these statuses:

> In thus introducing the name or capacity in which he speaks, the speaker goes some distance in establishing a corresponding reciprocal basis of identification for those to whom this stand-taking is addressed. To a degree then, to select the capacity in which we are to be active is to select (or attempt to select) the capacity in which the recipients of our action are present. (Goffman 1981: 145)

The central idea is that anyone co-present in the social situation in which conversation is occurring has some status, even if it is 'overhearer' or 'eavesdropper'. That status will determine how, and whether, any co-present person responds to any utterance's production format. Again, utterances are constantly monitored but, in this sense, not only for their meaning or the understanding they display, but for the roles they project (for both speaker and other participants), and participants make deft changes in footing as talk progresses. In this sense, footing is a collaborative interactive activity in the way participants in spoken interaction 'manage the production or reception of an utterance . . . participants over the course of their speaking constantly change their footing, these changes being a persistent feature of natural talk' (Goffman 1981: 128).

This wider consideration of spoken interaction brings in not only a myriad of possibilities as to who can be treated as being 'involved' in spoken interaction (and to what extent) but also the centrality of spoken interaction to the social encounter, situation and wider gathering in which that talk occurs. Thus, the focus extends to include what might be regarded as a 'situated contextuality' as well as a conversational one.

Conversational frames and performative drama

Goffman saw much of informal conversation as being not so much about the conveying of information, as about the *replaying* of experience. As we have noted above, informal conversation is full of stories and narratives about past, present or planned experiences and activities. Goffman argued that, in this sense, conversational moves allow for the formulation of various 'scenes'. To this end, what speakers call for from co-conversationalists, and monitor their conversational moves for, is not so much understanding in a substantive or factual sense, but such things as sympathy, approval, exoneration, amusement, appreciation and the like – signs that recipients show that indicate not so much that they have been informed, as that they have been in some way 'stirred' (all the things an audience to a staged performance would be expected to exhibit). This is a dramatic interpretation of the kind of phenomenon we termed 'normative overlap' above. Unsurprisingly then, Goffman's discussion treats speakers as akin to performers, and recipients as audiences. There are, Goffman argued, 'deep-seated' similarities between the structure of the theatre and the structure of informal conversation (Goffman 1974: 550).

Opening up the dramaturgical metaphor to understand spoken interaction as producing shared mental worlds, combined with a recognition of expressive moves and issues around changes in footing provides for a powerful and deeply layered analytical framework. In his work on the frame analysis of talk, Goffman showed how speakers use a range of 'framing' strategies and techniques to, in effect, 'signal' to co-conversationalists the nature of what is being replayed or performed, and how it should be interpreted. For example, conversation can move from serious to humorous frames in and through speakers' expressive stances. More sophisticated techniques include 'keying', and 'laminations', referring to the way in conversation we often engage in mimicry, mockery and role-play to pretend we are doing something we 'really' aren't (proclaiming "This bridge is now opened" at the dinner table) or pretending to be somebody we really aren't (in this case, the Queen of England).

Such framings are essential parts of conversational performances. Likewise, we can speak as ourselves, but do so in a way that signals it's not really us speaking at all, by talking in a sarcastically joking or teasing manner, for example. Co-conversationalists usually recognize such activities (although speakers can employ what Goffman referred to as 'fabrications' and temporarily fool co-conversationalists into believing something is happening that really isn't). If and when there is some ambiguity as to what a particular speaker is doing, brackets such as "just kidding" or "but seriously" can be used to explicitly account for misinterpreted or unrecognized framing activities.

As might be expected then, such conversational possibilities open up significant scope for, indeed allow us to view in a new light, the notion of identity in informal conversation in a way that is much more multi-faceted, multi-layered and dramatically and expressively manifest than, for example, membership categories. Key to understanding identity is the notion of 'embedding' in informal conversation. This refers to the fact that, in replaying scenes, speakers must invoke and place in those scenes various 'figures' (persons past, present, real or imagined). Such figures can (as in the case of solely personal experiences), but need not, be the actual speakers themselves. Thus, reporting as part of some dramatic scene that "Lucy laughed at John screaming at the spider" clearly invokes two figures (three if the spider is accorded equal status in the scene) who are not the speaker yet nevertheless have been cited and whose actions (albeit non-lexical – see above) are part of then current / now replayed talk. All this gives speakers considerable conversational licence in identity work in spoken interaction. One aspect is that we may use such replayings to attempt to present cherished identities – those with some recognizable positive traits or qualities. Another is that we may be able to 'distance' ourselves from some less positive identity. As Goffman noted, any embedded figure is, fundamentally, '. . . a protagonist in a *described* scene, a "character" in an anecdote, someone, after all, who belongs to the world that is spoken about, not the world in which the speaking occurs' (Goffman 1981: 147). What this gives us the ability to do is cite ourselves as in some way 'detached' from our current speaking self, referring to '. . .what we did, wanted, thought, etc., at some distant time and place, when, incidentally, we were active in . . . an identity we no longer claim . . . if we happen to be recounting a tale of something that happened many years ago, when we were a person we consider we no longer are' (148–9). This of course gives us some flexibility in how we can disassociate ourselves from or disavow past, potentially then-deviant/now-damaging identities (see chapter 7).

Recipients – as audiences of this talk – allow and encourage unfolding replaying to proceed through the various alignments that are required or projected. For example, at a general level, suspension of disbelief is often a requirement of conversational replayings, as might be feigned ignorance if this or that particular scene has been 'seen' once already. More specifically, utterance types such as 'tickets' (Sacks quoted in Goffman 1974: 508), 'back-channels' (Goffman 1974: 509) and appreciative 'whoops', 'gollies' and 'gee-whizzes' can allow speakers to hold the floor, encourage them to further develop their conversational scenes, and display that the scene is indeed stirring.

This all points towards ordinary conversation as a mutually supportive system, in which conversationalists seem to have as much of a hand – and stake – in dramatically presenting and supporting identity claims as they do in effectively communicating ideas and conveying factual information.

Conversation as ritual interaction

Remedial interchanges

As well as its expressive, dramaturgical and presentational features, Goffman regarded spoken interaction as having important ritual functions – indeed, had as one of its conditions ritual considerateness. The influence of Durkheim (1915) on Goffman's approach to spoken interaction can be clearly seen in his discussion of remedial and supportive interchanges. Durkheim distinguished between *positive* rituals and *negative* rituals: the former are marked by the paying of homage to some deity; the latter by avoidance of violation of the sacred rights and domain of such deities. Goffman showed how these rituals can be seen to operate as part of routine, everyday conversation and to be closely organized as part of conversational activity – as interpersonal rituals.

Goffman's notion of *remedial interchange*, for example, is based on shared cultural norms and the expectations about conduct of persons in contact with other persons, and the moral responsibility to recognize them, that regulate public life. Although not confined to spoken interaction, the formulation and sequential organization of utterances are a fundamental feature of this regulatory activity. As with the omni-present risk of causing some conversational trouble (see e.g. Schegloff et al. 1977), when involved in spoken interaction participants are at risk of causing some *ritual trouble* – that is, in some way violating a range of personal 'preserves' (Goffman 1972) that each adult member of society is assumed to have. For example, personal information, personal space and even the right not to engage in conversation if disinclined are preserves that, if ignored or violated, require some form of remedial recognition by the perceived 'offender'. So, if we feel we are about to cause, or have caused, some ritual violation to another – some 'offence' – we may make requests, provide accounts or offer apologies for having done so (as part of our 'ritual accountability', so to speak). Such conversational moves have a dialogistic quality, that is, they normatively lead to some expected next move on the part of the person to whom they have been directed – they are expected to be acknowledged in and through immediately subsequent acts by whoever has been offended. Thus, for example (before an offence has occurred), requests invite, 'stimulate' or provide the ritualistic 'environment' for offers, and accounts and apologies (after an offence has occurred) lead to an expectation that replies that 'sequentially' follow should recognize these moves *as* remedial work. As a result, both 'offender' and 'offended' engage in a ritually sequential interchange aimed at demonstrating ritual awareness and considerateness – 'offender and offended each get a chance, a turn at, ritual work and that an exchange or "round" . . . results' (Goffman 1972: 150).

Of course, persons may have much to lose and much to gain in being able to demonstrate – or not – their awareness of possible offences, ability to ritualistically attend to them, and, by doing so, display their normative relationship to the ritual conditions of interaction, their ritualistic competences, and their moral qualities.

Supportive interchanges

Analogous to Durkheim's notion of positive rights are *supportive interchanges*. Greetings – or what we referred to earlier as 'access rituals' – are a basic example of supportive interchanges. Again, dialogically, one "hello" in effect invites a return "hello". In doing this, persons in spoken encounters are orienting not so much to turn-taking rules as to the ritual recognition and ratification of the (positive) relationship that exists between them (but cf. Sacks 1975). Basic greetings can be extended to include "How are you doing?", "Whadda ya know?" and similar statements, again inviting conversational response from those to whom such enquiries are directed. Indeed, such access rituals are a routine way of beginning larger conversation (see our discussion above for how conversation analysis deals with such phenomena). More extensively and substantively, 'grooming talk' is routinely employed in conversation, such as inquiring into another's health, asking about a recent holiday trip or eliciting another's opinion. Other supportive acts include invitations, introductions and what Goffman calls 'reassurance' displays – showing others that our relationship with them remains positive in the light of some actions or event that might suggest it may not be. The concept even extends to rights to conversational turns, as Goffman so insightfully puts it: 'In conversation, let a participant whom others would rather see silent make a statement, and he will have expressed the belief that he has a full right to talk . . . thereby obliging his listeners to give a sign . . . that he is qualified to speak . . . Without such mercies, conversation would want of its fundamental basis of organization' (Goffman 1972: 95).

In the same way that conversations have ritualized openings, spoken encounters are normatively and routinely ritually closed (cf. Schegloff and Sacks 1974). Thus "Catch you later" or "Take care" function to signal not only that the current conversation has ended, but, more importantly, that the positive relation between participants is intact and is anticipated to remain so for future conversational encounters.

These ideas of positive and negative underpinnings of ritual interaction were later developed by linguists Brown and Levinson (1987) in their study of another concept central to Goffman's interpretation of spoken interaction – perhaps the central concept – that of 'face' and associated practices of 'facework'.

Face and facework

Goffman's classic study of the concept of *face* and how we manage this in spoken interaction – as *facework* – is central to understanding both the ritual underpinnings of spoken interaction and the relationship between the self and talk. We are all aware of the expression to 'lose' or 'save' face. Goffman reflected this everyday notion by conceptualizing it as the 'positive social value' we routinely claim in and through spoken interaction with others. When involved in talk, we inevitably take some *line* – for example, some stance on whatever is being spoken about. From this line, others make assumptions about the values we are claiming for ourselves and ultimately the 'image' we are seeking to project, as we do with others. Being both aware of this routine face-claiming and reliant on others to have such claims recognized and supported, we routinely work mutually and reciprocally to support each other's claims. Goffman (1967) referred to such a conversational state as 'ritual equilibrium'.

Like orientation to the conversational rules outlined in the discussion of conversation analysis earlier, facework is a normative expectation of persons in face-to-face spoken interaction – it is not a goal of interaction but a *condition for* it and, like orientation to conversational turns, it requires some degree of practical competence, along with some expressive control, on the part of those persons involved in spoken encounters. Behaving tactfully towards others and conducting oneself with poise in terms of one's own face claims are examples of (other-directed and self-directed) 'preventative' facework – that is, moves taken to avoid any face threat (see Goffman 1967 for a range of examples). However, as with the potential for conversational troubles outlined in the discussion of conversational repair above, there is always some possibility of some 'ritual' trouble occurring in face-to-face spoken interaction – that is, of some face threat occurring in spite of the best efforts of participants to avoid such a threat. Thus, gaffes, faux pas and the like, as well as information coming to the interactional fore that in some way contradicts or undermines the face claimed by one or the other participant, can result in a temporary state of ritual 'disequilibrium' – an uncomfortable state in which it is difficult to support current face claims. As with conversational repair, 'corrective' facework practices can also be employed to 'remedy' such ritual troubles if and when they do occur.

The key point about facework is that it not only helps participants in spoken encounters claim and mutually support face, but helps maintain the ritualistic conditions for spoken interaction to proceed. To that end it is not the turn-taking system or intersubjectivity that is being maintained, and, if necessary, repaired, but ritual equilibrium – not meaningful conversation as such, but more *ritual interaction*. However, its collaborative and routine nature, and the ritualistic moves that are normatively and routinely employed to sustain it, can be regarded as equally as co-ordinated as the sequential management of conversational actions discussed above.

Of course, the upshot of this for identity is that there is an intimate relationship between the self and the way spoken interaction is organized. Goffman's view of spoken interaction was not naively utopian, and he did recognize the possibility of aggressive facework whereby the niceties of face were exploited by conversationalists in order to, for example, criticize, ridicule or shame others. The point is that –

much like preference organization – what people say in their conversational turns / do with their ritual moves is not a direct indication of any subjective, psychological states or preferences, but rather (in the case of facework) often a kind of 'lip service' or 'working consensus' to abide by the normative, routine, conditions of interaction. Persons in conversation are 'motivated to preserve everyone's face, they then end up acting so as to preserve orderly communication' (Goffman 1981: 19).

Methods and methodology

Conversation analysis

As has been emphasized above, conversation analysis is highly empiricist in that it makes no claims about its data other than what is evident in that data (what conversational utterances display for both the person in talk and the analyst being identical). Sacks' work on conversation analysis coincided with the increasingly easy availability of voice recording devices, especially the cassette tape recorder, and to that extent, the approach was born out of new technological possibilities for data collection. This allowed for the capturing of all utterances said in real time. Moreover (and perhaps more importantly), not only did this allow for the capturing of social reality as it had happened, but as it was happening. This is perhaps the central thrust of the conversational approach in relation to its data collection method. Transcription – as a first form of analysis – is a central feature of the conversation analytic approach (see Atkinson and Heritage 1984). Not only does conversational analytic transcription allow for the writing down of all utterances for closer analysis, but it also presents to the reader the same data that both the participants themselves and the analyst are working with. As we have outlined above, conversation analysis strove for – and to a large extent succeeded in establishing – a formal framework for the analysis of the machinery of naturally occurring conversation. Although initially complex in terms of its premises, once the methods have been grasped, students can collect, transcribe and analyse in a consistent and systematic fashion, and have their observations subjected to repeated examination. To that extent, conversation analysis follows scientific methodological principles. Although spending several years in the analytical cold, membership categorization analysis moves somewhat more in the direction of analytical interpretation (of what conversationalists are doing with their talk and their identities). However, this approach to

understanding conversational orderliness is still reliant on the same
data collection and transcription techniques seen in more sequentially focused studies of naturally occurring conversation.

The interaction order

Goffman's techniques for data collection were more in line with
ethnographic and observational methodology, a well-established
approach to doing social research by the time Goffman started his
work. However, the perspective for understanding the interaction
order *sui generis* (Rawls 1987) was, like Sacks' project, new and innovative. Moreover, Goffman drew not only on observations of actual
(real) interactional data but included an eclectic array of illustrative
examples in his analysis, from etiquette manuals and newspaper
reports to 'made-up' vignettes.

In this sense, rather than presenting the reader with the 'evidence',
as such, Goffman appealed to 'experience' – what can be seen and
felt to 'ring true' to the reader. Consequently, Goffman's analysis
is full of "oh yeah", "he's right", "brilliant" moments as opposed
to the rather dry and sometimes seemingly laboured close analysis
of conversation analysis. Indeed, whereas a central focus of conversation analysis was on the self-evidential nature of the turn itself
(and nothing more), Goffman's inclusion of aspects of the social
situation and social world more widely, the possibility of 'unspoken
but heard' features of talk (for the participants, but not necessarily for the analyst) and identity issues (biography, role, etc.) that
may tacitly impact on the interaction or inform what wasn't done
or said meant that informal conversation (as an interplay of moves)
was 'not subject to systematic transformation into words' (Goffman
1981: 48). In this sense, the appeal to the reader's experience is an
extension of and essential element to Goffman's analysis (to some
extent, the reader and Goffman are themselves engaged in a sort of
collusive act of interpretation, giving each other a wink here, a nod
there, and a chuckle or two in between). Indeed, Goffman's work has
been accused of being not a sociology of spoken interaction, but a
psychology of the self (Schegloff 1988). The self is certainly a central
feature of Goffman's approach to understanding spoken interaction.
However, by revealing the ritualistic and dramaturgical bases of conversation and the reliance of the self and identity on these, Goffman
exposed the close relationship between the structure of that self,
and the structure of talk. Finally, although the conversation analytic
approach strove for – and to a large extent succeeded in establishing

– a formal framework for the analysis of the machinery of naturally occurring conversation, Goffman's approach was not developed in the same systematic manner (Rawls 1990). Indeed, whereas the student of conversation analysis approaches data armed with a bag of tools for transcription and analysis, the student interested in analysing data for the interaction order comes armed largely with enthusiasm, insight and inspiration rather than any detailed methodological procedure (Helm 1982). Of course, the problem may be not so much Goffman's inability or unwillingness to outline such a procedure, as the recalcitrance of the dramaturgical and ritualistic features of talk to neat formulation as formal rules or mechanisms (Manning 1989).

4

Status and Power

Introduction

How social divisions are managed and reasonable social order is maintained are concerns for all sociologists. These issues are central to interactionist approaches too, but – as with other sociological issues – they are treated somewhat differently by interactionists and their mainstream sociological counterparts.

No one would dispute the notion that there are significant differences between the ways different groups in society are treated and treat one another. Characteristically, any group member will be part of a group hierarchy, subordinate to some group members and superordinate to others. Ranks in the army or police would be formal examples of such a hierarchy. By virtue of his or her group membership, though, that group member is also likely to look up to or look down on members of other groups as a result of *their* group membership. Thus, for example, even very junior doctors tend to regard themselves as superior to very senior nurses – because 'doctors' are a higher status group than 'nurses', regardless of the responsibilities of any particular member of either category. It is these latter relationships, those between groups, that have been of greatest concern for mainstream sociologists. The analyses of social inequality and stratification conducted by Karl Marx and Max Weber form the bases of this concern.

Marx's fundamental insight about social inequality, status and power, was that its basis in contemporary (capitalist) societies was *economic* rather than social or cultural. Society, he argued, was moving towards a polarized class system, with a large working class (proletariat) confronting a small ruling class (bourgeoisie). These classes have contradictory economic interests, Marx argued. The ruling class rule because they *own the means of production* (i.e., businesses) and derive their income from the profits those enterprises make. It is thus in their interests to cut costs, reduce the wage bill, and seek to charge more for – or produce more of – the commodity they are selling. The working class, on the other hand, do not own much beyond what they need for themselves. To prosper (in good economic times) or simply to survive (in times of recession) they must *sell their labour-power*, their capacity to work, to an employer. In short, any member of the working class must work for a wage or salary, selling their ability to do things to someone else, being paid by the hour, day, week or month. Members of the ruling class, therefore, seek to make workers produce more and work longer, and to pay them less.[1] The working class, on the other hand, seek to increase their wages, to work shorter hours and to produce less. Ultimately, these contradictory interests, according to Marx, will lead to revolution and the end of capitalism and class society.

This is very much a thumbnail sketch of Marx's ideas. Work, in his thought, is not simply production, but is the thing that defines humans *as human*; there are gradations of status and power within and between the two classes; there are other classes which emerge or continue to exist in diminished form (e.g., the 'reserve army of labour', which would include people currently unable or unwilling to work; the petit-bourgeoisie, which would include those workers who are self-employed or who run small businesses; and the landed gentry, which may survive even though its members neither work nor derive their income from efficient capitalist production); and so on. Nevertheless, Marx's central insight about power and inequality is that, to a great extent, it derives from economic relationships in contemporary capitalist societies.

Weber broadly agreed with Marx's analysis, particularly with respect to the latter's argument that capitalist economic relations tended to sweep away other forms of social relationship. He disagreed with Marx, however, in three ways. Firstly, he argued that the *nature* or *form* of capitalism that came to dominate in any particular society was shaped by that society's existing culture and values. Thus, for instance, in Protestant countries like Britain and Germany, a rational, bureaucratic capitalism developed because this was congruent with the rational, bureaucratic way of life of the people who ran factories, mills and so on, in those countries. A particular outlook, based on saving, re-investment, the close scrutiny and maintenance of records, and a disapproval of personal wealth and ostentation, which emerged from a Calvinist form of Protestantism, shaped and informed the way capitalism came to dominate in those cultures. In contrast, he argued, in Catholic countries, capitalism developed in a more haphazard and less 'totalizing' manner. Indeed, modern, bureaucratically rational capitalist production did not develop in, for example, Italy and Spain until well into the twentieth century.

Secondly, Weber argued that, although economic relationships were important aspects of social stratification (the separation of social groups by hierarchy), they were not the sole, or even necessarily the most important, bases for such forms of inequality. Weber instead argued that there were three kinds of power, and it was possible for individuals to find themselves in different social strata depending on which form of power was being examined. These were class, party and status. Class represents the distribution of resources across groups, similarly to in Marx's definition. Those with greater access to, or ownership of, such resources will come to dominate those with reduced access or ownership. Party affiliations are a conscious and deliberate attempt to have shared interests represented in the political arena. By acting in an organized and strategic manner, parties (which can include extra-Parliamentary groups like trade unions, lobbying groups, business consortia and so on) seek to influence public policy to reflect their own interests more effectively. Parties can reflect economic interests – the early Labour Party in the UK was meant to represent the interests of the working class, for instance – but they do not have to. The Conservative Party in the UK and the Republican Party in the US both boast high numbers of working-class members, even though the policies of those parties may economically disadvantage that class *viewed as a class*. Because not all interests are economic, party organizations may cut across class interests, as, for example, in the case of some pressure groups such as Stonewall (representing the interests of gay, lesbian, bisexual and transgendered people) or the Campaign for Nuclear Disarmament (advancing the argument that nuclear disarmament should be a much more important aspect of government policy). Status is a more nuanced and complex cultural form of power. Those in a particular status group will typically restrict their communication to others in that group, will share traditions and resources as a consequence of their membership of that group, and will use their group membership to guide their economic and social decision making. Thus, for example, those from a similar educational background – such as people who went to public schools like Eton or Westminster – are likely to share social circles, join the same societies and clubs, engage in similar leisure pursuits, and orientate to a shared world view. Although it will not necessarily mean that they will act together, this shared status increases the likelihood that members of this group will seek to maximize their common interests, even if their class or party affiliations are different.

Thirdly, Weber argued that there are different ways in which power and domination can be exercised. There are, he argues, three forms of authority: bureaucratic, traditional and charismatic. Bureaucratic authority is that which claims its legitimacy on the basis of its independence from personal and particular interests. Provided appropriate procedures are followed and rules are observed, anyone can take a position of authority and exercise delimited power over others. Thus, for example, provided an individual has the appropriate qualifications and successfully applies for the job – where proper procedures for competitive recruitment are followed over the course of the recruitment process – anyone can become a senior university administrator, with the power to shape university policy and strategy, hire and fire staff, and determine priorities for teaching and research. In the event that it emerges that the person so employed has been hired inappropriately – because they do not have the correct qualifications or because proper procedures for recruitment were not followed – they can be disciplined or fired. Whether the person in question is good or bad at the job is less relevant than whether proper procedure has been followed: the person in question can only exercise control if they are seen as a legitimate incumbent in the role they occupy. Traditional authority, on the other hand, is that which is based on a person claiming power by custom. There is no reason why Britain could not be a republic, with an elected President, rather than a kingdom, with a King or Queen as head of state, except that it never has been. At the time of writing, the Queen (Elizabeth) will be succeeded on her death by her eldest son (Charles), who will in turn be succeeded by *his* eldest son (William) on *his* death, unless either Elizabeth chooses to abdicate or Charles declines the throne or abdicates in favour of his son. These facts are inevitable within the logic of traditional authority and, unless the legitimacy of that authority is undermined, it can maintain itself indefinitely. Finally, Weber argues, some forms of domination can be based on charismatic authority. This is where an individual claims the right to dominate others based on his or her personal biography or characteristics. Examples of such charismatic authority figures are post-revolutionary leaders, such as Robert Mugabe, who claim their legitimacy on the basis of their involvement in a revolutionary struggle, and leaders of cults, sects and closed communities, such as the Church of Scientology, who claim their leadership on the basis of their knowledge of hidden truths of which their followers are only partially aware.

For both Marx and Weber, societies are riven with inequality and contradictory interest groups. Neither, however, would argue that contemporary societies are characterized by open conflict between these groups. For Marx, the ideas of the ruling class – its ideology – come to dominate how members of society *in general* understand themselves and one another, leading them to believe that false unities and divisions (such as nationalism, religious affiliation and notions of ethnic superiority) are the 'real' problems they face. The class basis of inequality and conflict is hidden. Marx talks in particular about how political economy (now simply economics) *fetishizes* commodities and their attributes, such as stocks and shares, currency prices, etc., to make it seem as if these abstract products of human labour were themselves the social forces behind, and causes of, that labour. In short, open conflict is prevented through the indoctrination of the population with false ideas about how the world works.

For Weber, matters are more complex. To be sure, he acknowledges that particular ideas (such as those that underpin bureaucratic rationality) may come to dominate society more generally, instead of remaining the province of particular social groups, professions, etc. Conflict prevention for Weber is more about the heterogeneous nature of power and authority. Different parties, classes and status groups may form coalitions, and may work together in strategic and tactical ways to achieve their goals. Equally, different authority figures may find it useful diplomatically and practically to avoid open conflict. More centrally, the State acts as an authority of last resort: in the event that there are widespread conflicts in a society, it is the role of the State to arbitrate and, ultimately, physically overcome troublesome groups. The State, as Weber argues, has a *monopoly of legitimate violence* – it is the only institution in a society that can use violence to achieve its ends without that violence being ethically or legally 'wrong' – and so stands above all other power formations, even if it is itself, in fact, the bearer of a particular group's interests.

Marx and Weber, typically classified as 'conflict' theorists of social structure, therefore agree that divisions in society – power imbalances – can spill out into open conflict, but that there are mechanisms in place to prevent this from happening. While symbolic interactionists, ethnomethodologists and conversation analysts might or might not agree with Marx or Weber on a personal level, they share a sociological commitment to demonstrating how power and status are worked out, produced, managed and understood in everyday life. They share a commitment to the notion that to understand such sociological phenomena one must start from the interpersonal and interpretive realm, and that – although Marx or Weber may be right – power and status both manifest themselves in, and are produced through, routine and mundane everyday activities.

Symbolic interactionism, status and power

The symbolic interactionist approach to status and power is fundamentally Weberian in form, insofar as it recognizes the existence of social strata (status and class hierarchies) and institutional power arrangements (both within institutions and between them). Its central line of investigation concerns the ways power is exercised and inequality managed through the interactions of particular individuals.

Status dilemmas

As Weber points out, different individuals may find themselves in contradictory status positions: they may, for instance, be economically poor but of high status, as in the case of the 'respectable' landed gentry in Victorian England. 'Keeping up appearances' and 'maintaining a front', regardless of how exhausting these activities might be, were required by many in this position to maintain their social status – even though the wealth on which that status originally rested was no longer present.

The symbolic interactionists often referred to such disjunctures as *status dilemmas*. An individual with contradictory status positions could be treated as high status given one set of criteria or low status given another. Hughes ([1945a] 1971) illustrates this position with the example of a Black medic working in a predominantly racist society, the Southern United States in the late 1930s. As a doctor, such an individual is in a very high status group: medicine was, and to a degree still is, regarded as one of the most prestigious professions one can belong to. As a Black man, however, such an individual is in a low status group, African-Americans being, in that place and at that time, looked down on by White Americans. This is a status dilemma insofar as a White patient seeking treatment from such a doctor could treat him in two different, contradictory, ways: as a respected professional of high social status or as a member of an ill-regarded race of low status. Hughes' point is that how this dilemma is worked out in the real world depends crucially on the role-taking and ascription of parties to the encounter. There is no way of determining a priori how the patient will view the doctor, as this will be worked out in real time and in the course of the interaction. Similar dilemmas may appear for the doctor's White colleagues, and for the doctor himself – as someone who has to decide which status to base his role-taking on.

Furthermore, Hughes points out, the possibility of such a dilemma is not going to be a surprise to anyone: although its resolution is worked out afresh, *it will manifest itself on every occasion such a doctor meets such a patient*. Hughes, therefore, argues that *institutional* solutions to the dilemma are likely to exist, and will be designed either to prevent its occurrence or to minimize its effect. Black doctors might be assigned their duties in largely Black neighbourhoods or areas, for example, to make it less likely that they would be required to treat White patients (or that such patients would exhibit open race prejudice); in the hospital setting, such doctors might be required to undertake work that does not put them into direct contact with patients, such as research or administration, where their professional status can be honoured by their colleagues and their race status ignored. Such solutions, however, as Hughes points out, simply reinforce race segregation and inequality: in each case the 'solution' to the problem of a race-based status dilemma is one that reproduces the separation of individuals by ethnicity.

Hughes' work on status dilemmas further illustrates an issue taken up by many subsequent interactionists: the notion that there can be *master statuses*. These are status positions that universally override any other status position in any other social situation. Goffman (1963b) refers to these master statuses, in their negative forms, as stigma, 'spoiled' identity. Someone with a physical disability, with mental health problems, with a history of criminal behaviour, with a drug or alcohol problem, and so on, is likely to be viewed as 'just that' – handicapped, mad, a criminal, an addict – regardless of whatever else they might be. Such stigmatic identities require ongoing management both by the stigmatized individual and by those he or she interacts with, and this management can be more or less problematic depending on interactional circumstances, role requirements, the activity being engaged in and so on (see, for instance, Davis 1961). Some statuses 'count' more than others, in particular places and at particular times, and it is always possible for negative statuses to become neutral (as, for example, atheism has become less unacceptable over the years) or even positive (being 'in trade', once seen as an inferior status, now being lionized as being 'an entrepreneur').

Similar changes from positive to neutral, or negative, can also occur over time. Such changes are taken up further in chapter 7.

The ongoing management of status dilemmas in a less extreme form was investigated by Gold (1952) in his study of apartment block janitors. Such workers have a classic status–income dilemma: their work is dirty and of low status, but typically they earn more than the inhabitants of the apartments they maintain. Gold found that the ways janitors are treated by their clients, and the way they, in turn, treat their clients, tend to form fairly stable patterns. More well-to-do apartment dwellers tend to be respectful to janitors, addressing them formally and making requests for service in a polite manner. The janitors treat such clients reciprocally, being polite in turn and dealing with requests promptly and professionally. Tenants who are more marginal, on the other hand, often treat janitors peremptorily, referring to them simply as 'Janitor', rather than by name, demanding personal service beyond the janitor's normal duties, and resenting the janitor's income and conditions of work and accommodation. These 'fourflushers' (as the janitors call them) complain more, and attempt to make trouble with the janitor's employer. Janitors seek to improve their status position by behaving professionally, treating the things they know about tenants discreetly and without gossiping, and ensuring that they tailor their service (and the charges they can make for it) to the needs and ability to pay of each client. The status dilemma for janitors, Gold points out, rests on the fact that they have professional skills, which they carry out in a professional manner, and for which they are financially rewarded – but they are still the people who take out the trash, do the 'dirty work'.

Status and institution

As is apparent from Hughes' analysis, and Gold's exemplary study, individuals belonging to a particular status group are not necessarily treated one way or another simply because of that status. All people have *multiple* statuses, and different ones can be relevant at different times and for different people. What counts in any one instance is an *interactional achievement* – something which emerges from the understandings, relevances and activities of parties to that situation – rather than something which controls what will happen in the situation. Status, however, is not simply a personal or individual choice: it is institutionally located and framed, and its institutional forms are also of concern to symbolic interactionists.

Hughes takes the idea of 'dirty work' further in his examination of the ways low-status activities become institutionalized and marginalized. Status is not simply an individual matter, as Gold's analysis points out, but can be an *occupational* or *institutional* one. Janitors, as a collection of workers engaged in the same occupation, might appear to form a group, but this is not the case: each janitor looks down on his equivalents in other apartment blocks, and there is little or no social solidarity between different janitors or groups of janitors. From the outside, janitors can be seen as a particular occupational status group, but they are not organized as one: they communicate little with one another, and do not organize themselves collectively.

In many cases, however, people of a similar status are placed in the same institution, or membership of a particular institution can confer on its members a particular status. In the former case, for example, people found guilty of particular crimes may be institutionalized in prisons, people diagnosed as having mental health problems may find themselves institutionalized in mental hospitals, or people with transmissible diseases may be quarantined for the safety of others. In each of these cases, personal status attributions determine an appropriate institutional location for the person in question. This need not represent status degradation, however. People awarded degrees by universities become alumni, and are allowed to change their designation (by appending their degree qualification, 'B.Sc. or 'BA', to their name, or even by changing their title from 'Mr' or 'Ms' to 'Dr'); people who are ennobled may become eligible to join and take part in the proceedings of the House of Lords; others may be elected to join local authority Councils or the House of Commons; and so on. There are institutional 'homes' for people with particular status designations, therefore, and typically to get into such an institution requires a ceremonial process of status degradation or dignification.[2]

Sometimes, however, the opposite applies: membership of a particular institution confers upon the person a particular status designation *by virtue of their membership*. Any society is made up of a series of in- and out-groups (Hughes [1962] 1971). In-groups are those that any one member of society regards him- or herself as belonging to. These could be one's family, one's school or college, one's religion or church, and so on. These can be closer or further away: a Christian, for instance, is likely to be more closely affiliated to the particular church she attends than to the church it is a part of (e.g. the Roman Catholic Church), and again closer to that church than to the religion (Christianity) as a whole. Each of these groups are defined in contrast to others: to out-groups. Our Christian, for example, would define herself *against* atheists or followers of other faiths (e.g. Islam or Judaism), against other Christian churches (e.g. Anglicanism or Methodism) and against other particular churches in the area (those, for instance, of another parish). Being *against* an out-group does not mean disdaining it, disliking it or being hostile to it (although it can), but rather means being positioned *in contrast to* it. Hughes ([1948] 1971), for example, points out that differences between ethnic groups are not the result of cultural or lifestyle differences between members of those groups, but rather such differences are invoked to justify and provide a rationale for their separation and perceived difference.

Some out-groups, however, are ones that are actively disliked by members of their contrasting in-group. Criminals would be one example: typically people who are convicted of crimes, especially serious ones, are looked down upon by the law-abiding. Such groups are regarded as a problem for the in-group, who have to manage or otherwise deal with them. Hughes talked about such management as 'dirty work', the work of dealing with those who are regarded as outside and beneath an in-group. Typically those who have to deal with that out-group will *themselves* be regarded with some hostility or suspicion: although there might be calls for those doing such work to do it in particular ways (for prisons to be harsher, for instance, or the police to be more aggressive), members of the relevant in-group have little stomach for actually investigating what that dirty work entails, or how it should be organized.

It is, however, not the case that in- and out-groups map directly onto other social hierarchies. Becker (1952b), for example, discussed the relationships between Chicago schoolteachers and pupils from different social classes. A naive view of status hierarchies would suggest that those from higher classes would tend to be respected more and evaluated more highly than those from lower ones. This was true to a point, but not entirely. Teachers viewed pupils from the lowest class backgrounds as being the 'hardest' to teach: they were believed to be unmotivated, and their parents disinterested in their progress at school. Pupils from the *highest* class backgrounds, however, were also perceived to be problematic: '"spoiled", "over-indulged", or "neurotic"' (Becker 1952b: 458). Such children are allowed 'too much' leeway at home and so prove difficult to discipline and teach in school. Teachers were most comfortable teaching middle-class children, who combined discipline and commitment with a willingness to learn.

In these senses, then, status emerges from a society's organizational structures – from the interactions and relationships of those who have to work together. The existence of social groups *necessarily* implies the existence of out-groups (those who are either not members, or who are members of competing groups), and one's status as a member of any group – or of any occupation or profession that has to work closely with that group – can provide another way in which status can be made relevant to a situation. Go-betweens, people who are in neither one group nor another, often emerge as means of inter-group communication. As Hughes ([1949] 1971) argues, this is particularly apparent in occupational contexts where groups are separated by their ethnicity as well as by their status in the organization. In factories where the workforce are Black but management White, for instance, it is often the case that a 'straw-boss' is used to facilitate this communication. Such a person is typically Black himself and speaks the language of the workforce (sometimes literally, where the workforce and management speak different languages), so is able to represent the workforce to the management. Crucially, however, he is himself a manager of that workforce, albeit one who is of lower status (because of his ethnicity) than the 'real' management. Because the straw-boss knows he will not rise above his organizational status, he can be relied upon to impose management decisions on the workforce and to represent workforce concerns to management – without being fully accepted by either. His marginal status allows him to smooth over the more divisive occupational realities of such a situation. Just as organizations find ways of dealing with those members of their staff who could open up status dilemmas, such people also fulfil a key organizational role in smoothing over institutionally based status differences.

Conclusion

What should be visible here is the way in which the social-structural and the individual are both invoked and used in the course of interaction. Depending on the particular identities and statuses of parties to a situation, status differentials may or may not be invoked. Status derives its sense from group membership, whether that group is deliberately constituted and organized (like a religion or political party) or simply viewed as being a group by non-members (like janitors as an occupation). *Which* group membership will be invoked in any concrete situation is, however, impossible to predict: it depends on the biographies, plans and role-taking of the participants. Equally, however, one cannot advance any status one wants: membership of some groups is difficult to hide, and certain low-status occupations carry stigmata along with them (smells, dirt, injuries and so on). One must select from available roles and statuses, both in terms of presenting oneself and in terms of interpreting the identity of co-interactionists. Although attempts can be made to control what information is available to others, and to allow for only certain identities to become salient, the parties to an activity decide what does and what does not count.

Ethnomethodology, status and power

Resistance through rules

Ethnomethodologists, in contrast to symbolic interactionists, have typically studied status and power through the close examination of how status and power get done: the methods that members use to defer and dominate. Ethnomethodologists would agree with Hughes that there is nothing intrinsic or inevitable about different groups having different status locations, but wish to focus on the deeper question of how those status locations are achieved, challenged and undermined.

For ethnomethodologists and for symbolic interactionists, rules are central to the generation of in- and out-group differences. Differences are maintained through the application of rules for how (or whether) members of one status group should communicate with members of another. These rules are most apparent where status groups are clearly delineated, as for example in the caste system of Hinduism. In such a system, who can do what, who can communicate with whom and so on, are all clearly demarcated through a formal system of rules of etiquette.

Where ethnomethodology differs from symbolic interactionism is in its treatment of those rules. Rather than guiding behaviour, such rules are understood as being part of the behaviour itself: they are not 'external and constraining', but rather are internal aspects of interaction. They are *reflexively* tied to the activities they 'govern': they shape what one can and cannot do, but are invoked and used in the course of those doings. Wieder (1974) provides an example of how such rules obtain in the setting of a half-way house for convicted criminals, i.e., a place where criminals are contained and controlled after leaving prison but before re-entering the community fully.

In this setting, struggles between staff and inmates are ongoing: the former are required to check up on the latter, administering drug tests, checking working patterns and so on, while the latter are often not committed to the 'rehabilitation' they are meant to be undertaking. Viewed in a conventional sociological manner, staff have power over inmates – because they have the right and responsibility to do things that the inmates do not want done – but such a view neglects many nuances of the situation. Inmates view themselves as an in-group, in contrast to the out-group of staff, and much of their interactional work is devoted to maintaining this separation. This is similar to Wieder's (1974: 115–18) invocation of rules of conduct for inmates as means of organizing their behaviour. These rules are as follows:

1. Above all else, do not snitch (inform).
2. Do not cop out (defect to the staff side).
3. Do not take advantage of other residents.
4. Share what you have.
5. Help other residents (in covering for and facilitating their illicit activities).
6. Do not mess with other residents' interests (in particular their enjoying deviant activities).
7. Do not trust staff – staff is heat (cannot be trusted).
8. Show your loyalty to the residents (i.e., never take the side of staff or help them in their work).

These eight maxims allow inmates to maintain themselves as an in-group in opposition to the staff out-group and, indeed, to exercise some power over staff. Wieder points out that staff themselves orientate to 'the code', by recognizing that there are some things they cannot ask inmates to do, and not placing 'good' inmates in difficult positions by requiring them to do things that might be construed as a breach of one of the code's maxims.

Where Wieder goes further, however, is in his analysis of *how* this separation is maintained. The code, he points out, is not transparent as it stands. It is *talked* into being through inmates' use of its maxims to organize the ways they understand their own, and one another's, behaviour. The code depends on this *reflexivity* – its status as an explanation for activities that it is itself a part of – for its sense. It would be impossible to reconstruct what the code's maxims are from simply listening to talk or observing non-verbal behaviour in isolation from one another: the way talk and activities inter-relate produces and elaborates what the code means. Furthermore, just what 'counts' as an instance of following the code cannot be determined in advance: the 'rules' do not contain their own applications.

The point of this is that the code does not govern how in- and out-groups in the setting maintain themselves, but rather provides a way of understanding inmate activities and providing for different kinds of action to fall under 'the same' rule. Thus, for example, an inmate's refusal to organize a baseball team is expressed as '*You know* I can't organize the baseball team': staff members should know better than to ask inmates to do such things (which breach the maxim 'show your loyalty to the residents'). The general rule provides for the inmate to refuse doing the particular thing he is being asked to do. It also, however, informs *general* patterns of non-compliance and group maintenance: inmates do not volunteer *as a matter of course*, and staff generally do not ask them to do so. The code is used to account for these instances of non-compliance, and through its 'telling' its status as an objective and context-free description of behaviour is produced and maintained.

Membership and competence

The explicit nature of the convict code – its existence as a set of rules – makes it a clear mechanism through which 'in-' and 'out-' groups are produced and maintained, and by which the requirements of one group are forced upon the other. This is a very extreme case of imbalanced power relationships, though. In common with the symbolic interactionists, ethnomethodologists recognize 'power' and 'status' as interactional achievements. In one key way, however, ethnomethodologists define status into their definition of the social actor.

Garfinkel defines a 'member' as 'a mastery of natural language', the capacity to 'gloss particulars' and thereby mean 'differently than he can say in so many words'. This oblique definition hides an important feature of competent membership of society: the ability to be left to go about one's business without interruption. An example would be a learner driver: such a person may need to be instructed what to do in a number of circumstances, and may need to be told the names of many routine and ordinary features of the driving experience (e.g., the names of the car's foot pedals, the meanings of road signs, the proper way to pull into traffic or come to a halt). Such a person is being instructed in the language of driving – and, as long as such instruction is required, they cannot be referred to as a competent practitioner, a *member* of the driving community. On gaining enough experience, however, the same person may well be able to generalize from one set of circumstances to another, for example, be able to drive safely in icy conditions as an extension of being able to drive safely in wet ones, or to be able to manoeuvre along a narrow, winding street as an extension of being able to pull into and out of narrow parking spaces. The

driver does not need to spell out what he or she is doing at any particular time, but is simply able to identify correctly that any particular
situation is 'an instance of' a category of situations. Indeed, most
drivers forget much of what they learned, and may forget the names
of particular road signs, car controls and so on, while being perfectly
capable of observing them, operating them, etc.

This ability to 'gloss particulars' is a fundamental requirement for
any social membership. In terms of work and experience, however,
it takes on different connotations. Coroners (Garfinkel [1967] 1984:
ch. 1) operate on the basis of professional knowledge, but *exactly*
what they do – what the particulars of their job might be – is of little
interest to them. 'Although they would' talk about these details 'they
can have none of it'. This means such details are the unseen background to their work, and to make that background a topic in its own
right would mean questioning the taken-for-granted basis of their
professional knowledge and skills. It can be glossed, talked about in
shorthand, but that glossing itself demonstrates the ability to focus on
what is problematic, difficult, questionable and so on, in contrast to
what is generic, boring, routine and ubiquitous.

This membership accrues professionals a further characteristic.
Their membership in any profession means that non-members are
expected to leave them alone to get on with their work uninter-
rupted. Doctors may take advice or requests from patients about
many matters, but they do not take advice or requests *about specifically medical or surgical matters* from people outside their profession.
Their membership in the community of doctors means that they are
not answerable for their actions to 'outsiders' except in particular,
delimited, circumstances (e.g. if a professional inquiry extends into
criminal investigations). Status here is a seen-but-unnoticed matter:
something which is never referred to because its very status depends
on it *not* being referred to. It is the basis of members' capacities to get
on with their activities unmolested.

The politics of experience

Some actors, however, are denied their rights and privileges as
members. In many cases this will be a consequence of their having
these rights and privileges removed, as outlined in chapter 7. A
certain category of actors, however, have their *most basic* rights and
privileges denied them: the right to be a competent communicative
participant. Such people are the mentally ill.

The mentally ill are those whose mastery of natural language has been thrown into doubt: what they say is typically not trusted or taken as salient, and their right to be allowed to engage in everyday activities unmolested has been taken away or moderated. A problem for ethnomethodologists is that the mentally ill often have *alternate*, competing views of what is happening in the world, and it is empirically impossible to investigate the veracity of those views.

Pollner (1975), for example, refers to a famous case study of three paranoid schizophrenics (Rokeach 1964). At one point in the treatment, one of the patients claims that he had made a table levitate. On being asked to repeat this feat by his therapist, the patient chose a 'massive' table and 'commanded it to lift itself'. The therapist did not see the table move, and told the patient so, to which the patient replied, 'Sir, that is because you do not see cosmic reality.' The problem Pollner identifies here is there is no way of arbitrating between the two claims: for the therapist the patient *hallucinated* making the table rise up, while for the patient the therapist *cannot see* something which he can. Pollner refers to these phenomena as 'reality disjunctures', and argues that the fact that one version of events is almost always taken as justifying a line of action – in this case the patient requiring further treatment rather than the therapist requiring training in cosmic perception – demonstrates that they are resolved *politically*, through a 'politics of experience', rather than empirically. Pollner uses these 'disjunctures' to argue that 'reality' itself is something we experience in the way we do because we have chosen to see things in one way rather than another: ultimately, power resides in those who can define reality itself, and prevent competing versions from becoming the bases for further action. This is similar – but more extreme in form – to Smith's account in chapter 2.

Others disagree with such an extreme example. Coulter (1975), for instance, argues that many psychiatric patients can be convinced of the erroneous nature of their beliefs and perceptions *before* these can manifest themselves as full-blown reality disjunctures, and points towards the fact that many such patients *refer themselves* for psychiatric evaluation and treatment because they are aware that their sense of the world is wrong. Cuff (1993) takes the more mundane example of radio phone-in shows, and demonstrates that ordinary disagreement and differences of opinion are easily settled using the mundane mechanisms of conversation. Both would argue that Pollner's case is weak as he bases his argument about the 'politics of experience' and nature of reality-definition in society on extreme cases, and reasons that if a category of people can be judged defective in judgement and experience then it follows that our shared judgement and experience themselves are the result of domination and partiality. In order to assess these claims, closer examination of the operation of status and power relations through conversation is required.

Conversation analysis, status and power

Talk could be understood as a fundamentally competitive and conflictual system: there is competition for the next turn at talk at each turn-transition point, for example, and the majority of disagreements and disputes (as well, of course, as agreements) take place verbally. Conversation analysis' approach to power and status, conflict and dispute, however, can be divided into three. Early, Sacksian, approaches to the topic tended to examine the uses of status-based membership categories in talk. Middle-period approaches were based on the examination of how disagreement and dispute could be managed through turn-taking, particularly when the organization of talk 'prefers' agreement and concord to dispute and disagreement. It was only after Sacks' death that 'conventional' notions of power and persuasion were re-introduced to conversation analysis as ordinary sociological tropes. These latter two uses will be left for the subsequent section.

Status categories

In ordinary talk, status attributions are made through the application of categories. These attributions adhere to the format and organization of other membership categorization devices, as described in chapter 3. Where such categories are designed to place their bearers in higher or lower social or moral positions, however, they tend to take the form of contrastive pairs.

Sacks (1992a: 59) points out that the kinds of categories we use to distinguish between things are typically not measurements in a mathematical sense. When we say that someone is poorer than someone else, or less normal, or more ill, or dirtier and so on, we are not providing a location on an objective scale. There is no commonly recognized measurement of dirtiness, starting at zero (very clean) and going up to ten (utterly filthy), except where we as social scientists generate such measurements for the purposes of questionnaires, surveys and so on. This is in contrast to, for example, measurements of height: we can say that a person is shorter than another, and, *if we have to* we can then measure the two people to demonstrate the veracity of our claim. Some things that can be measured, however, are *zero-sum* phenomena: there is only so much of a thing to go around, and if someone has a lot of it there will be less left over for others. When eating food together, for example, someone who takes most of the vegetables will leave fewer for everyone else: there is a finite amount of this particular thing, and it has to be divided up between those present. Other things do not have this character. If someone has more money than someone else, that does not mean that the former has this money *because* the latter has less, or that there is a logical connection between someone having more and another having less. The amount of money in circulation can grow or reduce – through the government printing more money or through the banks generating money through loans – and the overall wealth of an economy can increase or decrease over time.

Sacks points out that the ways in which we think about power and status are ambiguous in these ways: when we talk about power we talk in *directional* rather than *quantitative* terms. This means we say someone is more or less powerful than someone else, or more or less powerful than they had previously been, where exactly *how* powerful they are is unspecified – and is not capable of being specified. Power and status, then, are *contrastive* categories: they vary either over time or between parties to a situation.

What is more, these contrasts tend not to be organized in minor ways: it is neither interesting nor newsworthy to point out that someone is higher-status than someone else (indeed, in most interactional settings, referring to status at all would be a strange thing to do). Where status is invoked, it is usually done in a radically contrastive manner: where one party is approved of by virtue of their having the opposite status characteristics to another. Lee (1984), for instance, discusses the way such contrastive status pairs are organized in newspaper headlines. 'Girl Guide aged 14 raped at Hell's Angels convention' and 'grandmother struggles with gunman', for example, both rely on the notion of moral culpability being located in one individual or group *contrasted with* a morally blameless co-interactionist. As with 'the baby cried' (see chapter 3), these headlines are linguistically ambiguous. It is possible that the Girl Guide was not raped *by* a Hell's Angel or group of Hell's Angels, or that the struggle between the grandmother and gunman was instigated by the grandmother. That is not how we hear or read such accounts, however. The activities 'rape' and 'struggle' necessarily imply categories of actors among whom blame can be allocated in a zero-sum manner: fault can usually be attributed to the assailant in a rape or the stronger or more aggressive party in an altercation. As in Smith's (1978) account of 'K' becoming mentally ill (see chapter 2), moral status is attributed by demonstrating one party's absolute culpability (a zero-sum phenomenon here) in an encounter.

Such contrastive categories, however, are 'illustrative'. The fact of someone being a Hell's Angel or a gunman does not necessarily imply that they will behave in particular ways in particular settings. Such low-status classifications do, however, imply that their bearers are 'the kinds of people' who might do particular kinds of things. Bearers of such classifications, or their allies, might seek to minimize the extent to which they are understood *through* those classifications (as in Hughes' account of master statuses, above). Such minimization is achieved through the use of 'modifiers' (Sacks 1992a: 44–5), through which a member of a class of people attempts to demonstrate that their membership of the class does not determine what they are *personally* like. In the expression 'I'm 48 but I look and feel younger . . .', for example, a member of the class 'middle-aged' attempts to demonstrate that the negative connotations of being a member of that class do not apply to them: their appearance and activities are those of a younger person. Members of all kinds of low-status classes of person attempt to use such modifiers (as in Davis' account of deviance disavowal; see chapter 7), but they come with a particular problem. 'Anti-modifier modifiers' can be brought to bear by other members to demonstrate that the original exception to the rule in question does not apply. Thus, for instance, 'Women will be women' acts to restate the notion that particular disapproved-of traits are common to *all* women, *including* those who have attempted to modify their gender attribution to argue that they are not 'like all the others'. Sacks points out that low-status attributions are 'sticky' insofar as, although one can demonstrate that one is not 'just' a member of a low-status category, it is possible for someone to invoke 'a set of things that can properly be said about that category, removing the modification under which they've been living' (Sacks 1992a: 45). A Muslim only needs to criticize Israeli policies in the Occupied Territories for her 'real' character – as a political extremist, anti-Semite or potential terrorist – to be asserted, regardless of how much work she had previously done to demonstrate the inappropriateness of those attributions to her as an individual. Such categorical status attributions are 'extremely deadly', because they can always be reasserted in such a way as to erase individual differences.

Handling status through talk

The organization of talk allows for status differences to be handled in very subtle ways. It is unusual for someone to complain of status differences manifesting themselves through higher-status members dominating lower-status interlocutors. Generally speaking, the organization of talk allows members of different statuses to get on with activities together by suspending the relevance of those differences. Sacks (1992a: 100), for example, talks about joke-telling as a means of overcoming status differences. Where a group of people from different status backgrounds are brought together, telling jokes is a means of overcoming those differences and 'breaking the ice'. One person, by telling a joke, provides a reason for each other participant to tell a joke in return, thus giving each person both 'a set place to talk' and 'something to say'.

More broadly, there is a *preference for agreement and contiguity* in conversation. When a speaker asks a question expecting a particular answer (e.g., "Is it okay if I take this chair?"), while providing the anticipated answer ("Yes") is enough to satisfy the requirements of conversational preference, giving a different answer requires explanation ("No, there's someone sitting there"). Sacks formulated this as questions with preferred answers eliciting '"Yes"-period' or '"No"-plus' answers. The organization of conversation requires unexpected responses to turns that have a preferred response to be accounted for: speakers are not supposed to say something that contradicts previous speakers' expectations without providing a reason for so doing. Furthermore, when statements are made, there is a conversational preference for avoiding direct contradiction. Thus, even in a simple question–answer exchange, there is a tendency to mitigate or attenuate disagreement:

A: So is this permanent?
B: Yuh it's 'permanent'; permanent until I get moved again.

(Sacks 1987: 62)

Here the response demonstrates that speaker B does not think 'this' is permanent at all but – rather than saying "No" – attenuates his response to avoid too overt a disalignment. An initial agreement is presented and then modified, rather than an open disagreement advanced.

These mechanisms allow disagreement and contradiction to take place without open breaches in the organization of talk occurring. Through its preference for agreement and contiguity, conversation actually facilitates argument and dispute. By *using* the features of conversational organization, furthermore, it is possible to impose one's view on co-interactionists. By avoiding taking a position on a subject, for example, it may be possible to elicit another person's position first, then providing one with the ability to pass judgement on that position. As Sacks (1992b: 346) points out, 'it's quite a different thing to develop a critique of someone's position than to develop a defence of your own'. Pomerantz (1984) illustrates this in her analysis of how 'assessments' (statements of opinion) are treated in conversation: the recipient of such an assessment can respond by providing an assessment of his or her own, a second assessment, by disagreeing or by agreeing (and in some cases disagreement rather than agreement may be preferred – as in cases where the assessment is self-deprecating). This provides the recipient of a judgement with a rich range of conversational resources. Avoiding giving an assessment, therefore, can provide a speaker with argumentative resources that allow for far greater persuasive and argumentative leeway as a conversation develops. Thus, for example:

K: I couldn't, I'm a weak[ling.
():   [hmh!
          (1.0)
K: I am. I'm comin t'that conclusion. I'm a damn weakling.
          (1.0)

(Pomerantz 1984: 91)

Here the self-deprecating assessment 'I'm a weakling' would 'prefer' a disagreeing second assessment (e.g. 'No you're not'). The absence of such a response provides K with an opportunity to redesign the assessment, but instead it is repeated in a stronger form ('damn weakling'), which elicits another long pause. Here, by providing a self-assessment with a preferred disagreement as response, K has left him- or herself open to a self-deprecation being confirmed by the other speaker. The power to decide whether or not K is a 'weakling' has become invested in his or her interlocutor.

Analytical power and the use of talk to dominate

Schwartz (1976) provides a final example of how the organization of talk can be used to exercise power and downgrade an interlocutor's status. In therapeutic settings, utterances can be treated simply as moves in a game, and their content ignored. Thus:

A: I keep getting these funny twitches.
B: Jesus, A, every time something real comes up you try to change the subject.

(Schwartz 1976: 59)

By construing the preceding utterance as 'changing the subject', it is possible to take the next turn at talk without responding to that utterance's content, and thereby make its producer out to be acting improperly (in this case, not taking a group therapy session seriously). Schwartz (1976: 67) goes on to provide 'rules' for the way this technique can be used:

1. Let X be some proposition about the world.
2. Skip to a metalinguistic level and consider 'X' as a conversational object.
3. Find some verbal activity which is 'done' by the statement, 'X'.
4. Find a personal motive, a reason why someone would do this activity. (Sometimes, as already discussed, the activity done by 'X', and the motive for that activity, will be one and the same.)
5. Evaluate the personal motive as healthy or unhealthy, normal or pathological, etc.
6. If the motive is found to be invalid or inauthentic, the statement, 'X', is false. Don't believe in the statement.

While these 'rules' are more ethnomethodological than conversation analytic they provide for two things. Firstly, they demonstrate how the ordinary ways of using conversation, in particular those concerned with the classification of previous utterances, can be used to dominate and undermine interlocutors. Secondly, though, they provide for a damaging critique of post-Sacksian conversation analysis, in which classifying utterances as 'instances' of particular analytical categories and speakers as 'bearers' of extra-conversational identities allows for the re-importation of conventional sociological tropes into this radical alternative to constructive sociology.

Later conversation analysis, power and mainstream sociology

Post-Sacksian conversation analysts have tended to talk more about power in terms of the use of conversation by different kinds of member. It has been argued, for instance, that women tend to find it harder to elicit conversation, have to do more support work to maintain topic and demonstrate interest, and are less likely to gain the conversational floor at turn-transition points (Zimmerman and West 1975). Kitzinger (2000) has taken this further by examining *gendered* talk as a topic in its own right.

Wowk (2007) elaborates the problems with these approaches. Standard sociological categories like 'gender' are reintroduced into the analytic framework of conversation analysis without their relevance being found in the data under examination. Furthermore, such analyses tend to reduce conversation analysis to being merely a method, like any other, which can be used for particular political purposes. The problems of 'importing' such 'conventional' notions are also criticized implicitly by Schwartz (above). The issue at hand is whether it is legitimate to blend a particular form of sociological analysis which stands opposed to (or at least disinterested in) the sociological mainstream with elements of that mainstream itself. Analytical privilege is reasserted, and the sociologist stands not as someone providing a description of what is occurring but as a commentator, explainer and critic (Anderson and Sharrock 1984).

Becker's (1967) comments about political engagement in studies of deviance, and Pollner's (1991) concerns about providing a 'radicalized' ethnomethodology demonstrate that these concerns are not restricted to CA. Ultimately, in studying power and status, the role of the sociologist is always ambiguous: simultaneously seeking to describe how power and status get done, while wanting also to take sides. The strengths of interactionist sociologists in this field have been to focus on the former while avoiding the latter, very much against the sociological grain. Developments in post-Sacksian CA, and tendencies in both SI and EM, demonstrate that this clarity of purpose may be difficult for some to maintain.

5
The Body, Health and Illness

Introduction

The naturalness of the body is widely taken for granted. The able-bodied can walk to the shops, their next class or meeting, they can look to see where the shortest queue is at a supermarket checkout, or they can hurry up the steps to catch the train that they have heard arrive and which they know will be leaving shortly from the station platform. When our body functions 'normally', it is an unnoticed natural condition, but when it becomes injured, impaired or sick, then that naturalness is questioned as our compromized capabilities move to the centre of our preoccupations. At such times the body can seem to have a will of its own (Frank 1991).

This chapter considers some of the distinctive contributions that sociologies of interaction offer about illness, disability and death. This chapter concentrates on studies in the sociology of health and illness in order to provide fresh insights about how bodies and their states are enduring sources of social significance. The embodied state of the human being has long been a key referent for interactionist sociology. George H. Mead (1934) underlined the importance of embodiment by frequently describing humans as 'minded organisms'. A first question might be to ask what makes humans distinctive as an animal species. At least five features distinguish humans from other species: binocular vision; the audio-vocalic system; bipedalism; hands; and expressive capacities.

Humans have two eyes placed at the front of the head. The *binocular vision* that results makes it easy for humans to judge the depth of visual fields. Human eyes have evolved so that they can distinguish the colours of the spectrum in fine detail. Humans have also evolved an *audio-vocalic system* so that speech is a universal method of communication. As Mead (1934) compellingly argued, speech is closely implicated in the development of the human mind. Humans walk upright on two legs. This *bipedalism* is another distinctive characteristic that means that walking is a very basic way in which we move around the world. The possession of *hands* that are made up of four fingers and an opposing thumb enables humans to wield tools and manipulate physical objects. Tool-use itself is often seen as a major distinctive feature of *Homo sapiens*. Certainly, no other species is so adept at manipulating the physical world through a range of tools that extend the hand's physical capabilities. Finally, humans have complex and finely developed *expressive capacities*. The capacity for language is the most outstanding of these, but humans also have a range of non-vocal expressive forms, at least one of which (laughter) seems to be unique to humans.

This, then, is an account of the body of *Homo sapiens* much as an evolutionary biologist might couch it. It works well as a general account that marks out how humans are different from hedgehogs or hippopotamuses. But it is very much an ideal type that abstracts from the real condition of actual human bodies in the world addressed by sociologies of interaction. Consider how our description leaves out many features of the bodies we routinely encounter. Very many humans have eyesight that must be augmented by spectacles. Some few may stutter or otherwise find difficulty in smoothly delivering their talk. Many others, especially older humans, may need the assistance provided by walking sticks, wheelchairs and other aids to mobility. Skill in the use of the hands for everyday tasks varies enormously across cultures and across the life-cycle. The management of one's expressive capacity can be a challenge for many, as anyone who has felt like laughing at a funeral or crying at a party knows. To develop a more realistic appreciation of bodily skills and capacities we need to examine them in their socially situated contexts – the actual situations in which a range of embodied conduct is sensed and interpreted. Here the work of Goffman (1963b) on stigma can prove instructive since illness, disability and dying constitute classic 'predicaments'.

Erving Goffman's celebrated book *Stigma: Notes on the Management of Spoiled Identity* addresses 'the situation of the person disqualified from full social acceptance' (Preface). More concretely, Goffman suggests that there are three broad types of stigma. He initially categorizes: (1) 'abominations of the body' (physical disfigurements and disabilities); (2) 'blemishes of individual character' (biographical features such as a criminal record or a history of mental illness); (3) 'the tribal stigma of race, nation, and religion' (the grading of people by their ethnicity, nationality or beliefs) (Goffman 1963b: 4). This initial categorization shows us that stigmas can concern matters of 'body' as well as 'mind', but, helpful as it is, will not take us very far sociologically. Goffman (1963b: 3) insists that for sociological analysis to proceed, 'a language of relationships, not attributes' is required.

Central to this sociological analysis is a distinction between the discredited and the discreditable. The distinction turns on 'observability' or 'evidentness' of the stigma. Those with an observable stigma such as a harelip or a stutter begin their encounters with others as discredited. The key issue for the discredited is the problem of stigma management – how to make the best out of a difficulty they cannot hide. Goffman goes on to propose that the 'mixed contacts' between 'normals' and stigmatized present 'one of the primal scenes of sociology' (1963b: 12–13). They dramatize what normality and departures from it amount to in actual situations in which a variety of feelings – fear, embarrassment and misunderstanding chief among them – may be mobilized.

The discreditable are in a very different position. They have something they can hide from others, if they wish – a divorce, a criminal conviction, their health status. Thus, the discreditable are faced with opportunities to manage others' awareness of their stigma. If they are skilful in how they control the discrediting information about themselves, they can 'pass' as normal. They constantly face a dilemma: 'To display or not to display; to tell or not to tell; to let on or not to let on; to lie or not to lie; and in each case, to whom, how, and where' (Goffman 1963b: 42).

What Goffman shows us is that certain embodied stigmas can be managed through careful disclosure. Being economical with the truth can be central to surviving as a normal. Goffman also underscores the relativity of what will count as a stigma. A stigma is responsive to the particularities of local contexts. It is easy to envisage situations in which a tattoo functions to stigmatize the bearer, and others in which the tattoo works as a basis for social inclusion. Goffman's analysis shows how stigma is experienced by everyone at some point – that stigma, understood sociologically, is less about membership of a particular category than it is about a relationship between normal and stigmatized in everyday social interaction.

The sick role

From Goffman's analysis, we can see how the social significance of human bodies is a deeply contextual matter. The particularities of the actual local context need to be specified if we are to reach a proper understanding of many aspects of human embodiment. Goffman thus has a general lesson to teach us concerning how features of embodiment are to be interpreted. Some of these implications for sociological studies of health and illness are explored below. Before we can address this relevance, we must first consider a study of pivotal importance for the sociology of health and illness, Talcott Parsons' famed account of the sick role and modern medical practice.

Talcott Parsons ([1951] 1991) was the first sociologist to apprehend medicine clearly as a social institution. His analysis centred on sickness as a social role, not just as a state or condition of the human body. Being ill meant having to act in certain ways: there are 'institutionalized expectations' with a normatively binding force. First of all, a person's incapacity due to illness was grounds for exemption from normal social-role responsibilities. You might be signed off from work or someone else would carry out your usual household duties. Second, the sick person was exempted from responsibility for their condition. The illness was not their fault and it could not be mended by a simple act of will. Third, the sick role was regarded as undesirable and therefore persons are under an 'obligation to want to get well'. Fourth, insofar as the person cannot get well by themselves, there was an obligation 'to seek technically competent help' (Parsons 1951: 437) in the shape of advice from a doctor or other appropriately qualified professional and to co-operate with those professionals in getting better.

Parsons ([1951] 1991: 438) emphasized that admission to the sick role was adjudged entirely on the basis of 'universalistic' criteria, the presence of symptoms of sickness. He suggested that it was a 'functionally specific' role, i.e. limited to health problems and the specific difficulties linked to illness. Further, the sick role's orientation was 'affectively neutral'. Irrespective of what the person felt about the illness, getting well was taken as an 'objective problem' to which medical solutions must be found. For Parsons the sick role was also 'collectivity-oriented' in that the ill person must cooperate with the doctor in the task of returning the person to full health.

Depending on the nature of the illness, the sick role can involve varying degrees of physiological, psychological and social malfunctioning. It can be considered a deviant role because being sick is not a normal or desirable state of affairs. But it differs from other deviant roles in that the person is not held responsible for their condition. A broken leg cannot be mended by resolving to do things otherwise, in the way that, for example, persistent thieving can be. This is why many legal codes make important distinctions between the criminal and the sick. The sick role is part of the institution of medical practice that is distinctive to modernity. The doctor occupies a professional role that is devoted full-time to the care of the sick (a role that did not exist in many traditional societies). This responsibility to care for the sick, along with the special training and expertise the doctor possesses, makes for a fundamentally asymmetrical relationship with the patient.

Parsons embedded the analysis of the sick role in a broader consideration of the modern institution of medical practice. Since it was the first major sociological statement on health and illness, it has subsequently become the target of criticism, some of which we consider below. Some critics felt that Parsons' model applied only to acute illnesses of temporary duration and not to chronic illnesses that are often incurable. Parsons (1975) responded that even chronic illness (such as his own diabetes), which demanded a degree of self-care by the sick person, was nonetheless overseen by professional medical authority. The basic asymmetry of the doctor–patient relationship was preserved.

The idea that the sick role is a kind of social correlate of physiological illness has been challenged by interactionists. Judith Lorber (1967) suggested that the social label of illness was not a transparent indicator of a biological condition of sickness. Lorber brought into focus the interaction occurring between patients and doctors. Patients frequently self-label that 'something is up' and needs checking out by a doctor, and the doctor, who is empowered to assign the socially consequential label of illness on the basis of their professional judgement, responds with a diagnosis and a proposal for treatment. But conferring incumbency of the sick role cannot be regarded as a simple process. There are several possibilities. Drawing upon Goffman, she suggests that, as a form of deviance illness is sometimes distinguished from crime by its 'accidental' character, and thus what is required is for the patient to put on a 'performance of innocence' in order to show that they are neither hiding symptoms nor manufacturing them. After all, the doctor may suspect the patient of deliberate self-injury (e.g. to seek compensation), or of feigning illness (e.g. malingering). Alternatively, the patient may conceal illness from their doctor or family members. All this underlines how illness may be a morally contestable matter.

Like Parsons, Lorber sees illness as a special form of deviance, but maintains that the deviant aspects of illness are best seen in Goffmanian performative terms. When illness is approached as a performance, then becoming ill is less a matter of straightforwardly taking the sick role than it is a mobilization by the patient of the arts and techniques used in everyday presentations to convince a medical practitioner that the label of sickness is justified. Occupying the sick role does not happen unproblematically, as Parsons' account seems to suggest. Rather, this interactionist account emphasizes the social processes involved in assigning the sick label – a sequence of actions following a broad pattern of 'self-label, awareness of societal reaction, performance, social label, revision of self-label, performance in the role implied by the social label' (Lorber 1967: 309).

Going to see the doctor

Interactionist sociologists have studied the processes involved in making the decision to go to see the doctor. It might be thought to be a simple matter of rationality: the person experiences a troubling symptom that does not go away and so seeks aid. However, studies show that people from all social groups often experience symptoms worth clinical investigation that they do not take up with a doctor. Also, delay in seeking medical advice is very common whether the symptom is perceived as serious or slight (Zola 1973). The normal state of affairs is for persons only to seek medical consultation when there is a 'break in the accommodation to symptoms' occasioned by an interpersonal crisis (a divorce or bereavement, for example) or by perceived interference with interpersonal relations, with work or physical activities, or by direct sanctioning by family and friends.

There are variations, typically along class, gender, age and ethnic lines, in what it takes to prompt the person to go to the doctor. For example, women tend to have higher levels of medical consultations than men (in one popular saying, 'women get sicker but men die quicker'). This has prompted interactionist-oriented sociologists to inquire into the sources of these differences in order to understand better how illness is socially constructed. Eliot Freidson (1970) examined the lay constructions of illness – that is, the non-technical beliefs and perceptions of people about being sick. Freidson examined the 'lay referral structures' people use – the social networks of persons that can be turned to routinely for advice about worrisome symptoms. Typically these 'consultants', as Freidson calls them, are the family members and relatives, the friends and co-workers, with whom an individual can discuss their current symptoms and worries. These networks may be loose and truncated, for example among White middle-class professionals, or they may be cohesive and extended, for example in established working-class communities. Since White middle-class professionals have few consultants in their lay referral network, and because their cultural values are broadly consonant with those of medical professionals, they will more quickly seek formal medical attention than members of working-class communities, who have a richer range of consultants to provide guidance about the significance of their symptoms and some cultural values dissonant with those of professional medicine.

Medical encounters

Parsons was very aware of the special nature of the relationship when a patient presented their body to a doctor for examination. Interactionist sociologists have developed the understanding of the doctor–patient relationship through studies that have directly observed patients consulting doctors. Consultations may be very infrequent or, in the case of chronic conditions, very frequent. Plainly, the doctor–patient encounter is the primary source of professional medical diagnosis.

Consider the potentially difficult social encounter that occurs during gynaecological examinations. Traditionally, gynaecology has been a male-dominated area of medical work and, while this is now changing (increasing numbers of women have trained in recent decades so that they will soon predominate in the specialism in many parts of North America and Europe), there remains the interactionally delicate issue of a male doctor having access to female genitalia, something that usually only occurs in a sexual context. Thus the study of the gynaecological examination considers what Emerson (1970, riffing on the title of one of Goffman's books (1963a)) calls 'behaviour in private places'. The doctor is usually accompanied by a female nurse, and singly and jointly they engage in practices of 'dramaturgical desexualization' (Henslin and Biggs 1971) of the patient and the situation. The examination takes place in a setting that is self-evidently medical in character (medical equipment in the room, professional qualifications on the wall). The dignity of the patient is respected by the strategic use of screens and covers to minimize the amount of the patient's body that is physically exposed. Throughout the examination there is extensive use of a depersonalized language instead of vernacular usage to desexualize the encounter. If events threaten the medical definition of the situation, they will be diplomatically dealt with by the doctor and nurse (e.g. sexual arousal may be re-defined as 'ticklishness'). In these ways, a medical definition of reality is sustained in the gynaecological examination and alternative designations (a sexual advance, an assault) denied.

The medical consultation is a special type of 'social occasion' that is 'more formal, more public and more artificial than everyday events' (Strong 1979: 6). Strong's study of paediatric clinics where parents (most often the mother, sometimes the grandmother) bring their child for diagnosis and proposed treatment underlines how patterned these occasions could be. Both doctors and mothers ascribed idealized roles to each other. Doctors were seen as virtually unchallengeable sources of wisdom and expertise while all mothers were assumed to be good mothers with their child's best interests at the forefront of their concern. Strong found that the most common patterning of the consultation approximated a 'bureaucratic format'. By this Strong drew attention to the doctor's civil, business-like and reasonable demeanour. Medical routines were blended with the doctor's polite, economical and impersonal self-presentation. The doctor controlled the pace of the consultation and patients deferred to the doctor's professional expertise. Patients were given little scope to air their fears and anxieties. Their unease was subsumed under the polished workings of the bureaucratic format.

Ethnomethodology has provided insights about how common-sense knowledge figures in decision making in medical encounters. Hughes (1977) challenged the view that medical work simply consisted of trained and specialized medical personnel applying their medical knowledge to the patient. In a study of a hospital casualty department, he looked at how staff categorized patients. 'What everyone knows' (where 'everyone' includes porters, reception workers, escorts of patients – not just doctors and nurses) about identifying a patient's condition is important for medical staff in deciding an appropriate line of treatment. A man is admitted having been hit on the head by a ball. His escort is quizzed by medical staff about whether he lost consciousness, did he appear dazed, what sort of ball was it? It was a golf ball. Here everyday, not medical, knowledge is deployed about the meaning of loss of consciousness, dazed states and the effects of golf balls hitting the human head. Everyday and medical knowledge intersect in the process of categorizing patients. Medical staff often find that diagnosis is facilitated if they can construct a 'story' to account for the circumstances of the case. For example, a man in his late teens with long hair is admitted in a comatose state. Nurses attempt to revive him, but act with a certain unseriousness because they can see that his condition is not life-threatening. As news of a more urgent case arriving comes through, they leave the young man in a recovery room. Then, a few minutes later, a second man of the same age, appearance and state arrives. This seems too much of a coincidence to the nurse in charge who begins questioning the young man's escort about what he's taken and begins to look for needle marks on his arms. Here the inferences made by medical staff are everyday, common-sense inferences, not those based on a command of an esoteric body of knowledge.

Control in doctor–patient encounters

Freidson's notion of lay referral structures was developed in order to identify the sources of power that were alternate to those represented by the medical profession. The notion of lay referral challenges the monopolization of power by professional medical authorities. The institutionalization of 'professional dominance' was often seen to stem from the medical profession's control of its practitioners and its relation to the State. But studies of medical encounters have suggested that it is also evident at the level of the doctor–patient consultation. Typically, there is a pronounced power imbalance that emerges from several features specific to the medical consultation. The doctor controls the timing, duration and conduct of consultation. Also, the normal rules about touch and personal space are routinely broken. Importantly, there is a knowledge asymmetry motivating the encounter, which simply means, as Becker (2006: 65) put it: 'If you know why I'm sick, and I don't, if you know what to do so that I'll get better and I don't – then the power lies in your hands.'

As has been widely observed in medical consultations generally and doctor–patient encounters specifically, the medical specialist or doctor controls the interaction: he or she sets the agenda, opens and closes the encounter, and asks the majority of questions to which the patient is required to give candid answers. How can the doctor's control be explained? At least three views can be identified: (1) a symbolic interactionist view that conceptualizes professional dominance as the outcome of a negotiation that the doctor invariably 'wins'; (2) an ethnomethodological view that sees professional dominance as a widely taken-for-granted matter acknowledged by patients and doctors; and (3) a view that draws upon CA methods to develop the idea that differential competence is the key to understanding how the doctor's dominance is produced.

(1) A common view in interactionist sociology is that there is a process of negotiation in which both parties seek to define the situation but where the doctor's definition invariably prevails. In Wadsworth's (1976) study of childhood epilepsy doctor–patient–parent encounters, the negotiated character of the dealings that parents and doctors have with each other was emphasized. Parents had to make sense of the various interactions they had with doctors while, for their part, doctors were trying to cope with genuine clinical uncertainties as they attempted to maintain the legitimacy of their expert role. The picture painted is a long way removed from the simple enactment of the normative expectations of the sick role.

(2) Sharrock (1979) re-casts Freidson's concept of professional dominance in an ethnomethodological direction. He argues that analyses like Wadsworth's are mistaken because there is little observational evidence of a 'negotiation' or debate in which the doctor routinely triumphs. Transcripts of doctor–patient encounters do not show unambiguously that the doctor's dominance in medical encounters is best understood as an interactional contest in which the doctor always triumphs over the patient. Instead, there is much evidence of the doctor's agenda smoothly unfolding. Sharrock proposes that medical dominance is better regarded as a recognition of the legitimacy of medical authority that is embedded in patients' common sense. Patients are aware that 'they are meant to take up as little of the professional's time as possible, that they should confine themselves to things that he deems relevant, that they find doctors fearsome people, that they expect that attempts to get answers will fail or be frustrated' (Sharrock 1979: 143). These ideas are widely accepted and treated as a matter of course. There is no general process of interactional challenge by patients who are then defeated by doctors. Institutionalized professional power is an accountable matter at the level of the consultation that is assumed by the doctor and acknowledged by the patient.

(3) Sharrock's interpretation of medical dominance is disputed by Hughes (1982) who maintains that there are interactional issues at stake as well as the normative ones that Sharrock identified. Drawing on a body of transcripts of consultations in a cardiology clinic, Hughes shows how many features of professional dominance are

rooted in the necessity that 'a series of topics had to be raised and organized in relation to a body of specialist knowledge with which one party was not familiar' (Hughes 1982: 361). Patients acquiesce in simply answering the questions that doctors put to them because they do not know what may be relevant to a diagnosis of their condition. This knowledge differential between the doctor as expert and the patient as layperson goes some way towards explaining the long chains of adjacency pairs in doctor–patient transcripts where doctors ask all the questions and patients provide answers to those questions. Hughes' analysis grounds the understanding of doctors' control of medical consultations in the work that is done in these consultations (arriving at a diagnosis and plan of treatment) which itself is premised on the knowledge differential existing between doctors and patients. The approach taken by Hughes applies some of the concepts and techniques of CA to address the issue, although Hughes hesitates to classify his work as CA proper.

Another example of 'applied CA' that can be brought to bear on the problem of the doctor's control of medical consultations is West's (1984) study of interruptions. An interruption is a violation of a speaker's turn at talking that occurs when there is a deep incursion into the speaker's turn space. The use of interruption by one party to a conversation is an exercise of dominance over the other party. Routinely, adults interrupt children, men interrupt women, and doctors interrupt patients more frequently than vice versa. But what happens 'when the doctor is a "lady"'? The gendered dimension to the doctor's control is explored in West's (1984) study of doctor–patient encounters in the southern USA. West transcribed the entirety of 21 consultations, 17 of which were with a male doctor and 4 with a female doctor. In the 17 encounters with male doctors, there were 188 interruptions, 67 per cent of which were initiated by doctors and 33 per cent by patients. In the 4 encounters with female doctors there were 59 interruptions, 32 per cent initiated by doctors and 68 per cent by patients. In the female doctor encounters, the two male patients interrupted much more than the two female patients. In other words, with the female doctors there was a more or less equal pattern of interruption in the same-sex consultations but a highly unequal one in the cross-sex consultations. These findings, albeit on a very small sample, indicate a gender biasing of the pattern of interruption in medical consultations. The status of being a woman seems to undercut the authority of being a doctor. West links this finding to the ideas presented by Everett C. Hughes ([1945] 1971) about status contradictions and dilemmas (see chapter 4). She suggests that her study shows how gender works as a master status that creates a dilemma when it is found alongside the potent status of doctor. The dilemma is whether to treat the person in terms of the 'woman' or 'doctor' status.

This study is controversial within CA. The definition of an 'interruption' as a violation seems unduly 'moral' to some conversation analysts. They would prefer a more neutral term like 'interjection' and point out that some interjections can be supportive, as when a listener uses an interjection to encourage the speaker's development of a story ("So what happened next?"). Also, the study represents a mixture of CA methods with the approach of variable analysis that CA eschews. West recognizes that her analysis focuses on outcomes rather than processes – that she could have analysed how dominance and control are constituted through acts of interruption in her transcripts. This direction is taken by her later work on doctor's 'directives', the instructions and orders that doctors issue to patients. West (1990) found marked gender differences in the ways in which patients responded: women doctor's directives were more likely to elicit a compliant response from the patients. West found that male doctors tended to use statements that told patients what they 'ought to' do or 'needed to' do. They also issued directives to patients by saying what they 'wanted' or 'didn't want' the patient to do, or they made quasi-questions ("Why don't you just . . .?") or they suggested what they would do if they were the patient ("I would do that, I would drink plenty of fluids"). These speech acts, West maintained, serve to underline the distinctions between doctors and patients. Women doctors tended to use 'mitigated directives' that minimized the difference between doctors and patients: they used "let's" and "we" frequently ("Let's get a fasting sugar next time", "if we can control it") and they used "can" and "could "more frequently than male doctors. Thus, built into the way turns were constructed in doctor–patient encounters were gender differences in speaking. In the face-to-face arena of the consultation, West found evidence of women doctors enjoying greater success than their male counterparts in getting patients to do the doctor's bidding.

Encouraging a patient to accept the medical point of view can involve matters that may be better conceptualized as persuasion than as control. More recent studies in the CA tradition have refined sociological understandings, further qualifying the Parsonsian model of the authoritative doctor and the expertise-dependent patient. One example can be found in Douglas Maynard's (1989, 1992) study of encounters between doctors, parents and children in a clinic for children with mental development issues. Maynard concentrates on the phenomenon of the 'perspective-display series'. Very commonly, before a doctor will give their diagnosis, parents will be invited to speak about their understandings and observations of their child's difficulties, as in the following example:

1 Dr: →   What do you see as Donald's difficulty?
2 Mom: → Mainly his – the fact that he doesn't understand every-thing, and also the fact that his speech is very hard to understand what he's saying lots of time
3 Dr: →   Right . . . okay I you know I think we basically in some ways agree with you insofar as we think that Donald's MAIN problem you know DOES involve you know language
   Mom: Mm hmm
   Dr: you know both his being able to understand what is said to him and also certainly to be able to express his thoughts.
                                (Adapted from Maynard 1989: 93)

The perspective-display series is a sequence consisting of three features (identified by arrows in transcript above): (1) a 'perspective-display invitation' in which the doctor invites the parent to set out their view of the child's difficulties; (2) the parent's assessment of those difficulties; (3) the doctor's clinical diagnosis, which builds on and elaborates the parent's assessment. Using this perspective display series, the doctor is able to 'co-implicate' the parents into his previously established clinical view. How this process is carried out can be quite complex. A key distinction, Maynard suggests, is between perspective-display invitations that are 'marked' i.e. take for granted the presence of a problem ("What do you see as his difficulty?" "What do you think is his problem?"), and those which are 'unmarked', i.e. more open and general ("How do you see Johnny now?"). Maynard shows how marked invitations presume the existence of a problem and the ready co-implication of the parent's and doctor's views, enabling the doctor to progress smoothly to the clinical assessment. Sometimes, unmarked perspective-display invitations can also facilitate parent–doctor co-implication but, in addition, unmarked invitations leave more scope for parents to disagree with the clinical assessment ("I don't think there's anything wrong with him"). Maynard's study shows how the workings of power, control and their contestation are, in such instances, an interactional matter to be worked out through the activities of the interactants.

Another CA study that indicates how the parents of patients may challenge doctors' clinical judgements is Tanya Stivers' (2002) examination of how parents pressure their doctors to provide inappropriate treatments for their children. A common form of inappropriate treatment is the use of antibiotics for viral conditions (colds, flu). Conditions that are viral in origin are not responsive to antibiotics, which are effective only for bacterial conditions. Yet the parents of children who are simply showing signs of viral infection nonetheless pressure doctors to prescribe antibiotics. How is this pressure manifested in conversational encounters between parents and doctors?

Most transparently, parents can ask doctors directly for antibiotic treatment. However, this happened quite infrequently (only around 9 per cent in Stivers' sample). More common were indirect communicative forms such as 'inquiring about antibiotics'. In line 4 of the following extract, the father designs his question as an inquiry (not a request, not a demand). The inquiry elicits an explanation from the doctor about the appropriate use of antibiotics.

```
1  DOC:   She: doesn't have anything right no:w,
2         any symptoms of mucus
3         or vomiti[ng that's contagious.
4  DAD:           [Are you gonna give her ana- antibiotics?
5  DOC:   Yeah- uh No : I don't have anything tuh treat right now
6         for antibiotics. Her ears look really goo:d, .hh she has
7         no sign of bacterial infection right no:w?
8         .tlkh and that's (what) she'd get antibiotics for
                              (Adapted from Stivers 2002:1117)
```

Another practice that parents use to communicate pressure for antibiotic treatment is mentioning past occasions when antibiotics were used. For example:

```
1  DOC:        So : – Let's take uh listen to 'er che:st,
2  MOM:        (Alright) ,
3             (.)
4  MOM: →     Remember she– she:=uhm_ had something like this: in
5       →     December?
6  DOC:        Uh huh,
7             (0.5)
8  GIR:        Hhh. = .h
9  MOM: →     (n') She was on an antibiotic.
10            (1.0)
11 DOC:        Doo doo.      ((to girl))
12 GIR:        Ksh : : : : : , uh.
13 DOC:        Yeah: Well I think that she probably got:= similar
14            type of thi :ng, ya know [some sort of a secondary–=
15 MOM:                            [Mm hm: ]
```

16 DOC: = .hh uh: respiratory infection in her ch<u>e</u>s:t, like
17   uh bronchitis an'_

                                  (Stivers 2002: 1120)

Here the mother draws attention to an earlier similar problem that led to antibiotic treatment. The doctor examines the girl and agrees that the current illness is a 'similar type of thing', thereby warranting use of antibiotics. In addition, the mother positions herself as knowledgeable about her child's unique biography, allowing the doctor a space in which to reach a treatment recommendation different from general treatment guidelines.

Many contemporary health policy statements stress the importance of patient (and parent) participation. One consequence may be that doctors find their clinical judgements increasingly open not so much to direct challenge as to subtler forms of pressure as parents seek to secure forms of treatment better attuned to their perceived circumstances than to the medical knowledge and practice in which doctors have been schooled.

Chronic illness and disability

A chronic disease is one that lasts a long time, sometimes defined as more than three months. It is named after Chronos, the Greek god representing time. In medicine it is usually contrasted with an 'acute' disease, which has rapid onset and a short course. Chronic diseases include arthritis, asthma, various autoimmune diseases (colitis, Crohn's, etc.), cancer, cardio-vascular diseases, diabetes, HIV/AIDS and Parkinson's. The term 'chronic illness' covers a range of conditions – some are life-threatening while many threaten the quality of life. Chronic conditions are becoming increasingly common in the Western world.

Chronic diseases vary in terms of their severity and stability. The management of the disease can be affected by the nature of its onset: (1) if a child is born with a chronic condition then it is the parents who must make the initial adjustments; (2) sudden onset, which is most common among teenagers; (3) slow onset, where symptoms gradually worsen, is the most common type of onset and is often regarded as part of the ageing process. Different 'illness trajectories' are associated with each type of onset. The idea of illness trajectory was introduced by symbolic interactionist Anselm Strauss (1916–96) to characterize 'the total organization of work done over that course of illness plus the impact on those involved with that work and its organization' (Strauss et al. 1982: 257). What Strauss and his colleagues wished to alert us to was not only the physiological course of an illness but also the work done by medical staff, carers and family, their relationships, and how this work and these relationships then affected the management of the illness and the fate of the patient.

Thus there is a heavy emphasis on notions of temporality and process in the work of Strauss and his colleagues: they analyse how activities linked to illness unfold over time and how understandings and relationships change. For example, they suggest that there are three key lines of 'work' in the management of chronic illness at home: illness work, everyday work and biographical work (Corbin and Strauss 1985). 'Illness work' concerns various methods of treating pain, taking of diagnostic tests (blood sugars, blood pressure) and doing physical therapy. 'Everyday work' involves all the activities associated with running a household, maintaining family relationships, pursuing one's own interests. Chronic illness serves to make problematic those activities previously taken for granted as routine. Stairs become obstacles, opening food packaging a challenge, and family meals just too much trouble to do. 'Biographical work' focuses on reconstructing the narrative of the chronically ill person's life. This includes incorporating the illness into the fabric of one's life, making sense of it, explaining it to others. Symbolic interactionists have studied the problems and consequences of each of these types of work among the chronically ill. We will sketch just one of these areas, biographical work, in order to examine the key themes highlighted by interactionists.

Broadly, people tend to experience chronic illness in one of three ways (Charmaz 1991): as an *interruption*, where people treat the illness as time out from their lives, to be resumed when the illness plateaus; as an *intrusion*, where the illness demands to be accommodated as something either acknowledged or hidden from view; and as *immersion*, where people lose their sense of self as the illness becomes the overriding fact of their lives. Often, as the problems created by the disease become more prominent, the sick person's experiences shift from interruption to intrusion to immersion.

Mike Bury considers that 'disrupted biography' typically follows onset of a chronic illness in teenage or adult years. He suggests that 'the structures of everyday life and the forms of knowledge that underpin them are disrupted' (Bury 1982: 169). Individuals need to make sense of their illness in terms of their biography yet the illness may not fit in with their lives so far, and has obvious implications for their future in terms of shortened life and compromized activities. The chronically ill must come to terms with the meaning of their illness. Bury (1988) distinguished 'meaning as significance' from 'meaning as consequence'. 'Meaning as significance' refers to the cultural associations and perceptions the illness has for the sufferer and others. Often elements of stigma are involved but such cultural meanings are open to revision and testing in everyday interaction. 'Meaning as consequence' refers to the effects of illness on the life of the sufferer – incorporating treatment regimens into daily life, living with pain and restricted mobility, loss of independence, money and employment difficulties, and so forth.

Kathy Charmaz (1983) argued that 'loss of self' was a major form of suffering faced by the chronically ill. In addition to physical pain and psychological distress, individuals experience a 'crumbling away of their former self-images without simultaneous development of equally valued new ones' (Charmaz 1983: 168). Self comes under assault in four main ways:

(1) leading a restricted life. Typically, the chronically ill face a shrinkage of their social lives, which become more home-centred than before; often the capacity to own and drive a car is regarded as a source of freedom and choice and its loss can be a serious blow.

(2) social isolation as a consequence of leading a restricted life. The chronically ill experience difficulties in maintaining social relationships that involve outside participation (in work or hobby or sports groups for example). People have to come to visit the ill person rather than vice-versa.

(3) being discredited. This can occur in interactions with others or result from the ill person's own 'unmet expectations' (Charmaz 1983: 181). In public places children can be particularly cruel in vocally deriding an oddity or departure from conventional appearance, such as an amputated limb. But discrediting can also have its basis in the person's own standards and expectations, which can lead them to avoiding participation in activities. Difficulties here can be compounded by significant others not shifting their own expectations to accommodate the ill person's current condition.

(4) guilt and dependency. The chronically ill often feel guilty for burdening others to help them carry out activities they could once accomplish independently, like washing, dressing, toileting, etc. As the ill person's immobility increases, there follows

a greater dependency on others and the sense of becoming a burden, often expressed as feeling 'useless', intensifies.

The suffering by the chronically ill is largely seen in negative terms involving notions of loss. The exceptions, Charmaz notes, are those who had improved and whose suffering was no longer as intense as it once was. They were able to see their earlier suffering in a more positive light, as trials through which they had endured. They were able to draw lessons about themselves and human nature from their experience. In contemporary American society, such learning from the past, Charmaz concludes, seems only possible when the current position has become more hopeful.

These interactionist accounts derive from many hours of interviewing, observation and reflection on the situation of the chronically ill. The points summarized in the present discussion are developed in ethnographic detail in the studies cited, which we encourage you to read. While interactionist accounts attempt to discern the broad patterns evident in and through the ethnographic illustrations provided, ethnomethodological studies make the organization of the details of particular instances the focus of analytical attention. As one example of this approach, we will consider Albert Robillard's (1996) analysis of the anger a chronically ill person feels when he becomes the object of exclusionary practices.

It is important to note Robillard's own identity as someone with severe muscular dystrophy, who cannot speak, and who is a wheelchair user. Robillard describes himself as an expert in anger. That anger is often occasioned by communication difficulties between Robillard and his interlocutors. These 'interpretive asymmetries' arise because Robillard (1996: 17) fails 'to effect the talk and understandable body moves to create, sustain and dissolve social engagements'. Robillard's ethnomethodological approach treats his anger as a situated, locally achieved outcome of ongoing interaction. He seeks to analyse the specifics of what created anger on his part by examining the specifics of actual instances of interaction. The article's title ('Anger in-the-social-order') is designed 'to indicate not general social order but the social order achieved through *just* this talk and bodily behaviour, with *just* these people or social members, and with *just* what these members make of the talk and bodies' (1996: 19).

Robillard analyses an encounter at the shopping mall. A friend he once used to sail with came up behind Robillard's chair, touched his back and greeted him with 'I haven't seen you in a long time – I see your kids but not you.' Before Robillard could respond, the friend was racing up a stairwell away from Robillard, calling back 'Er, it was nice seeing you.' Robillard explains how his anger arose from his frustration at not being able to sustain a more satisfactory encounter. This was due to several features of the encounter: the friend's greeting was accompanied by a movement that meant that no eye or facial contact was possible. Robillard's own restricted movement did not allow him to position his body or his wheelchair in a way that would have permitted direct face-to-face contact and his inability to speak did not allow him to catch the attention of his friend and issue an invitation to talk. In addition, Robillard's disinclination to be interpreted by methods such as lip-reading the spelled-out letters of individual words effectively compounded the difficulties of sustaining the shopping mall encounter. Lip-reading letters is a tricky process that often leads to the person looking like a cultural dope, or the translator looking like an idiot, or both.

Robillard's analysis of his communicative difficulties might be regarded as an 'ethnomethodological demonstration of the embodied commonsense knowledge used to "do" a chance meeting in the mall' (Robillard 1996: 28). In it, Robillard meets Garfinkel's 'unique adequacy requirement' in that he is a practitioner of the behaviour he is analysing. He shows us the working detail of an exclusionary practice by drawing upon his own first-hand lived experience.

Death and dying in hospital as social processes

Based on extensive ethnographic studies of hospitals in the USA in the 1960s, interactionists Barney Glaser and Anselm Strauss (1964, 1965) and ethnomethodologist David Sudnow (1967) presented distinctive characterizations of dying as a social process. Exiting this life may seem a grossly physiological matter. These studies show that how persons pass from the living to the dead in the context of the modern hospital involves actions that are fundamentally social in form.

The analysis provided by Glaser and Strauss turns around the key concept of 'awareness context'. This is 'the total combination of what each interactant in a situation knows about the identity of the other and his own identity in the eyes of the other' (Glaser and Strauss 1964: 670). It is a way through which the sociologist can formulate the sum total of who knows what about whom in any situation. Applied to the situation of the patient thought to be dying, four possibilities emerge:

- closed awareness context: patient unaware of coming death while staff know
- suspicion awareness context: patient suspects oncoming death but staff stonewall
- mutual-pretence awareness context: both staff and patient know death is imminent but pretend it is not
- open awareness context: candid recognition of what is to come by both parties.

This is clearly the simplest outline of possibilities, which become more complicated once the relatives and friends of the dying person are brought into the picture. While generated out of a study of how hospitals care for and manage dying patients, the concept of awareness context has a broad applicability to any situation in which there is a difference in knowledge, such as disclosure to a person of their adopted status or the interpretation of early signs of Alzheimer's disease.

Sudnow's (1967) study of two US hospitals, one ('County') a charity institution on the West Coast, the other ('Cohen') a private hospital in the Midwest, is an ethnomethodological ethnography of how the dying and dead are dealt with by these hospitals' staffs. The ethnographic Sudnow (1967: v) 'seeks to depict the heretofore undescribed social organization of "death work"' from the point of view of hospital staff, while the ethnomethodological Sudnow (1967: 8) investigates illness, dying and death '*as constituted by the practices of hospital personnel* as they engage in their daily routinized interactions' within the organization. Sudnow distinguishes clinical and biological death, referring to the presence of death signs and the cessation of cellular activity, from social death, whereby the patient, although clinically and biologically alive, is nonetheless treated for all intents and purposes as a corpse. Sudnow gives a great deal of attention to recording the details of the practices surrounding how death is dealt with in the two hospitals – how bodies are wrapped and ticketed, how death is catalogued, where bodies are placed once removed from the ward and so on. Thus we learn that at County Hospital the boundary line for deciding whether an expelled fetus is considered 'human' is '550 grams, 20 centimetres, and 20 weeks of gestation. Any creature having smaller dimensions or lesser embryonic "age" is considered non-human . . . and if "born" without signs of life, properly flushed down the toilet, or otherwise simply disposed . . . [while larger or older foetuses] . . . cannot be permissibly flushed down the toilet, but must be accorded a proper ritual departure from the human race' (Sudnow 1967: 176–7).

Sudnow concentrates on the routine practices associated with the care and treatment of the dying and dead. He also notes departures from the routine and exceptional events, as when, for example, a nurse attempts to feed a patient who is already clinically and biologically dead. There are conspicuous contrasts between the two hospitals that Sudnow's study documents. In summary, social death occurring prior to the clinical and biological types was more common at County. Part of the reason for this was the heavier application of routine procedures and the poorer, often more socially isolated character of the patient population. The patient's family was not as conspicuous a grouping to which staff felt accountable at County. Sudnow's study thus can also be read as documenting social-class inequalities in health care worked out at the level of the situated practices of hospital staff.

Conclusion

Parsons' highly influential account of the sick role has largely been superseded by more detailed, qualitative, ethnographically informed accounts of issues around health, illness and the body. Concepts of 'embodiment' have also been informed by a range of other social theorists, in particular Foucault and Bourdieu. Nevertheless, the distinctive approaches of interactionist researchers provide a set of alternative ways of considering these issues. To the extent that they are compatible with what are now mainstream sociological understandings, they can be understood to have succeeded in penetrating the research field in ways they have been unable to elsewhere.

6

Work

Introduction

When different sociologists talk about 'work' they often mean quite different things. Some deal with what anyone would recognize as work – paid employment – while others deal with the organizational and institutional structures in which that work takes place. Some address the relationships between different occupations, either in terms of the class and status positions of their members (nursing, for instance, was reclassified as a 'middle-class' rather than 'working-class' occupation in the 1990s), or in relation to how different trades and professions co-operate to produce complex contemporary goods and services. Others extend the definition of 'work' to include things that would not normally be included in the category, such as domestic labour (childcare, home maintenance, washing and cleaning, and so on). Others, still, extend the definition even further. Interactionist sociologists reflect this ambiguity, with ethnomethodology and conversation analysis in particular mirroring the divisions about what constitutes 'work' and how it might best be understood. As elsewhere, though, all three interactionist traditions can locate their investigations in established sociological understandings of the term.

Early sociological definitions of work tended to emphasize two opposite ends of a spectrum of activities. Durkheim focused on the ways in which *mechanical* solidarity has come to be replaced by *organic* solidarity when considered from the point of view of society as a whole. In the earlier 'mechanical' form, each unit of society (a village, a tribe, etc.) was self-sufficient and had a similar structure and organization to each other unit. Thus, for example, one feudal village in England would be fairly similar to any other village: each would have the same personnel (a blacksmith, a carter, a herder, and so on) to maintain the same kinds of social requirements. Under contemporary conditions, each social unit *specializes* in particular tasks: thus, for example, Sheffield used to rely on steel production, Manchester on trade, Bradford on woollen manufacture and so on. Through this specialization, overall production (and so social wealth) could be increased enormously, but this required each town, city, village and so on to be mutually dependent on one another. For Durkheim, then, the division of labour in society means that units of production become more specialized and thus more differentiated, but this allows for greater productivity and wealth overall.

Marx, on the other hand, emphasized the ways in which social progress depends on greater homogeneity. As feudal societies are superseded by capitalist ones, he argued, there is a tendency for work to become deskilled and monotonous. The need for enterprises to compete with one another means there is a drive towards reducing labour costs and increasing productivity, which in turn leads to technological developments to effect these changes. Production line work, the replacement of craft skills with mass-produced items, and an increased control over what workers can do while at work (restricting breaks, enforcing constant rates of work and so on), are all examples of the kinds of changes Marx discussed. Although Marx would agree with Durkheim that the overall wealth of societies is greater in capitalist than in feudal arrangements, he argues that this is not an end in itself but a by-product of capitalist competition: each enterprise in any society has to have lower costs and higher revenues than its competitors to survive, and, *as a consequence of this*, specialization and deskilling are introduced.

The difference between Durkheim and Marx is not simply that the former is (relatively) optimistic about contemporary social trends in work, while the latter is more critical. The definition of work and the value accorded it are different between the two writers as well. For Durkheim, the utility of activities derives from their utility for *societies as a whole*. Thus, the measure of social change is the extent to which it benefits social organization and social structures, not just the individuals who are affected by (or who advance) this change. For Marx, on the other hand, there is something greater at stake: he argues that what defines us as human beings (what distinguishes us from other animals) is our capacity to *transform nature* through work. We alone can make the environment what we want it to be. When work is imposed on us by others, who control both the nature and the value of that work, our 'species-being', what makes us human, is alienated or estranged: we cease to be fully human, as we can no longer freely do the thing that makes us what we are.

The sociology of work has tended to be split between these two approaches. Durkheim's successors in structural-functionalism have examined how different professions work together and how different kinds of work serve to maintain social structures. Parsons, for example, examined the role professional medics have as 'gatekeepers', people who can determine who is legitimately allowed to opt out of their usual social duties and responsibilities as a result of illness (Parsons [1951]1991: ch. 10). Doctors simultaneously serve a function – by determining who can legitimately expect what treatment – and reproduce the social structure – by allowing employers, family members and others to make reasonable social demands on those who are not deemed to be unfit. Marx's heirs have tended to examine the ways in which work is dehumanizing and deskilling (Braverman 1976), removing its sense of value and stripping autonomy from workers. They have also examined the ways in which workplaces are sites of conflict and disagreement, wherein groups of workers may resist management demands (e.g. Cleaver 2000) or be persuaded to put their personal, class interests aside in favour of management-determined 'common interest' (e.g., Beynon 1973).

Sociology's different understandings – between work as having a particular function and work as having particular effects on workers, and between work as a means of creating and transforming the world and work as a specific category of paid effort – are reflected in the different approaches to work taken by symbolic interactionists, ethnomethodologists and conversation analysts. Each perspective has a distinctive approach to the topic and, as we shall argue, the disagreements about just what 'work' is play themselves out in and through these approaches.

Symbolic interactionism and work

Careers and turning points

Following their Chicago School predecessors, symbolic interactionists have tended to examine work in terms of the *spatial* and *temporal* distribution of activities in society. There is, literally, a time and a place for everything. Activities are *spatially* distributed because certain things are done in certain places: funeral directors, for example, organize their workspaces in such a way as to provide for families a specific area for bereaved family members to 'participate in the ritual of funeralisation' (Habenstein 1962: 233). Similarly, the 'dirty work' of preparing deceased persons for funerals is undertaken (sorry!) in 'backstage' (Goffman [1959] 1991) areas where relatives and others will not be able to see the work of preparing the corpse for viewing or disposal. Activities are similarly *temporally* distributed because different people have different uses for the same space at different times. At night, for example, homeless men use the spaces in which apartment block refuse is dumped and stored through the day to search for discarded magazines and books which they can sell second-hand on the street the next day (Duneier 2000). The uses of the space – to discard and to collect items – are *reversed* over the course of a short period of time.

These distributions also apply to the activities people undertake in the course of their working lives, and the identities these entail. Hughes ([1952] 1971) pointed out that narratives about people, biographies, take the form of *careers* with particular *turning points*. A career is a progression from one social position to another. It can apply both in the world of work and elsewhere. Goffman, for example, used the concept of 'career' to account for the ways in which psychiatric patients move from exhibiting odd behaviours to being institutionalized. Careers are not, however, smooth transitions. They are characterized by periods of unchanging routine activity punctuated by sudden changes in status and role: turning points.

Children at school, for example, do not progress day by day from reception class to GCSE, but go through a number of turning points between the ages of five and sixteen. Each year, for example, they change school class, often having a different teacher and being made a part of a different class of peers. They will often change school, either as they progress from one age group to the next, or in the event that schools are closed, opened or reorganized. Furthermore, they may be selected to move into more or less advanced sets depending on how they perform academically and the scores they get on standardized tests. Each of these changes punctuates the child's transition through school, and each can mark changes in all kinds of other things: friendship groups, ambition, performance and so on. These examples presuppose that the child in question has little say in his or her own career: the turning points outlined above are routine, bureaucratic ones that affect any child. The child's own actions and those of his or her parents, however, can be equally important: illness can affect the child's performance in tests and examinations, for example, or his or her parents may have to move home, leading to the child having to develop an entirely new friendship group and fit in to a new and unfamiliar environment. Parents may be pushy or ambitious, or more relaxed in their attitudes, leading to different kinds of demands being placed on teaching and administrative staff, and different peer groups may orient in very different ways to the school, its activities and its value system.

In terms of working life, careers and turning points retain this joint quality: they are a working-out of both organizational imperatives – how particular institutions do particular things – and the effects of individuals' actions and decisions as members of those organizations. Becker (1952a), for example, described the ways the careers of Chicago public (i.e., state) school teachers depend on those teachers knowing when to make changes in their working life to move upwards through the teaching hierarchy. Such teachers, Becker argued, typically take jobs in poorer, less well-equipped schools following qualification. This is largely because better-established schools are less likely to take new staff without extensive experience. As they gain this experience, however, they have a choice of remaining at the 'poor' school and rising through its staff hierarchy or moving to a 'better' school but starting out again at a low level. The problem with this choice is that it has to be made *at the right time*: if the teacher remains at the 'poor' school too long he or she will find it more difficult to gain work elsewhere – other potential employers will suspect that the teacher has become fixed in doing things the way they are done at the school – but attempting to move too early will appear disloyal to the 'poor' school and potentially overambitious or pushy to the 'better' one. Career progression is not automatic, therefore, and it is not simply something workers ask for and get: it requires the right circumstances to be present at the right time in the worker's career. Symbolic interactionists, therefore, emphasize the sense in which socialization is not just something that happens to children but, through career progression and its punctuating turning points, a constant aspect of adult life as well.

Identification with work

People identify with their jobs. Often we will introduce ourselves by saying what we do, or where we work, and this information may be concealed if it is felt to be embarrassing or discrediting. Rather than taking for granted the notion that some occupations are 'superior' to others – either in terms of status or with respect to the responsibility invested in such jobs – symbolic interactionists examine the ways in which a person's occupation is tied in with their sense of self.

Becker and Carper (1956), for instance, discuss the ways different professionals understand their role and status with regard to their institutional position. Physiologists, for instance, see themselves as occupying a narrow and esoteric academic specialism, and are hostile to the notion of moving beyond it: to move into management, or the private sector, is, in some ways, to cease to be a 'real' physiologist. Engineers, on the other hand, see themselves as being much more independent: they can work anywhere, and understand their career progression as being about choosing between potential employers (rather than avoiding unemployment). This means they have less of a sense of group loyalty than the physiologists, and greater heterogeneity of activities in their actual work. Contemporary examples of similar professions might be sociologists, with their professional associations and almost universal employment by further and higher education institutions, and software developers, for whom large companies have to compete to make it worth their while not to operate simply as self-employed consultants.

These identifications, again, are neither fixed nor permanent. Occupations can become more or less prestigious, and the movement of individuals *through* an occupation often requires them to change their self-perceptions and identifications as they progress. Medical students, for example, typically go through several different ways of understanding themselves and their profession before settling on the 'correct' self-identification. Becker and Geer (1958) described this progression as concerning the 'fate of idealism' in medical school. Initially, student doctors are drawn by the idea of helping people, saving lives and so on – but their notion of what this will actually be like in real life is not very realistic. Because of the demands placed on them by their studies and placements, these trainee doctors move through a phase of being disillusioned and cynical with their profession, and – more particularly – with many of the patients they end up having to deal with. This phase is then replaced by one in which the doctors, now ready to practice, become more realistic, and prepared to accept both the positive and negative aspects of their profession. The self-identification of medics as particular *kinds* of professionals depends on this movement through idealism, cynicism and realism: it produces doctors who are able to practise in the ways that are required.

Formal features of work

Everett Hughes ([1951] 1971: 316) oversaw many of the classic interactionist studies of work, and emphasized the *formal* and *comparative* importance of those studies, as we saw in his remarks on the matter on p. 32. Work, in this sense, is not something just to be studied for its own sake. The comparison of different trades, and the identification of their formal similarities, allows other sociologically interesting features of the world to be identified. Notions of loyalty and group identification, for example, are particularly strong at work. Becker (1952b) discussed the ways in which staff at a school typically expect their managers to take their side in conflicts with pupils and their parents. For managers to manage such institutions successfully they must be seen to understand the needs of staff members, and the particular pressures they are under – they show this understanding and sensitivity through not taking seriously clearly frivolous or unreasonable client demands.

Other client-based work has similar features: Becker elsewhere (1993) discusses 'crocks', those patients who do not respond to treatment despite being seen and treated by all relevant personnel. Identifying such a patient means being able to demonstrate that their illness is not due to any mistake on the part of the medical team, reinforcing a sense of professional expertise – after all, if the patient's failure to improve is because of his or her personal characteristics, it does not reflect badly on those treating that patient. Loyalty is also important in less 'professional' jobs. Roy (1952), for example, discusses the ways in which production line workers orientate to what is for them a 'reasonable' level of productivity. Although they could work faster, and produce more, and be paid more as a consequence (the workers were on piece rates), the production line workers he studied enforced a set level of productivity on themselves and one another. Working too slowly or too quickly brought unwanted management interest, and so the group maintained and enforced the level of daily productivity it viewed as acceptable – and those who worked faster or slower than this norm were subjected to negative sanctions by their peers.

Negotiation and disagreement at work

Loyalty is often an ambiguous term in the workplace. Strauss et al. (1964), for example, investigated the ways in which different professionals working together in a psychiatric hospital have to manage their professional identities – as doctors, nurses, social workers and so on – in conjunction with their professional responsibilities – to treat patients effectively and quickly. These loyalties are made more problematic by the fact that different professionals will often legitimately have different notions about what constitutes appropriate treatment: psychiatrists will often emphasize physiological interventions, for example, while social workers may be more concerned with social relationships and lifestyle. These differences are *negotiated* through interaction, typically in staff meetings. Precedents are cited, the correct way to understand cases argued about, differences of opinion aired – but, universally, decisions are made and treatment is administered. The different workers' professional understandings do not get in the way of their work – because the centre of their professional status is their ability to practise effectively. Even though ideological and other differences exist, to allow those to get in the way of routine organizational workings would be to cease to act in a professional manner. It is here that ethnomethodological understandings of work begin.

Ethnomethodology and work

The ethnomethodological definition of a 'member' (of society) is 'a mastery of natural language'. As we discussed in our chapter on status and power (chapter 4), this translates as the capacity to be left alone to get on with one's affairs without interruption by others. A member is someone *competent* to practise the activities they are engaged in, and who should not be disturbed or interrupted in their conduct unless there are good reasons for such an interruption. In short, a member is someone whose conduct is manifestly *rational*: it makes good sense and it would be unreasonable for anyone else to question it.

This definition informs and underpins the ethnomethodological understanding of work and work practices. Work activities are understood to be rational, to make good sense, and it is the job of the ethnographic investigator to demonstrate how that good sense is produced and recognized by participants. In common with Marx and the structural-functionalists, however, ethnomethodologists do not just understand 'work' to mean 'paid employment'. Instead, ethnomethodologists define *any* activity that is productive of the social world as 'work'. Unlike structural-functionalists, however, ethnomethodologists do not define this 'productivity' as meaning that activities generate social structures – instead, they take 'productivity' to mean the generation, maintenance and recognition of meaning, the production of sense. This means that ethnomethodological studies of 'work' often seem quite strange: indeed, ethnographies of Kung Fu (Girton

1986) and the occult (Eglin 1986) were included in Garfinkel's edited collection *Ethnomethodological Studies of Work*.

The concept of work is therefore something that ethnomethodologists use to refer to the generation, production and maintenance of meaningful settings and activities. Like the symbolic interactionists, many ethnomethodologists have orientated to the fact that this generation, production and maintenance has certain formal characteristics that are found across radically different settings. These include the retrospective–prospective sense of activities, an orientation to rules, and the concept of *Lebenswelt* pairs.

The retrospective–prospective sense of activities

Garfinkel ([1967] 1984: 41) argues that work activities have a 'retrospective–prospective' sense. This means they are not carried out in the way a computer might manipulate an input to produce an output, but are undertaken with an orientation to what the possible effects of different results might be. What this means is that when we are working, what we do is constantly being considered in relation to how other people might take it, what difference it might make to ourselves and to others, whether it could be subject to complaint or grievance procedures, whether others might argue that we did it the wrong way, and so on. Possible future states of affairs are invoked to allow us to make sense of current actions.

Garfinkel ([1967] 1984: ch. 1) illustrated this with reference to the work of coroners deciding how someone died. Each case can be 'found' to be the result of an accident, a homicide (murder or manslaughter) or suicide, and the coroners have to work out which is the 'correct' interpretation of any particular death. As well as examining the corpse for signs of one mode of death rather than another (such as the 'hesitation cuts' that suicides often exhibit, marking the points where they tentatively cut themselves shallowly before administering the final, killing, cut), the sense that will be made of different decisions is also used to reach a verdict. A verdict of homicide, for instance, will necessarily require police and court involvement, and so such a verdict will not be reached lightly: doubt about the correctness of such a decision is far likelier to rule it out than doubts about a verdict of accidental death.

Garfinkel and his colleagues Michael Lynch and Eric Livingston (Garfinkel et al. 1981) took this approach further in their study of the discovery of the first pulsar, an astronomical object that emits a regular 'pulse'. Astrophysical knowledge indicated that such objects should exist, but none had ever been observed. Garfinkel and his colleagues were able to get hold of the audio recording of the night the first pulsar was discovered. They found that, in the scientific reports of this finding, the pulsar's existence was taken for granted and the work done to 'locate' it succeeded or failed on the basis of whether equipment was properly calibrated, the telescope was pointing in the right direction and so on. The pulsar existed all along, and the earlier failures to observe it were the result of not knowing how such an observation could be made. In fact, on listening to the audio recording, it was found that something quite different happened: the scientists looking for the pulsar were systematically going through different settings on their equipment *until* the point they 'found' the pulsar. On discovering it, they *retrospectively* classified their previous activities as 'unsuccessful' because they now had a 'successful' observation with which to compare them. The sense of some work activities can only be derived after the fact, once an outcome has emerged – and what these activities 'were' can then be read back from that outcome.

In some ways the retrospective–prospective sense of activities is ethnomethodology's 'version' of the symbolic interactionists' concepts of careers and turning points. Rather than emphasizing the momentous points at which lives change, however, ethnomethodology focuses on the ways that possible futures are invoked at all points in the work process, to make sense of what is being done and to ensure that it is being done correctly. 'Doing correctly', however, also requires a notion of normative orderliness.

Orientating to rules

Most work activities are based on the application or interpretation of rules. Organizations are *formal* because they are based on proper procedures, guidelines, policies and standards. There are usually particular ways of doing things, and for those things to have been deemed to have been done *correctly* they have to be done in the correct ways. Those rules do not *govern* activities, however: rules do not contain their own application. Proper procedures are followed when workers can demonstrate to interested others that rules have been orientated to. Rules are not taken as descriptions of what people do in ethnomethodological studies of work, but as features of the setting in which people do their work – and like any other feature of that setting they can be *used* in different ways, and different kinds of actions can be *shown* to come under their auspices.

Bittner ([1965] 1974), for example, lists three ways in which rules can *practically* be shown to have been followed in organizational work. Firstly, 'the gambit of compliance' can be used. In this, whatever needs to be done to get a job done *is* done, but it is done in such a way as to allow workers to be seen to have followed the organization's guiding principles. A police officer, for example, may not arrest someone who is committing a crime if, by doing so, he or she might make the situation worse: the rule 'keep the peace' is used to justify this action, even though it clearly breaks another rule, 'arrest lawbreakers' (Bittner 1967a). Secondly, 'stylistic unity' can be invoked to justify an action. Complex organizations depend on lots of people acting in similar ways, and so decisions and courses of action can be shown to 'make sense' if they align with the ways other people get things done. Even if doing something apparently breaches a rule, the fact that everyone works in that way allows for precedent to be cited and the action to be undertaken anyway. Thus, for example, staff working in a halfway house for drug users released from prison often do not ask inmates to take part in the activities they are meant to, as they know such requests will be rejected. Although this entirely reverses what staff should be doing, it serves as a means of showing an orientation to the normal workings of the establishment: not wasting time asking for things to be done that clearly will not be (Wieder 1974). Finally, 'corroborative reference' can be deployed. This allows workers to refer to the organization as a whole in justifying their actions: it is always possible to justify something in terms of the interests of one or more aspects of the organization, even if it apparently breaches rules. Thus, for example, police officers can invoke the notion of 'discretion' in justifying their activities, where 'discretion' is seen to be something important to the police force as a whole (Bittner 1967a).

Bittner's emphasis on the *uses* rules are put to in organizational life is the ethnomethodological riposte to symbolic interactionism's emphasis on the formal features of different kinds of work. While ethnomethodologists do not dispute that working practices have formal similarities, they emphasize the ways in which those formal features are the outcomes of interactional work, and are produced and maintained by members. Although sociologists can describe rules, regularities, formal similarities and so on, when they are doing so this is always a matter of describing what members themselves are producing and managing: there are no 'real' formal features sociologists can point to existing separate to the circumstances of their use. Ethnomethodologists have glossed this emphasis on process by using the term '*Lebenswelt* pair'.

Lebenswelt *pairs*

Garfinkel uses the concept of *Lebenswelt* (life-world) pairs to refer to the difference between producing something and the outcome of that production process (Lynch 1993). When we talk about a book, a report, a film, a piece of music, a telephone and so on, we are always referring to the outcome of processes of work: these things are always produced, usually by a large group of people. The sociology of work – including symbolic interactionism – is meant to look at these activities of production, the ways in which objects, services and so on get made. In reality, however, the mundane details of manufacture, of production, are rarely examined: there is a tendency to ignore the everyday, even though the everyday is the stuff of work. Garfinkel insists that the manufacture of *anything* should be of sociological interest, and the subject of sociological description, starting from the smallest and most 'trivial' of things.

Thus, for example, the sociology of culture (as dealt with by, amongst others, Becker, 1982, in his *Art Worlds*) often describes how works of genius are actually the outcomes of lots of different people doing lots of different things. As Becker points out right at the beginning of the book, without someone to bring him coffee in the morning the Victorian novelist Anthony Trollope would not have been able to write: because of this servant he was able to get his writing for the day done before breakfast, and thus maintain a good level of productivity. Here, however, the sociology of work tends to stop: demonstrating that work is a collective enterprise, even if it might seem otherwise, is 'enough' to show that it is a sociologically legitimate area of study.

Garfinkel insists that this is insufficient. To write, it is not enough to have coffee, light, a desk and so on – one must also have the equipment and ability to make inscriptions, either by writing with a pen or pencil, by typing, or by manipulating a keyboard or other input device. Exactly how these inscriptions are made, and how they are combined to make up a 'book', 'article', 'poem', 'short story' and so on, is as important as anything else – and these doings should be topics for sociological study as much as anything else. Sudnow (1993) described how learning to type and learning to play the piano are remarkably similar activities, and how a feature of both is forgetting that they involve the movement of fingers on a keyboard: a competent typist is not aware of his or her hands moving, but focuses entirely on the words being written and their output on paper or a screen. The description of these 'ways of the hand' is an example of the ethnomethodological description of work activities, insofar as an 'output' – a performance or typed document – can be shown to emerge from the artful deployment of such mundane abilities.

This emphasis on the 'just this-ness' of a social activity – its haecceity – the thing that makes it what it is rather than something else, is, as we have seen (in chapter 2), a fundamental concern for ethnomethodology. The notion that orderliness can be found in the slightest details of social activities is its other key finding. The idea that work itself can be found in such fine-grained details is, of course, the province of conversation analysis.

Conversation analysis and work

Sacks' interest in the production of orderliness ran throughout his work. Introducing one of his lecture courses he said:

> Whatever we may think about what it is to be an ordinary person in the world, an initial shift is not to think of an 'ordinary person' as some person, but as somebody having that as their job, as their constant preoccupation, doing 'being ordinary'. It's not that someone *is* ordinary, it's perhaps that that's what their business is. And it takes work, as any other business does. And if you just extend the analogy of what you obviously think of as work – as whatever it is that takes analytic, intellectual, emotional energy – then you can come to see that all sorts of nominalized things – personal characteristics and the like – are jobs which are done, which took some kind of effort, training, etc. So I'm not going to be talking about an 'ordinary person' as this or that person, or as some average, i.e., a non-exceptional person on some statistical basis, but as something that is the way somebody constitutes themselves, and, in effect, a job that they do on themselves. They and the people around them may be co-ordinatively engaged in assuring that each of them are ordinary persons, and that can then be a job that they undertake together, to achieve that each of them, together, are ordinary persons. (Sacks 1992b: 216)

Much of Sacks' early work can be understood as being about the doing of ordinary activities – categorizing things, describing, asking and answering questions, asking for and providing accounts, and so on – but his later sequential analysis appears to be a move away from this. As we have seen (in chapter 3), Sacks' later work emphasizes the *machinery* of conversation, the ways in which different elements are assembled and organized around one another in tightly arranged ways. His emphasis on the context-dependent nature of conversation, however, provides us with a way of bridging his earlier and later approaches. The notion of 'context-free' rules for turn-taking does not provide us with a mechanistic, automatic system for organizing sequences of conversation. Rather, these elements make up the machinery of conversation itself, with the *work* of operating this machinery being that of participants to any specific interaction. 'Doing being ordinary' and 'doing turn-taking' are different elements of the same set of procedures: deploying elements of talk, and operating the machinery of turn-taking, to achieve interactional goals. This may well be the strongest and most detailed form of ethnomethodological description.

More colloquial understandings of 'work', however, are often brought to bear in conversation analytic work. Studies of the relationships between talk and work fall into two categories: studies of 'talk at work', and studies of membership categorization in the work setting.

Talk at work

In the 'simplest systematics' (Sacks et al. 1974), it is suggested that conversation is just one form of 'speech exchange system'. Others might include ceremonial talk, debates, chaired meetings and so on. Sacks et al., however, do argue that conversation is the basis for these other systems – it is the home ground from which other ways of organizing talk are developed – and that this should be borne in mind when conducting comparative studies of these different forms of turn-taking and speech exchange. The study of how different speech exchange systems operate in different settings is the main area of interest of the 'talk at work' programme (Drew and Heritage 1992).

In their collection *Talk at Work*, Drew and Heritage take a more mechanistic line. While they acknowledge that talk's organization is both context-free and context-dependent – rather than simply context-free – their comparative analyses, in which different work settings are considered from the point of view of the different kinds of turn-taking organization they 'contain', tend to emphasize the normative and institutionally stable features of work talk over the details of their local production. Thus, for example, they argue that:

> if it can be shown that the participants in a vernacularly characterized institutional setting such as a courtroom pervasively organize their turn taking in a way that is distinctive from ordinary conversation, it can be proposed that they are organizing their conduct so as to display and realize its 'institutional' character over its course and that they are doing so *recurrently and pervasively*. (Drew and Heritage 1992: 26)

Thus, for example, Atkinson (1992) points out that proceedings in a criminal court are often very different from the ordinary conversations studied by earlier conversation analysts:

Counsel: Did you ever receive any telephone calls from him?
Witness: No.
Counsel: Did the defendant ever request a date with you?
Witness: No.
Counsel: On February 14th, 1975, you were what, eighteen years old at that time?
Witness: Yes.

(Atkinson 1992: 201)

By acknowledging answers only by asking a further question, the counsel here is able to make it difficult for the witness to establish what has been made of the previous answer. The uses to which those answers might be put is something that will only emerge later in the cross-examination, or in the summing-up.

While it allows for different kinds of turn-taking to be examined, this approach is problematic as it assumes that the interactionally generated turn-taking system in, for example, a courtroom is a 'thing' which can be analysed in relation to other 'things': the system of turn-taking is taken as a unit of analysis, rather than treated as the result of analysing conversation analysis' *real* unit of analysis, interaction through talk. Although the 'talk at work' approach was popular, and generated a number of studies, it will not be considered further for the purposes of this text. As Schegloff (1992b) points out, there is a tendency in such analyses to 'jump' from the examination of talk to the presumption of the existence of a particular kind of social context or structure (e.g. a court, a classroom) and make attributions about each by using the other. While this is not necessarily 'wrong', it does diverge considerably from the original aims and objectives of conversation analysis.

Debates about how 'context' or 'structure' can or should be incorporated into conversation analytic work are typically somewhat fraught. Wilson (1991: 27), for example, argues that 'externality and constraint are members' accomplishments, and social structure and social interaction are reflexively related rather than standing in causal or formal definitional relations to one another'. This sounds reasonable, and seems on the surface to fit with existing ethnomethodological and conversation analytic notions of context as locally produced and recognized (see, for example, Zimmerman and Pollner 1970). A problem with this approach, however, is that the context of 'work' is often applied by the sociologist doing the investigation rather than by parties to the interaction themselves. In studies of medical encounters, for example, lots of things may get done: evasion, revelation, questioning and answering, and so on. No one would deny that these things may be done differently in a medical context compared to a different one. That does not mean, however, that one can unproblematically state that the organization of talk is done to maintain, produce or orientate to its status as 'consultation talk'. Rather, that has to be *shown* through close analysis of the talk itself.

In their analysis of the generation of applause by politicians, for example, Heritage and Greatbatch (1986) provide a typology of the different techniques speakers can use to signal to an audience that an applause-relevant point is coming up. These include the employment of conventional turn designs (such as three-part lists) and conventional rhetorical devices (such as attacks on opponents). The fact that these techniques are used to elicit applause does not, however, mean that they will necessarily work – or, indeed, that their main function is to generate applause. 'Applause' is not necessarily one coherent phenomenon, and it is unclear whether one can treat the utterances that precede applause as necessarily being designed to elicit it. By treating 'applause' as a context-independent phenomenon, and by treating the utterances that precede it as being 'designed' to elicit it, Heritage and Greatbatch are able to come up with their typology. There is not, of course, any reason to believe that this typology either is comprehensive or allows for the successful generation of applause in any particular case: it is a very conventional sociological list of activities, rather than something produced in the Sacksian conversation analytic tradition.

The invocation of 'context' and 'structure', then, is problematic in the 'talk at work' approach, as it tends towards reducing talk to its more context-independent and mechanical features, and allows analysts to substitute their descriptions and categories for those that may be found to be being used by parties to the talk themselves. An attempt to return to the earlier, more context-sensitive, forms of conversation analysis, and thereby to avoid such problems, is offered by membership categorization analytical approaches to work talk.

Membership categorization and work

Work often involves the classification, categorization and evaluation of objects and persons. Thus, for example, in a neuroscience laboratory, slides of rat brain are classified on a continuum from 'good enough for publication' to 'good enough to use as data' to 'not good enough' (Lynch 1982). These categories are explicitly used by laboratory workers in their evaluations of brain lesion material: one scientist explicitly says to another, "They're users but they ain't lookers", referring to an electron-micrographic 'montage' of brain materials. Such categorization also extends to making judgements about other people. Baker (1997) examined the ways a 'ticketing' system for rewarding good behaviour and punishing bad was used to make moral assessments about children in school staff gatherings. This added complexity to the decision making of staff, as discussions were constantly ongoing concerning whether 'good' pupils were receiving 'enough' motivation from being given 'good' tickets, whether there was consistency in ticket-giving between staff and across similarly behaved pupils, whether 'good' pupils were 'rewarded' (demonstrating that the categories 'good' and 'bad' are not the same as the categories 'highly positively ticketed' and 'highly negatively ticketed', respectively), and so on. Issues are embedded in the teachers' use of categories:

Jon: I can't see why you're trying to make it harder to go up. Positively=
?:   =No, I agree with that, I I think
?:   Well, [I think
?:   [I think it's a good thing that so many kids <u>were</u> (up)
Al: Because I think it- a lot of kids are up on Plus 3 now, and at the end of the year they're gonna be knocked right back down to nought. So if you can make it harder to get up there, you're only going to get the good kids and they're going to be demoralised come February when they're back to zero.

                                                            (Baker 1997: 88)

Here we can see an interesting variant on the notion of measuring: the tickets are meant to act as rewards for good behaviour and as punishments for bad, and also to provide a measure of a pupil's progress over the course of a year. This *should* mean that 'good' pupils are those with a high score, and 'bad' ones are those with a low one. In fact, as we can see from Al's comment, 'good kids' might not be rewarded properly by the system, leading to them becoming demoralized. The issue here is that the teachers already know who the 'good' and 'bad' kids are – and they are attempting to organize the ticketing system in such a way as to reflect that knowledge. The system, in short, is not 'objective' but needs, in order to be understood as rational, to map onto what 'everyone already knows'.

In studies of complex work settings, the ways in which categories, identities, motives and activities are co-related are far more revealing. In a courtroom setting, for example, testimony should be clear and unambiguous: witnesses should be able to state that either something happened or it did not, as we saw in Atkinson's transcript (above). When they are unwilling to make such statements – because it will impact negatively on their reputation or image – they may find the requirement to speak in such unambiguous terms problematic:

> Nields: Did you suggest to the Attorney General that maybe the diversion memorandum and the fact that there was a diversion need not ever come out?
> North: Again, I don't recall that specific conversation at all, but I'm not saying it didn't happen.
> Nields: You don't deny it?
> North: No.
> Nields: You don't deny suggesting to the Attorney General of the United States that he just figure out a way of keeping this diversion document secret?
> North: I don't deny that I said it. I'm not saying I remember it either.
> (Lynch and Bogen 1997: 113)

Through the classification of North's testimony as 'not denial', and the invocation of the 'Attorney General *of the United States*' (my emphasis), the cross-examiner, Nields, is able to demonstrate from North's testimony that – even if he cannot remember whether or not he suggested covering something up – the fact that he *could not remember* whether or not he had made such a suggestion to such a powerful and, one might assume, morally upright character has seriously negative implications for potential assessments of his moral character.

While the study of membership categorization in work contexts avoids the problems of the 'talk at work' programme, it is fundamentally just membership categorization analysis conducted in a work setting. To be fair, its practitioners do not claim it is an alternative to sociological studies of work, but rather that it stands as a particular way of examining conversation. It may be the case that 'work', in the sense of paid labour, is simply a different setting in which routine talk takes place. This would resonate strongly with Sacks' early formulation of 'doing being ordinary' as 'work', and chimes with the ethnomethodological understanding of all social activities being 'work'. As in Macbeth's (1990) account of how a teacher uses a 'quiet reproach' to calm down a disruptive pupil, it is possible for sequential and membership categorization analyses to be brought together to show how a particular work activity gets done, but it seems unlikely that this will 'add up' to form an alternative sociology of work in the ways that the ethnomethodological and symbolic interactionist approaches attempt to do.

Computer-supported co-operative work

Macbeth's analysis does point towards something interesting about work, however: the fact that it is made up of temporally organized mundane activities. In recent years, informed by conversation analysis and ethnomethodology, examinations of technologically mediated working practices have had a major impact on the design and implementation of new technologies. Suchman's (1987) book *Plans and Situated Actions* is the canonical text for this approach, sometimes referred to as 'human–computer interaction' or 'computer-supported co-operative work' (although studies in the tradition are not strictly just about computer use).

In this approach, video recordings of people working with technology are studied to determine what 'works' and what 'doesn't', which aspects of the technology allow people to get on with their jobs and which do not. Feeding these findings back into technology design has facilitated improvements in interface design, and most major technology companies (such as Xerox, Microsoft, Hewlett-Packard and Apple) now employ interactionist sociologists, usually trained in the conversation analytic tradition, as part of their research and design departments. Although there seems to be no convincing conversation analytic sociology of work, the methods Sacks initially employed and the findings he and his colleagues made have found a home in one of the most cutting-edge and highly funded sectors of the economy.

Conclusion

Symbolic interactionist, ethnomethodological and conversation analytic studies of work have often been useful to employers, organizers and others, as, for example, in the case of computer-supported co-operative work. Nevertheless, the strength of these approaches is in their ability to ground debates about what constitutes work, how it gets done, and how it is organized *by its participants*. Symbolic interactionists have successfully demonstrated that 'structural' and 'demographic' features of the working population are the product of artful and rational activities on the part of workers. Ethnomethodologists have 'respecified' work more radically than even the Marxian tradition, and found unexpected logics and rationalities in the mundane details of how people organize themselves. Conversation analysts have convincingly shown the ways mundane skills are brought to bear to undertake complex and difficult occupational requirements, from hearing evidence to keeping order in a classroom.

7
Deviance

Introduction

A range of academic disciplines and dedicated professions have developed whose business is 'the deviant'. Underlying much of their work are attempts to identify what 'causes' persons or groups of persons to become deviant and what might be best 'done' about – or with – them. The body of sociological and criminological literature that has accrued over the twentieth century on this issue is huge, but has displayed some clear directions, perspectives and explanations.

From the nineteenth century 'classical' criminologists emphasized the idea that deviant acts are a matter of 'choice', based on the premise that all persons possess 'free will' and act according to principles of cost–benefit ('how will I benefit from some deviant action and what will it cost me if I get caught?'). We are all capable of committing deviant acts, but normally refrain from doing so, on the basis of the pain we may suffer by being identified as having done so. Deviance in this sense is a breach of the 'social contract' that benefits all members of society and which, when breached, should be responded to with force appropriate to meeting the extent of harm caused. In effect, members of society operate under the same contractual conditions and must expect similar punishment for their wilful misdemeanours.

The idea that absolutely anyone might equally commit deviant acts was undermined by the more 'positivistic' criminology of the late nineteenth and early twentieth centuries. These approaches looked less at choices, and more at the 'causes' of deviance. The idea underlying these approaches was that society did not consist of persons operating under equal conditions, or even with equal degrees of free will. Rather, certain 'forces' – over which individuals have limited or no control – exert particular influences that may predispose them to, or push them towards, deviance.

Of particular interest to sociologists was the identification of 'social' forces (social, cultural and economic conditions) that, although perhaps not strictly deterministic, can be seen to have a significant impact on whether, why and in what form, persons or groups of persons engage in deviant behaviour. Sociologists taking this line imply that any person could become deviant, if subjected to similar social, cultural or economic 'conditions'. In this sense, then, deviant identities could be regarded as an embodiment of wider social ills, shortcomings and inequalities.

Taking Durkheim's notion of anomie, for example, the sociologist Robert Merton argued that persons were presented with shared cultural values, but some were denied legitimate 'opportunities' to achieve them. The only choice left open for many was then to take alternative routes, which would often manifest in and through deviant activity in a variety of forms, depending on available deviant opportunities (see Cloward and Ohlin 1961). Simultaneously, the Chicago School (see Bulmer 1984; Kurtz 1984) produced a wealth of studies focusing on rapid urban change, and its effect on contemporaneous urban deviance. Rather than free will or internal drives, the emphasis focused on such things as social (dis)integration and (dis)organization as mapped out across the spatial, social and moral arrangements of the modern city (see Park 1925; Shaw and McKay 1942).

Bubbling away in these studies was the recognition that social groups as well as structural conditions could be the loci of deviant behaviour. On this latter point, scholars such as Sutherland (1947) recognized the power of 'association' – that is, the way in which face-to-face interaction allowed for the transmission of deviant values between social actors. This perspective allowed sociologists to demonstrate how persons with similar deviant values could ultimately form collectives with similar others as deviant 'subcultures' (Cohen 1955).

Although several of these early approaches to understanding deviance did recognize the importance of societal reaction and response in *dealing* with deviance, the recognition of the actual role that such response might play in the *development* of deviance marked the start of what we know today as the interactionist approach to deviance (Tannenbaum 1938; Lemert 1967). Ideas around 'secondary' deviance emerged from this literature – that is, deviance that comes about not from, in the first instance, free-will, structural conditions or differential associations, but as a result of persons or groups being in some way identified and publically known *as* deviant by the wider community. Developing from this, Becker's (1963) classic study of labelling showed how societal definitions of deviance and identification of perpetrators could have a powerful (potentially all-consuming) impact on persons' biographies, conceptualizations of selfhood, and identity.

Against this backdrop of criminological theory, one might be tempted to equate deviance solely with 'criminal' and 'delinquent' behaviour. However, interactionist studies of deviance do not restrict their focus to deviation from formal rules (laws), but include breaches of less formal 'norms', 'expectations' and 'proprieties'. Non-normality and non-ordinary-ness are of equal interest. Qualities such as morality and competence alongside delinquency and criminality can thus be opened up for close examination. Moreover, this focus on the non-ordinary allows us to move away from the spectacular to the everyday, routine, mundane and taken-for-granted ways in which deviance can be identified and may reveal itself.

Much of social life places on us all the demands of 'being ordinary' (see Sacks 1984b). We are expected to neither *attract* unnecessary attention from nor *pay* unnecessary attention to each other (Goffman 1963a). Indeed, we are under some obligation actively to 'demonstrate' our normality (Goffman 1983a). This working agreement allows us to go about our everyday lives largely unnoticed and unmolested. Moreover, it allows the social world to function as a group of persons who can rely on – and to some extent predict – each others' 'ordinary' competences, co-operation and moral integrity across the various episodes of interaction that constitute social life. Much of this agreement, and many of these expectations, rests on our desire to avoid being noticed or 'picked out' in some way as *being* or *behaving* 'differently'. There are good reasons for wanting to stay 'unnoticed' in many social situations. As Sacks noted, 'For Western societies, at least, being noticeable and being deviant seem intimately related' (Sacks 1972a: 280). Moreover, 'deviant' is a heavily loaded concept in everyday life. When we think of, or sociologists generally talk about, 'deviant identities', we usually refer to undesired and undesirable ones; to be exceedingly beautiful may indeed be noticeable, but it is not usually thought of as 'deviant', whereas to be 'butt ugly' is! We have much to gain then by being unnoticeable and spend much of our time during the course of our daily rounds sustaining this 'unremarkable' status, and according it to others.

'Deviant identity' can arise from a myriad of 'sources'. Indeed, we may even experience some degree of deviant identity by mere 'association' with 'deviant' individuals. However, even though we can readily identify potential sources of deviant identities, as we shall see below, there are few (if any) aspects of identity that can be seen to be universally 'deviant' per se. What seems to be the case is that the nature, status, extent, duration and evaluation of deviant features relies upon how these things are defined as such. Relatedly, the significance for and impact on any given social situation depends very much on what the participants in those situations are prepared to 'make of' such features. What 'counts' and 'is noticed' as deviant, then, becomes an interactional issue and one most often specific to this or that social gathering, situation, particular encounter or group of persons.

This opens up the area of the everyday plight of the deviant. What constitutes deviant behaviour or characteristics, how these are managed, and public perceptions of them are not fixed and pre-given notions. In fact, just as deviant identities can arise in and impact on interaction, so they can be – and often are – negotiated, challenged and contested *through* interaction. Indeed, as we shall see below, a range of interactionist studies have looked specifically at that – how deviance becomes the 'football' of interactional games, negotiations and strategies.

Like any other system of order, there are limits or 'boundaries', beyond which certain actions 'must be' responded to. Certain deviant acts can, do, and are socially expected to lead to a range of negative sanctions. Although we are suggesting that there is no condition or aspect of behaviour that is deviant per se, there are certain aspects of behaviour that are the focus of legal or moral imperative to 'do something'. Although punishment, treatment or rehabilitation may be potential responses to deviance, public reaction tends to focus more on the former of these (rarely does the public react 'as sociologists would do' in a measured and critical manner). Indeed, there is a tendency for public reaction (often fuelled by media reporting) to be highly simplified and exaggerated and often panic-stricken (Cohen 1972). Even though often irrational and distorted, the sheer 'swell' of such collective sentiments can result in 'real' consequences such as changes in laws, and regulation of monitoring and control of particular groups, professions or persons (reflecting Thomas and Thomas' (1928) much-cited dictum: 'If men define situations as real, they are real in their consequences').

In focusing on this array of deviant acts, identities and interactions, the question of what 'causes deviance' (at least for interactionists) becomes somewhat meaningless. Instead, questions such as how deviance is defined, responded to, managed and, sometimes, contested in interaction become more salient.

Symbolic interactions and deviant identities

In chapter 1 we examined how, in interaction, 'things are acted upon according to their meaning' (Blumer 1969). 'Things' in this sense can be taken, in effect, to be any-thing that persons in interaction decide to attribute some meaning *to* and then follow some course of action *towards* based on that meaning. Features and characteristics of, information about, and behaviour and actions by persons can count as things. The possible number of things and potential consequences for interaction is too numerous to list. However, a useful way of drawing this myriad of possible sources together is by looking at three salient aspects of deviant identity – bodies, biography and behaviour.

Bodies, biographies, and behaviour

The body is perhaps the most tangible indicator of non-ordinaryness. At the start of his book *Stigma*, Erving Goffman relays part of a heart-rending letter sent to a magazine column by a girl with no nose. This single tragic example points to a wider discussion of what Goffman refers to as 'abominations of the body' (1963b). Goffman's observations, and those made by numerous other sociologists, point to the centrality of the physical embodiment of persons in interaction, and the ease with which deviant meaning, and deviant identity, can be ascribed due to certain features of the body. To be physically disabled, abnormally short, tall, fat, thin, to have some visible scar or disfigurement, to have blemishes, marks or unusual features of the skin, to 'give off' particular smells or sounds, or to have limited control over one's bodily movements – in interaction – can lead to the attribution of deviant identity, as can more subtle aspects of embodiment, such as having overly tanned skin or possessing red hair. Indeed, throughout history the body has been used as a marker of deviance. The word stigma itself originally referred to a mark burnt into the body to signify some deviant aspect of the possessor that might otherwise go unseen (see Goffman 1963b; obvious contemporary examples include such things as the tattooing of concentration camp prisoners).

Although embodied indicators provides us with an immediate

physical manifestation of definable deviance, much of what we conceive of as deviant relates to 'behaviour'. Behaviour that appears to be voluntary, volitional and motivated can be damaging to persons' identities. Behaviour in this sense points more in the direction of norms, expectations and 'rules', and apparent breaking of, 'faulty' relationships to, or inability to abide by those norms, expectations and rules. Moreover, there is a strong moral dimension to behaviour in this sense (how we might be judged or evaluated in terms of our moral worth, integrity, trustworthiness, etc). Indeed, for all of us, the morality of our behaviour is a minefield through which we have to pick our way carefully, and often 'mask' our tracks. Rule-breaking behaviour is most obvious when one considers 'formal' rules, that is, rules that are in some way written into and punishable by laws and legislation. As we have already noted, much criminological theory looks at this type of 'formally' deviant behaviour. Many formal rules are underpinned by moral expectations. For example murder, rape, assaulting the elderly or abusing children are taken to be not only legally sanctionable but also morally abhorrent. Others, although punishable by law, may be less morally reprehensible (e.g. vandalism, urinating in public or fiddling insurance claims). There are also, of course, many moral expectations that are not so formally prescribed, expressed or sanctionable. For example, a sexually promiscuous female or philandering husband, work-shy layabout, liar, cheat or binge-drinker may well behave in morally questionable ways but are not – all other things being equal – open to formal sanctions.

As Goffman (1967) noted, we are all susceptible to making gaffes or faux pas. However, one source of deviant identities is behaviour that is perceived as or deemed to be in some way 'odd', 'irrational' or 'inexplicable'. Quite often there is a situational element to this, pointing to what is 'proper' and 'improper', 'appropriate' and 'inappropriate' in particular social situations, or even at particular points in interaction. Although the inference might be that actions that are not based in physical incapacity or incompetence are always volitional, this latter aspect of deviant behaviour opens up the possibility that this may not always be the case, i.e., that persons may be understood not to be fully in control of their own actions. If this is determined to be the case, different meanings are likely to be given to actions and persons, different identities invoked and, ultimately, different responses and consequences may follow. Deviant 'minds', for example, tend to be treated with much more suspicion than deviant bodies.

Irrespective of the source, nature or extent of volition, if persons become 'known' for particular behaviours, or acquire a 'reputation' of some sort, then the consequences for their identity can be severe, and long-lasting. Here, the 'biographical' aspects of deviant identity can stretch far beyond the immediacy of illegality, incompetence, impropriety or indiscretions in a particular act. Indeed, as we shall see below, the mere fact of such a person's presence (if the 'biographical facts' about them are known) can be problematic not simply for them, but for all those co-present, and ultimately the social 'situation' as a whole.

Information management and impact control

It is quite obviously in our interest to guard potentially 'discrediting' facts about ourselves and, as we move through various social situations, we (when possible) will try to manage information that might negatively affect our identity. There are, of course, 'official' records of information kept on all of us, some which may well compromize us in the eyes of others. Indeed, the tension between 'data protection' and 'freedom of information' marks an interesting site in contemporary society where information is concealed and revealed on a daily basis (from credit and criminal record checks to targeted mailing and web-use profiling). Certain categories of persons (celebrities, politicians and other high-profile figures) have entire industries devoted to 'dishing the dirt' or finding 'skeletons in cupboards', and scandalously discrediting reputations; the rest of us usually have less proactive social forces intent on 'revealing' who we are or can be proven to be. Crucially, much of what others know about us does not come from published or leaked official sources, however, but is revealed, concealed or managed in the flow of everyday interaction.

When one thinks about the idea of 'managing' information, one presumes a couple of things: first, such information is not already (at least not fully) available to others; and second, one has some degree of control over that information. To highlight this point Goffman (1963b) made a nice distinction between what he termed 'virtual' (who others assume one is) and 'actual' (who one can be proved to be) identity. We all possess both aspects of identity and the facts and information – 'things' – persons know about who we 'actually' are varies from person to person, situation to situation and time to time (indeed, we are never sure what others do or do not know about us at any point time and in any episode of interaction). Due to the centrality of information to how we are perceived – and the negative consequences that any potentially discrediting information may have – we enter into social situations with the possibility of facts emerging about us that may in some way impact negatively on our identity. Goffman (1963b) distinguished between the statuses of the 'discredited' (ones about whom discrediting information is known) and of the 'discreditable' (ones about whom discrediting information has the potential to be revealed). Those persons with the former status may exert varying degrees of influence on the interaction and may in some way attempt to mitigate or even challenge the meaning attributed to some stigmatic aspect of their identity (see below). For the latter category, interaction with 'normals' (Goffman 1963b) may present the need for a different set of strategies, either to manage the release of information about any deviant aspects of their identity, or even to attempt to 'pass' as normal. For discreditables then, the pressures on the interaction may be reduced, but the pressures on the individual may be markedly increased.

As we noted above, there are not only personal reasons for managing deviant identities in social situations, but also social ones. In social situations, possessing some deviant identity can cause problems not only for those individuals whose bodies, biographies or behaviours lead to such imputations but also for the capacity of others to 'perform normally'. Such persons can significantly impact on the smooth running of social gatherings, situations and encounters and, ultimately, impact on social order itself. Indeed, the threat need not be spectacular in nature or degree, as simply being awkward or unkempt can be analogous in its impact to being a 'dangerous giant, a destroyer of social worlds' (Goffman 1961b: 81).

If we must carry with us into or reveal / have revealed the potential sources of deviance in encounters with others we can employ certain strategies to mitigate the impact of these. For example, if and when we can prevent them, 'sudden realizations or revelations' are something that we tend to avoid in the immediacy of the there-and-then real-time encounter (we can often 'fish', 'test the waters' or 'make ambiguous claims' if we wish to make revelations that might potentially be conceived as deviant). Even those obviously discredited can employ strategies to mitigate the impact their condition might have on the normal running of the social situation. Davis (1961) describes, as an example of this, the case of an interior decorator with facial disfigurement who would 'position himself' so that his disfigurement was visible from a distance, thereby giving anyone approaching him time to 'compose themselves' for the imminent interaction.

However, when and if such information is disclosed or 'leaks' out, the ascription of a deviant identity is not an automatic consequence. As we noted earlier, any issue of deviance is only an issue insofar as it is 'made' one by persons co-present in any particular social situation. Indeed, much of what Goffman (1963a) termed 'civil inattention' which we give to 'normals' can be extended to those who have been shown or can be shown to deviate in some way. This may, on occasion, reach a level that can in itself be perceived as 'wilful disattention' (see, e.g., Smith 2011). In fact, we all carry with us the capacity to 'violate' social interaction and social situations (Goffman 1972). As noted above, gaffes, faux pas and the like are common features of interaction, and, as Goffman noted in his discussion of 'facework' (see chapter 3), social interaction allows for the tactful overlooking of such incidents (in a "you overlook mine, I'll overlook yours" fashion). To that extent, although social situations are often fragile affairs, susceptible to violation on the part of witting or unwitting offenders, participants in those situations are particularly accommodating and competent in dealing with such social infractions, and the identities that may be responsible for them.

However, sometimes, work is required on the part of the deviant to, in effect, help or convince others to accept or define as normal what might otherwise be difficult to accommodate as 'anything other than' deviant. This necessarily involves attempting to alter the prevailing meaning accorded to some otherwise deviant status.

Negotiation, neutralization and normalization

As we noted in chapter 3, we are ultimately held to be 'accountable' for social action, in interaction. Thus, we may be expected on occasion to 'explicitly' account for behaviours or actions that might otherwise be construed as deviant (and non-accommodatable). Strategies available for doing this are not simply descriptive, but definitional in nature – in other words, they attempt not simply to account for, but to change the meaning of, potentially deviant actions and, in doing so, 'align' behaviour with that which is both recognizable and acceptable as normal. Some classic sociological studies have examined these interactional strategies from an interactionist perspective. Scott and Lyman (1968), for example, examined how we provide 'accounts' in order to mitigate any negative interpretation of our actions and behaviours. In advance of any actions or behaviours that might be construed as in some way deviant, 'disclaimers' may be offered (Hewitt and Stokes 1975). Sometimes, quite specific techniques can be employed to attempt to 'neutralize' potentially deviant actions and

behaviours (Sykes and Matza 1957). A key point about such strategies is that they function as 'aligning actions' (Stokes and Hewitt
1976) in that they attempt to normalize and neutralize not only
the act, but also the 'actor' – that is, are as much about potentially
deviant identities as they are about particular acts and behaviours,
(see chapter 8 for further discussion of some of these strategies).

Attempts to alter the meaning of actions and events that might
point to potentially deviant identities need not only be the concern
of those persons whose identity is 'at stake'. Indeed, as we have seen
above, much of social interaction rests on others working to normalize or neutralize (by, for example, 'overlooking') deviant identities
for those whose identity is at risk. A nice example of this type of
symbolic (re)definition is seen in Goffman's (1952) discussion of
'cooling the mark out'. To lose one's job, be jilted or be conned/
duped out of money can leave persons feeling morally threatened,
stigmatized, and occupying – if only temporarily – some deviant biographical space ('fool', 'sucker', 'failure'). In such situations 'cooling
out' such persons can help them to achieve a positive interpretation
of what is in fact a negative event by, in effect, putting the best gloss
on it. Thus, an employer may suggest a job loss is an opportunity to
seek out employment more suited to a person's particular skill set
(which the current job hadn't provided them with the opportunity
to do), a partner may claim "it's my fault", or those conned/duped
may be reassured by others declaring a similar fate had – or would
have, if they had been in the same situation – happened to them (the
con being highly sophisticated and therefore something 'any normal
person' would have fallen for).

Interventions, institutions and deviant 'careers'

Although much of what might be construed as deviant behaviour
can be – and routinely is – managed 'in interaction' (by 'ordinary'
members of society), there are some cases when what might be
classed as 'institutional' intervention is (deemed) necessary. Symbolic
interactionists have focused not only on the interactional but also on
this institutional aspect of deviance and the role it plays in responding to and impacting on the development of deviant identities. This
involves considering the role of particular 'persons', 'agencies',
'organizations' and 'institutions' authorized and 'qualified' to 'deal
with' deviant persons (see our earlier discussion of Hughes's ([1962]
1971) notion of 'dirty work' in chapter 6). In modern society, a
range of professions has sprung up to identify and deal with various

deviant identities that can't adequately be dealt with or overlooked in and through the routine process of everyday interaction. What we referred to earlier as 'agencies of social control' include the police and those in the criminal justices services, whose job it is to 'punish' deviant behaviour, alongside the professions whose job it is to 'treat' those responsible for deviant actions and behaviours.

As we suggested in the introduction to this chapter, symbolic inter-actionists look more than anywhere else to societal reaction to actions that are deemed to be worthy of intervention (by those with the authority to do so), and to the subsequent impact this has on persons so defined as deviant (see Tannenbaum (1938) for an early explora-tion of societal reaction to deviance). Edwin Lemert (1967) made the oft-cited distinction between 'primary' and 'secondary' deviance. The former refers to deviance that many of us may engage in, for whatever reason. The latter is of more interest in that it comes as a 'result of' being identified for deviant behaviour of some kind and, more importantly, 'known as' a deviant. Howard Becker's (1963) examination of labelling theory explored the impact of officially ascribed labels on persons' identities and the impact that this could have on their subsequent behaviour, and treatment at the hands of others, in social situations.

The interaction between the institutional and the deviant is seen perhaps no more saliently than when one considers what Goffman (1961a) referred to as the 'tinkering trades' (medical professionals whose work focuses on the mentally ill) and the establishments they often operate in to work on deviant identities. Goffman (1961a) employed the concept of 'total institutions' to refer to confined physical establishments and their organizational practices dedicated to working with deviant identities. We have already seen how 'insti-tutional solutions' can be provided to deal with potential deviant statues and the dilemmas they can cause (see the discussion of Hughes [1945] 1971 in chapter 4). However, rather than simply accommodating to deviance, such total institutions are 'purposely' designed, organized and managed to deal with deviant identities.

We have so far, in part, addressed the salient revelation of 'being' deviant in the immediacy of interactional encounters. However, symbolic interactionists are equally concerned – if not more so – with more longitudinal changes and symbolic transformations and the process of 'becoming' deviant. Goffman's (1961a) study of the 'moral career of the mental patient' provided a seminal study of these processes. Key to Goffman's study was the observation that persons pass through various stages on the way to becoming deviant.

These stages require not only the involvement, focus and definitions of the tinkering trades, but also a symmetrical set of definitions on the part of the deviant, and their families and friends. In the context and confines of lunatic asylums, for example, persons move through and out of 'pre-patient' phases, enter total institutions via 'degradation ceremonies' – a set of practices applied to persons to transform their 'total identity' – which reconstitute them as a lower social object and cast them as outsiders (see Garfinkel 1956), then through 'in-patient' processing before being released. The journey is marked by procedural and definitional features. These observations point to a central concept in the study of deviance for symbolic interactionists more widely – that of the 'career' (see Becker 1963), along with the related notion of 'turning point' (Hughes [1952] 1971). As we noted above, morality underpins much of what is classed as deviance, and the concept of 'moral career' advanced in Goffman's study and elsewhere is central to many readings of becoming deviant.

Finally, although various agencies, professions and institutions exist to define, impose and manage deviant identities, the idea that identity rests on the meaning given only by those bodies and 'normal' others was problematized in Goffman's study. Although such external social forces may be overwhelmingly powerful, persons do make attempts to resist, or at least 'adjust on their own terms' to, deviant identities – what Goffman referred to as 'secondary adjustments' (finding ways to live some sort of 'underlife' that runs parallel or even counter to institutional aims, objectives and doctrines).

Affiliation–disaffiliation, embracing and resisting

So far we have discussed interaction in what are essentially 'mixed contacts' (Goffman 1963b), that is, between those with some identity issue that is potentially deviant, and those whose identities are taken to be non-deviant, normal or ordinary. The interaction of persons with similarly deviant identities is something that is also of concern to symbolic interactionists. The relationships between the deviant individual and the 'deviant group' is important to symbolic interactionists from two directions: interaction in deviant groups leading to deviant identities, and deviant identities leading to affiliation with deviant groups, or subcultures.

Deviance and non-deviance are often seen as being 'learnt' in and through interaction. As we noted earlier, Sutherland (1947), for example, developed the idea of 'differential association' early on in the twentieth century. In associating with deviant others, corresponding values can be learnt, definitions formed and activities pursued. A fine example of how deviance is learnt in interaction with others from a symbolic interactionist perspective was provided by Becker (1963). Becker showed how becoming a marijuana user involved a series of stages through which smokers passed before they could reach the point of smoking the drug 'for pleasure'. These involved such things as learning the 'technique' of smoking marijuana, knowing how to perceive and recognize 'effects', and being able to 'attribute' these effects to the drug use. Becker's text contains wonderful examples of how 'regular' smokers guided 'beginners' through this learning process. Moreover, this learning to smoke the drug ran parallel to learning how to re-define the activity itself (as, for example, morally right or wrong) and smokers' changing attitudes to self and others.

Certain types of deviance may actually preclude associating with 'like' others. For example, Lemert (1958) showed how cheque forgers engaged in criminal activity as a solitary activity, avoiding association or affiliation with criminal groups or morals in favour of middle-/upper-class ones (forgery being historically associated with education and high levels of skill). However, although some deviant identities do not lead to affiliation with large deviant collectives, many do. Indeed many persons, once 'labelled' as belonging to some wider deviant 'population', have little choice but to associate with similar others. This, of course, is an obvious and unavoidable consequence of incarceration in total institutions discussed above, when one is 'forced' to live one's life in the close proximity of, and co-presence with, similarly deviant others. This affiliation may also be a more volitional matter. Becker (1963) noted that an option (sometimes the 'only' option) for persons labelled as deviant and excluded from contact with 'normals' is the seeking-out of, and affiliation with, 'like' others. This does not just soften the burden of being classed an 'outsider', but can also normalize what wider society would mark as deviant. Indeed, a point made by Becker was the way in which those classed as deviant, or engaging in deviant activity, could themselves cast wider societal members as outsiders – 'condemning the condemners', so to speak (see Sykes and Matza 1957). Thus, marijuana users might launch a critique of those who would condemn them yet engage in equally harmful acts such as drinking alcohol, and jazz musicians can easily identify and label those who do not possess their musical abilities and sensitivities as 'squares'. Both these groups can be regarded as conventionally deviant, yet each finds its own ways of defining its own actions and castigating wider societal behaviour, and those who abide by it (see also Young 1971).

Ethnomethodology and deviant identities

Ethnomethodology's focus in looking at deviant identities is on the procedures used by persons to make visible and identifiable what can be regarded as recognizably typical features that point to particular kinds of deviance, and normality. Thus, whereas symbolic interactionists focus on meanings, ethnomethodologists focus on 'methods', and the rules that seem to guide and are 'evident in' those methods. Their studies have shown that much of the work of identifying deviance and ascribing deviant identities rests on common-sense interpretations and shared stocks of knowledge as much as any uniquely expert or official methods and procedures that might ostensibly be operating.

Recognizing, defining and theorizing deviance

As part of their work, members of law enforcement organizations we referred to earlier (the police, the courts, probation officers) must find ways to 'know' delinquency and delinquents 'when they see it/them'. Cicourel ([1968] 1976) showed that, as they come into contact with juveniles and attend 'social scenes' where delinquency may have taken place, members of such organizations (most notably police) are faced with the task of 'making sense' of events and social identities (e.g. 'delinquents' or 'good kids'). In order to do this, police officers and the like draw on a stock of knowledge, which includes notions of what might constitute normal or delinquent behaviour, who might qualify as the 'typical' delinquent, and what natural features of things like background may be at play (based on a wider sense of social structure). Such typifications and sense-making practices allow for a practical solution to these interpretive problems. Moreover, whilst informed by such, these understandings find their way into official documents and statistics and allow for the construction of historical records, which, when read *as* documents, can be read *as* fact. Thus, what emerges as a 'factual picture' of delinquency is in fact a documentary version of more subtle, practical and common-sense interpretations and practices. This examination recognizes the phenomenon of labelling, but examines exactly how this labelling takes place at the level of routine practice and interpretation.

This idea that common-sense reasoning informs (constitutes) professional procedures and specialist practices was also highlighted in Atkinson's (1978) study of suicide. If we take the suicide victim as perpetrator – and in that sense deviant (see our discussion of Sacks

1992a below) – we can again see that the attribution of deviant identities via organizational practice has as much to do with everyday
sense-making as it does some 'specialist domain' of knowledge or
procedures to which 'lay' persons are not privy.

The job of defining suicide – of coming to an 'official' verdict – falls
to coroners. Unlike in courtroom settings where inferences may be
drawn about the defendant in and through what he/she says or how
he/she says it (see below), the suicide victim, by definition, cannot
incriminate him/her-self in such a fashion (can't be cross-examined,
etc.). Thus, coroners must draw inferences about the person and
reach a verdict as to 'what happened' in and through an examination
– the reading and interpretation – of what 'remains'. This in effect
involves sense-making practices in finding some sort of order out of
the initial chaos of those remains.

Atkinson showed that, although coroners worked as experts to
arrive at 'official' verdicts, much of their work also involved common-
sense interpretation and theorizing – similar if not identical to lay
interpretations. For example, notions such as 'obvious' accident/
suicide were employed, and, in less 'obvious' cases, 'typical' features
and 'classic' patterns were identified, alongside more subtle yet
equally mundane notions of 'strangeness' and 'normality'.

Over the process of an investigation into whether a sudden death
was a suicide or accident/misadventure, coroners in effect tried to
build up some sort of picture of the events leading up to the death
and its immediate circumstances. This included in what sort of circumstances and via what sort of mode of death the deceased would
be suitable candidates for suicide.

Coroners identified particular 'cues' in their investigations which
pointed to possible or probable suicide (e.g. threats made, mode of
death, location and circumstances, victims biographical and psychological details). Importantly, once read as indicators of suicide, these
were treated 'for all practical purposes' as facts about the case. Such
cues provided subsequent guidance on what further particular forms
of evidence to search for. Similar to the work of what jurors do (see
below), this meant the 'selective' inclusion and exclusion of facts.
Thus, once the investigation started down the trail of suicide, factors
seemingly pertinent to that conclusion were examined and others
that might suggest accident, for example, were gradually ruled out.

What this showed was that, in going about a practical problem
of arriving at a verdict that is not only 'accountable' but also objective, factual and definite for practical purposes, coroners used
common-sense methods not dissimilar to those used in other realms

of everyday life (including the media) where suicide can be understood as being done by particular types of person, in particular ways, places, times, etc. – what 'anyone' would be able to see. This reflects a shared understanding of what constitutes suicide, or how suicide is socially organized.

Whether or not one is categorized as delinquent, guilty of some crime or the other, or a suicide case then rests as much on common-sense reasoning, cultural stocks of knowledge and practical application of methods for arriving at those decisions as it does some reality external to those decision-making processes. The truth isn't found or discovered, it is done in and through the procedures for ostensibly finding it.

Rules, roles and the practical accomplishment of truth

Similarly, in their study of courtroom settings, Atkinson and Drew revealed how the law 'provides practical ways of achieving what is impossible in principle' (1979: 229) as they put it – that is, deciding between truth and falsehood, fact and fiction, vice and virtue, guilt and innocence (problems that have plagued philosophers for centuries – see our discussion of Wittgenstein in chapter 3). One procedure for allowing courtroom members to achieve this seemingly impossible task is to in some way control or restrict the particular topics or sort of utterances that may be permitted in the courtroom context (e.g. topics determined in and through questioning, exclusion of hearsay – in effect, 'occasioned' and relevant talk). However, a key activity that courtroom members engage in revolves around not simply considering the factual content and relevance of what is said (by defendant, witness, etc.), but the moral implication that can be drawn about this or that person from their spoken interaction with other members of the courtroom setting. In fact, Atkinson and Drew suggest that much of what goes on in courtrooms is the pursuit of 'moral inference'. The courtroom, although to a large extent controlled and restricted, allows defendants, witnesses and the like, by providing them with the opportunity to talk, sufficient leeway to freely incriminate themselves in and through what they say (enough rope to hang themselves, so to speak). Not only what but 'how' something is said can be treated with equal moral redolence (e.g. a pause may, in this context, signal hesitation and ultimately undermine credibility). Thus, establishing falsehood, fiction, vice and guilt is as much a matter of moral implications and inferences as it is about ascertaining factual truth (indeed, due to the impossibility of this, perhaps such

morally grounded activity is the only way for courtrooms to resolve
the dilemma of reaching the truth). A key point about this is that
much of what goes on in courtrooms is the sort of inferential work
and practical reasoning that takes place in everyday life.

A similar point was made by Garfinkel ([1967] 1984) in his examination of jurors' work. Like the courtroom, the jury room is a central
site in which social interaction between its members can – *must* –
lead to the ascription of guilt or innocence, deviance or normality.
Garfinkel examined how members of juries go about their deliberations in arriving at a legitimate, justifiable and 'correct' verdict.
Garfinkel showed that, in one sense, jurors go about – and are aware
they should go about – considering cases *as* members of a jury. That
is, following various directions and instructions provided for them
by the court, they are aware that they are both able and expected to
act as particular types of persons – as jury members. Jury members'
activity then involves the consideration, acceptance and rejection of
evidence in the sorting of truth from fiction, fact from fancy. In going
about their deliberations, jurors use 'rules' of proper judicial practice
to examine evidence, build up a corpus of knowledge of 'the case'
and arrive at a verdict, as the outcome of these proper jurors' procedures. However, again, Garfinkel argued that 95 per cent of what
jurors do is not some specialized type of reasoning, but common-
sense, everyday reasoning. This connection between the world of the
jury room and the world of the everyday is not insignificant as, for
the jurors, if the common-sense models of interpretation appear to be
correct, 'then that's what happened' (Garfinkel [1967] 1984: 106).
Indeed, it is an assumption and expectation of jurors that they do not
suspend 'what any competent member of society knows that anyone
knows' (106). In this sense, jurors are '95 per cent jurors' before they
enter the courtroom context, and apply those pre-armed cultural
competences in and through the jury process.

Garfinkel conducted interviews with jurors to explore the rules
they had followed and practices employed. This revealed a contradiction of sorts, in that, although retrospective accounts were given of
idealized practice, these could be seen to run counter to what actually
happened – retrospective accounts indexed an official set of procedures rather than simply indexing common-sense, practical, everyday
reasoning. Moreover, retrospective idealized accounts of what jurors
did to reach their verdict were something that could only be provided
after the verdict had been reached. In other words, jurors did not in
fact enter jury rooms with a full knowledge of what they must do to
reach a valid verdict, this was only something that could be articu-

lated after the event (in effect, the verdict came first, after which the full picture of how it was arrived at could be fully accounted for). Thus, verdicts were revealed as emerging, practically accomplished things based on everyday reasoning, cultural stocks of knowledge and routine competences.

Deviance and normality: the power of versions

Versions are powerful things. As might be evident from the previous examples, arrived at and presented in the right way, by the right persons, versions of deviance can be read as being 'the' version (the truthful, factual account of some real person, event or wider social reality). As we have just seen, from an ethnomethodological perspective versions are interesting as they index stocks of shared cultural knowledge, are practical achievements, and are often done using common-sense methods. Versions are important because they can not only provide accounts of things, but give us the ontological and interpretive framework to understand actions that are framed as belonging to the particular version of reality being advanced.

The power of versions, and of using information to in some way index those versions, is a useful way to understand deviance. As we saw in our earlier general discussion of ethnomethodology (see chapter 2), the indexical nature of action means that it in some way documents some wider frame of understanding. Once 'invoked', this frame of understanding allows us to interpret subsequent actions as being part of that 'thing' that is now being done.

A quite explicit example of how versions are presented, are constructed to work as factual accounts, and provide interpretive frameworks was provided by Smith (1978). She showed how a third-party account of mental illness was constructed and crafted in quite a sophisticated manner in order to provide a 'valid' version of things, and allow for the interpretation of a range of – otherwise innocuous – behaviours. Rosenhan's (1973) classic study of professional diagnosis of mental illness and subsequent interpretation of action provides another fine example of the power of versions. In this study, researchers faked certain symptoms that might indicate mental illness in order to enter mental insitutions. Once categorized as potentially psychotic by staff and admitted to these institutions, future behaviour could be incorporated into this diagnostic version (another 'symptom'), even if, in itself, it was quite innocuous (e.g. 'note-taking').

Of course, as we saw in our discussion of frame transformations (see chapter 3), we can play around with versions during the course of spoken interaction. 'Keying', 'fabrications' and the like, discussed earlier, are, however, laminations – fictional layers on top of the primary reality of any given social situation. However, a problem comes when persons take some 'version' of reality that would otherwise be treated as some lamination or keyed version (Goffman 1974) to be the 'primary' one. In his (1993) text, Cuff cites the character Don Quixote from the Cervantes novel of the same name. In one episode, Quixote observes what he takes to be giants and rides headlong into them. When thereafter entangled in the sails of what in fact turns out to be windmills, he provides a version of what has just happened as being the giants having turned themselves into windmills to deny him his victory in defeating them (giants possessing the power to effect such a metamorphosis). The point here is that Don Quixote inhabits a world of chivalry, which includes giants and their various powers, so his version stands as a correct explanation of the events. If and when versions 'compete' – just as Don Quixote's competed with the versions of the windmills that those around him may have had – persons may not only refer to them as being the correct versions, but may also draw on them to 'ironicize' (depict as faulty) competing versions. A good example of this is Pollner's (1975) discussion of 'reality disjunctures'. In his study of discourse in psychiatric settings, Pollner describes a patient who believed he could levitate objects with his mind. When challenged to do so and told by the psychiatrist the table selected for movement did not move, the patient's version of events was that the reason why it had not appeared to move to the psychiatrist was that he could not see 'cosmic reality'.

Spoken interaction and deviant identities

Conversational foundations of deviant identity

In chapter 3 we pointed out some key features of conversational orderliness and the Interaction Order in terms of persons' ability or willingness to abide by the underlying rules, norms and expectation of these orders. One idea that crops up in the writing of Sacks and other conversation analysts, as well as in Goffman's work, is that of 'competence'. 'Members' possess a mastery of how to use spoken interaction collaboratively to both achieve intersubjectvity and ensure interaction proceeds in an orderly manner. To that extent, an ability and willingness in terms of competence is something we all expect and rely on from each other in interaction. It follows that any unwillingness or inability to abide by the rules and conditions underlying the conversational and interaction orders may lead not only to perturbations of those orders, but also carry implications for one's identity. As we noted earlier, 'doing ordinary conversation' can be seen to be analogous to 'doing being ordinary' (Sacks 1984b). It is this that in no small part marks one as a 'member' (Garfinkel and Sacks 1970) of wider society.

As discussed in chapter 3, we have certain expectations from co-conversationalists (children are to some extent an exception – see MacBeth 1990 – although, on the downside, they are often denied full 'conversational rights') in terms of things like turn formulation (coherent, recipient-designed and occasioned) and sequential cooperation (utterances timed and placed appropriately, when 'conditionally' relevant, etc.). Even non-lexical items and laughter can be seen to be sequential in nature.

We are, in this sense, accountable for conversational actions and can be 'held to account' for them ("Why that now?", "Why not that now?" etc.). As we noted earlier, perturbations in conversation routinely occur, and are routinely and 'locally' dealt with. Things such as false starts, factual errors, tenuous topic links, not responding to greetings, etc., usually carry no significant or long-lasting implications for identity. However, certain categories of persons may find that their failure to abide by the rules and conditions of these orders can have significant and far-reaching implications for their identities. For example, those classed as mentally ill may have their mastery of natural language doubted, or may orient to the rules of turn-taking, or expectations of turn design and placement, in sequentially inappropriate or unpredictable ways, e.g. butting in, randomly changing topic, 'suddenly' ending conversations (Goffman 1983a). Such conversational behaviour can be used as 'evidence' for deviant identities. For example, we saw earlier how utterances made in the context of therapy sessions can be cast not as meaningful turns in themselves, but as attempts to 'change the subject' (Schwartz 1976) and, as we noted above, such things as pauses in courtroom talk can lead to inferences that a person is, for example, not sure about what he/she is saying or even is deliberately trying to mislead.

Conversely, sequence can also be 'exploited' to resist or manage the potential ascription of deviant identity. We discussed preference organization and its relationship to identity in chapter 3. Looking at this in terms of what we know about normative turn formulation and sequential organization, we can see how this can be drawn on to avoid deviant identities. For example, although somewhat less significant for our biographies than some of the examples cited above, being 'turned down' following an invitation can cast us in a negative light. However, by virtue of dispreferred turn design, a refusal of such an invitation can be 'seen coming', allowing us to, for example, backtrack, thereby avoiding any negative implication for us. Indeed, as we argued in chapter 3, the use of a range of dispreferred actions in conversation allows us to engage in this face-saving activity. Hutchby (1992) points to this anticipation of upcoming deviant identity ascription by virtue of knowledge of turn construction and normative sequential ordering, albeit in quite a specialized context. Hutchby noted that, during listener phone-ins to radio shows, radio hosts routinely adopted a stance of 'routine scepticism' ("You say x, but what about y?"). This quite often included attributing some position to callers that may have carried negative implications for their identity (e.g. undermined their knowledge on a topic, authority to speak about it, or cast them in a bad light). Aware of this, callers often interjected to ward off such an upcoming attribution, in a manner similar to the way emerging dispreferred turns can be warded off before they have actually occurred.

More significant deviant identities have also been shown to have been managed through the exploitation of conversational sequence and turn formulation. Sacks (1992a) showed how this operated in his study of calls made to a Los Angeles suicide prevention centre. Of course, in talk, persons may want to avoid being known to personally belong to some (potentially deviant) category. An observation Sacks made in his analysis was the way in which callers 'avoided' giving their names during the opening phases of their call to the centre by perturbing the normal sequential flow of the talk, thereby disrupting the sequence of turns in which personal identifications (names) are normally given.

A similar exploitation of opening phases of talk was highlighted by Widdicombe and Wooffitt (1995). During interviews for a research project on youth subcultures (in this particular case, 'punks'), in response to an opening question along the lines of "How would you describe yourself?", interviewees would often resist making immediate claims to punk identity, preferring to talk about more individualistic or general aspects of their identity, or might in some way problematize this initial question (which was in fact quite deliberately aimed at eliciting comment on their punk affiliations). One way of achieving this was to provide a conditionally relevant 'second-pair part' (see chapter 3) to the initial question (in the form of an answer), but choose to focus on aspects of their identity that were not necessarily subcultural (such as hair length, etc.). Interviewees would also initiate 'insertion sequences' (again, see chapter 3) by, for example, requesting clarification on what was meant by the question (marking it out as in some way 'troublesome' and thus in need of repair work on the part of the interviewer). This could involve what was in effect a selective re-formulation of the initial question on the part of the interviewee, mentioning in the request for clarification only those parts of the question that he/she wanted to answer. Interestingly, these selective requests for clarification would focus on things that 'anyone' might be legitimately asked about. Thus, a question along the line of "Can you tell me about your dress, your style, your attitude to life?" might be met with a request for clarification along the lines of "You want to know about my attitude to *life*?", after which the interviewee would be free to talk about any aspect of his/her attitude to life (whilst ignoring the 'punk' dress/style component). This allowed interviewees effectively to re-direct the specifics of the question to allow them to follow up on particular parts of the initial question that may not necessarily be associated with subcultural identity and in fact may be aspects of 'ordinary' identity.

Of course, recipients of talk that might index deviance for their interlocutors can themselves conversationally act to in some way negate this. One way to do this of course is simply to 'overlook' whatever has been said (and the inferences and implications of it). Another is to recognize but redefine preceding turns at talk. This was also evident in Sacks' work on calls made to the suicide prevention centre. Upon listening to calls made to and received by the centre, Sacks observed that some threats to commit suicide were met with laughter. What might seem to be a callous response in fact was revealed to be something else. By laughing at a suicide threat, centre workers worked to transform an action in a previous turn (a threat) into a different one (a non-serious threat, or joke). Moreover, because jokes 'invite' and make relevant laughter in subsequent turns, once jokes have been recognized and appreciated as such, that particular part of the conversation – that 'sequence' – is over. Thus, a claim made to some potentially deviant identity (potential suicide victim) is taken to be something different in and through the design and sequential organization of turns at talk.

Inferring and invoking deviant identities in conversation

As we noted in chapter 3, membership categories are explicit ways in which we can typify and classify persons and their activities and thereby directly and indirectly ascribe, claim, refute, etc., identities.

Deviant identities are a class of such categories that are regularly used in conversation as well as in other non-interactive contexts (such as in newspaper headlines see, e.g., Lee 1984).

We saw in the discussion of juvenile delinquency earlier how police and others could clearly identify good and bad (delinquent) kids. Hester (1998) explored the identification of 'deviant' kids through/as a membership category in a school context. School staff, when referring children to educational psychologists, used various contrast devices to describe problem children in terms of how they deviated from 'normal' pupils of that age (in, for example, excessive or uncontrollable behaviour, being under/over developed compared to other children). Baker (1997) explored similar 'moral categorizing', showing how teachers viewed 'good' kids (and those who may be 'problems') as independent moral categories and, subsequently, were prepared to work reward and punishment systems differentially towards those categories (not being unfairly or disproportionately hard on good kids, for example).

As with sequential exploitation, persons are also able to employ membership categorization to attempt to avoid deviant identity. Interestingly, this can sometimes involve ascribing some deviant category to others. Travers (2001) highlighted this by citing Watson's (1997) work on murder interrogations. In one case involving the murder of an African-American, the suspect (who was White) gave his reason for shooting at the victim as being because he was a 'nigger'. 'Nigger' itself is a membership category and one used, in this context, pejoratively, presumably to try to mitigate, account for, or disavow the act of shooting at someone. Of course, by using this category, the defendant cast himself as 'racist', and thereby potentially incriminated himself in self-ascribing a deviant identity.

A second case examined by Watson showed how a (male) defendant accused of murdering a female victim described that victim in terms of (category-bound) activities that could be heard to be associated with sexual promiscuity. In this sense, the successful ascription of a deviant identity to the victim may have helped to mitigate the offender's actions.

Such strategies can also be used to resist less severe deviant identities. Widdicombe and Wooffitt (1995) again showed this in their study of punks. When talking about their treatment at the hands of the police, publicans or the public in general, interviewees cited not aspects of their punk identity, but routine, mundane, 'normal' ones. Thus, in describing being refused entry to a pub, interviewees might describe their actions as simply 'going for a quiet drink' – the type of thing 'any person might do' (Widdicombe and Wooffitt 1995: 118). In other words, the claims made were simply to 'doing being ordinary' (Sacks 1984b), and the occasioned identities ordinary ones. Accounts such as "minding my own business" and the like were used to provide the normative backdrop to reported actions. Additionally, interviewees used what Pomerantz (1986) called extreme case formulations such as "always" (e.g. get abused), "everyone" (e.g. does that), or "never" (e.g. treated fairly) to describe behaviours and events further in an attempt to normalize their behaviour and resist any ascription of negative identity. To bolster further such claims to normal identity, interviewees would also contrast their normal behaviour with the irrational, unwarranted and extreme behaviour of others (the police, publicans, etc.), thereby, in effect, implying some degree of moral fault on the part of those others.

Deviant ascriptions in everyday talk

Several studies have shown how ascriptions of and imputations about identities routinely crop up – and are handled and managed – in and through recognizable conversational sequences. 'Teasing', for example, is a ubiquitous feature of ordinary conversation, and it is sequentially managed. Although 'meant' non-seriously, teases can carry some more serious imputations for those being teased. Exaggerated claims, verbosity or some aspect of known biography, for example, can be used as a reason to tease persons and 'say something' about them. Perhaps because of this, teases are routinely received in a 'po-faced' manner, i.e., they are taken to be at least partly serious (Drew 1987). More malign forms include criticizing, accusing, arguing and character contests (see Malone 1997).

Ritual, drama and situational propriety

The Interaction Order makes room for deviancy, and for deviants. From this perspective, however, deviant imputations are not located in conversational formulations or sequences, but in the interpersonal rituals, dramaturgical expression and expectations and norms concerning situational spoken propriety. Like Sacks and his colleagues, Goffman recognized what might be construed as 'non-deviant' troubles. Gaffes, faux pas and slips of the tongue are examples of this type of normative trouble and are not taken to indicate anything other than an 'interactional hazard' of being a participant in spoken encounters. Again, like Sacks, Goffman was keen to point out the accommodative nature of interaction. More specifically, like conversational repair, Goffman saw the Interaction Order as being remediable through routinized practice and conversational moves. Nonetheless, events can sometimes occur that may lead to the competence or even moral integrity of a person being called into doubt, and for which he/she can be held accountable.

As we have outlined in chapter 3, when in spoken encounters with others, we are expected to be considerate, tactful, modest and polite, etc. We are expected to give attention to other speakers, avoid interruption, stay on topic and properly terminate conversational encounters and so on. In his (1983a) paper 'Felicity's Condition', Goffman explored further these interactional demands – in particular, how a failure to demonstrate them whilst in conversational encounters with others could carry significant and quite negative consequences for identity. Goffman noted that, in spoken encounters, topics of conversation provide the shared resource around which talk can develop, and towards which utterances can be directed. Echoing comments by Schutz, Goffman asserted that, whilst involved in such conversational activity, if only for the duration of any given social encounter, participants can be conceived as not simply conversing around some shared conversational topic, but as jointly inhabiting some shared 'mental world'. An expectation of oneself and one's co-participants is not simply that this world is shared, but that 'aliveness' to it is somehow demonstrated. Evidence for aliveness is judged in terms of conversationalists' ability both to understand and interpret correctly other's utterances and to construct their own utterances, which may be equally interpretable, relevant, meaningful and so on. When thought of in this way, conversational utterances respond not to the preceding turn, or to any turn at all, but to the other participants' 'minds'. The implications of this for identity are not insignificant. This is evident on occasions when utterances made by one person or another may appear somehow odd, make no sense in the context of the current state of talk, seem to lack relevance, or no meaningful account can be provided for them. On such occasions, person responsible for such utterances can simply run the risk of being perceived as somehow incompetent, even if only temporarily, for example through tiredness, pre-occupation, inebriation, even self-consciousness (see 'Alienation from interaction' in Goffman 1967). However, a more significant interpretation, and one that carries the risk of a deviant identity being ascribed, is that that person is potentially 'defective', 'deranged', 'nutty'. Thus, through the management of our own words or the display of our understanding of the words of others, we display – and are expected and obliged to demonstrate – not simply our conversational competence, but our sanity (Goffman 1983a: 27; see also Goffman 1961a).

In terms of ritual aliveness, and the consequences for identity of not demonstrating this, Goffman's (1972) notion of remedial interchange is instructive. Face-to-face interaction with others always carries the risk that we may – deliberately or inadvertently – breach one of several 'preserves' or 'territories' that others possess. 'Bumping into' another, blocking their view, jumping the queue in front of them, requesting personal information from them, or even attempting to initiate conversation with them are such examples. If and when such infractions occur, and have been attributed to us as the 'offender', we must initiate what Goffman referred to as 'remedial interchanges', to both account and recompense for the offence, and, as importantly, demonstrate our recognition of and relationship to the rules or proper and moral behaviour.

Finally, as with conversationalists' ability to draw on sequence to resist or disavow a potentially deviant identity, so too can participants in face-to-face encounters use aspects of the Interaction Order to similar effect. As we noted earlier (see chapter 3), persons also have the ability to take up some stance to their spoken behaviour, other than being inevitably tied to and accountable for it. For example, by virtue of 'footing', speakers may utter words, but claim no ownership of them, nor attest to the position they are advancing. One thing persons can also do is not only take up various stances vis-à-vis utterances, but also take up stances towards selves. By referring to 'past' selves, participants in spoken encounters can claim that that person – that self – spoken of *belongs* to the past. Thus, present selves can disassociate from past selves – cast them off (see also Goffman 1967).

8

Leisure

Introduction

'Leisure' can cover a variety of activities, behaviours, pastimes and (depending on one's point of view) sins. In this chapter we want to examine briefly how the sociologies of interaction outlined in chapters 1–3 can shed light on the multitude of leisure pursuits, recreational activities, pastimes, hobbies and entertainments with which we occupy ourselves as part of our everyday lives.

It seems undeniable that, in contemporary Western society at least, leisure often involves consumption of some sort. The sociology of consumption and 'consumer culture' includes a vast range of theories, critical commentary and empirical studies that stretch far beyond the remit of possibilities for the current chapter. For the better part of a century, sociologists have critically examined the way we consume products, goods and services as we go about our various leisure activities. In these discussions, although not interactionist per se, leisure and consumption practices are often tied in with notions of identity. Indeed, several commentators see consumption practices as being a central part of the 'construction' of identity as, for the majority of us, 'whatever we wear, own or do [is] an expression of our choosing [and] our ethical and social identity' (Slater 2005: 180). The clothes we choose to wear, for example, act as 'metaphors for identity' (Davis 1992: 27). The critical stance taken towards contemporary cultural practice by many sociologists and cultural theorists often paints a bleak picture of modern society and the situation that persons find themselves in when seeking to pursue identities. The sociologist Anthony Giddens has suggested, for example, that 'we have no choice but to choose' (Giddens cited in Slater 2005: 179).

Indeed, exercising choice about what to consume in the construction of identities has even been conceptualized as more akin to 'work' (than 'play'), what the sociologist Zygmunt Bauman has described as 'a sentence to lifelong labour' (Bauman 2007: 110–11). One consequence of the relationship between self, identity and the ever changing and renewing nature of consumer culture has been argued to be the fluidity and instability of contemporary identity. Thus, although traditional bases for identity still apply (social class, gender, age, race, ethnicity), in modern society, consumption practices (leisure activities and the like being a core part of these) allow us to pursue multifaceted and sometimes fantastical identities, that extend beyond those characterized by twentieth-century modernity (of course, as we shall discuss in part below, even 'traditional' identities such as class, age and gender can be seen to be themselves constructed out of our consumption practices and leisure pursuits). This feature of contemporary society could be argued to allow expressive creativity and some degree of emancipation. As Bauman has further noted, 'The main attraction of shopping life is the offer of plentiful new starts and resurrections (chances of being "born again")' (Bauman 2007: 49).

Many approaches to understanding leisure practices point to macro concerns, such as social class, age, gender and ethnic differentiation, or issues of globalization. These are important aspects of leisure. However, our main concern here is to try to interpret leisure practices from a range of interactionist perspectives. Indeed, from the perspective of the sociologies of interaction, leisure practices, identities and interactions become important data for investigation.

Leisure is frequently treated as antithetical to work (see chapter 6). For example, leisure usually involves breaking away from fixed 'roles' and work-based identities (as we shall see below, there is often a normative expectation that work-based identities be 'kept out of' the arena of leisure). In this sense leisure provides a conventional way of freeing oneself from often all-consuming roles associated with work. Leisure activities are also often characterized by a breaking-away from formal(ized) 'rules' which govern us in the workplace. In fact, much leisure is marked by spontaneity rather than prescribed behaviour. Additionally, leisure provides a way of freeing ourselves from status-based (usually hierarchical and power-laden) 'relationships', often seen in work. The term 'letting one's hair down' (whether one has any or not!) encapsulates this emancipatory quality of leisure. Indeed, much of what we choose to do as part of our leisure pursuits is not only leisure- but pleasure-based, enjoyable, even hedonistic, as compared to the controlled, functional and potentially alienating behaviour and experiences of work (again, see our discussion in chapter 6).

While leisure often involves consumption and participation in formally organized activities such as foreign travel, sports clubs or hobbyists' circles, one needn't participate in the 'exotic' or 'spectacular' to engage in moments of leisure. For example, a quick chat at the photocopier, a flick through a magazine, or even a 'daydream' can provide a temporary leisure experience. We have discussed at length elsewhere the centrality of experience in a range of contexts (see chapter 2). For many of us, leisure is synonymous with experience. Be it a ride on a roller-coaster, cold-water swimming, visiting the zoo, or simply watching a movie, our leisure activities provide us with new, different and stimulating experiences. Of course, experience relies heavily on the meaning attributed to it. As we noted in chapter 1, things are acted on according to the meaning they have for persons. In this sense, 'leisure things' can include actions, persons, places or even ideas, and of course may mean one thing to one person (or set of persons) and quite something else to another. As has been noted, what is play to the golfer is work for the caddy.

Leisure can involve lone pursuits, but more often than not involves interaction with others, either focused (collaborating 'with' others in some joint leisure activity) or unfocused (acting 'in the co-presence of' others; see Goffman 1963a). To that extent, leisure often involves shared meanings and shared experience. Indeed, many leisure practices – and even the experiencing of them (see our earlier discussion of Becker's work on marijuana smoking) – need to be learnt. As one would expect, this learning routinely takes place in interaction with others.

Leisure pursuits often also require some sort of practice. That is, sometimes, some knowledge-base, expertise or competence is involved. For example, much of what we display about our leisure and consumption choices expresses our ability to make distinctions between available choices – our 'taste'. The sociologist Pierre Bourdieu (1984) examined this notion of taste and argued that we classify the objects and activities available for our consumption. One important consequence of this is that, in going about the act of classification, we are ourselves classified – the expression of taste 'classifies the classifier', as Bourdieu put it. Through building up a 'stock of knowledge' about leisure practices, we not only are able to appreciate the experience of them and participate meaningfully in them, but can also distinguish, for example, the precious from the profane, the authentic from the fake, or the playful from the serious.

Although somewhat antithetical to formal roles, rules and relationships, many leisure practices do have a normative dimension to them
– from tacit expectations, through 'unwritten' rules, systems of codi-
fication, to what we more formally think of as rules (of, for example,
games). Indeed, as we shall see below, even informal leisurely sociable conversation (the chat around the photocopier mentioned above)
can be seen to have a strong normative dimension to it.

Of course, there is also a strong expressive, sometimes 'performative' dimension to many leisure pursuits. Much of what we do when
we consume (including leisure) is done 'conspicuously' (see Veblen
1925), that is, so others can 'see' what we are doing – indeed, what
particular identities we are claiming. Consumption, in this sense, is
as much about the 'display' of what we choose to buy, for example,
or the leisure activities we participate in. Leisure in this sense can be
used as a vehicle to express who we are (and who we aren't), who we
would like to be (and be seen to be affiliated with / disaffiliated from),
as well as sometimes providing modes of expression that might otherwise have no outlet.

Finally, due to their antithetical relationship to work and focus on
enjoyment, pleasure and even hedonism, many leisure practices can
be regarded as not in the first instance (mass) 'cultural' ones (going
to the cinema, watching Manchester United play, taking a two-week
trip to the coast each year), but subcultural in nature. Moreover (as
perhaps with all leisure practices), there may be moral undertones
to such practices and moral inferences drawn about the 'type' of
persons who participate in them. Such practices may come to be
regarded as in some way deviant (see chapter 7), to the point of being
threatening or even dangerous. This can lead to the identification
of deviant or stigmatized identities, and ultimately a negative social
response, sanctions of punishment for those involved in particular
leisure pursuits and practices. 'Youth' subcultural leisure practices
(see Brake 1980) provide many classic examples of this (see Cohen's
(1972) definitive text for an examination of societal responses to
leisure-based identities, and Hebdige (1979) for a discussion of how
subcultures creatively participate in the construction of 'subcultural
identities'). Indeed, having a particular hobby or interest as a leisure
pursuit can, in some contexts, reach almost the level of master status
(again, see chapter 7) – 'trainspotters' being the archetypal example.
Even more 'specialist' leisure pursuits can carry with them potentially
negative connotations for identity if they stray too far from what is
considered the norm, or 'normal'. Such deviations from the norm
are not simply based in the pursuit itself, but can also be affected by

characteristics of the person(s) taking part (e.g. age, gender, job), who else might be involved, where the activity takes place, etc. A group of all-male geriatric vicars cycling naked through a town centre at night might seem like an innocent 'naturist' leisure pursuit to those involved, but may come across somewhat differently to persons not participating in such activity and may well have quite dire consequences for those doing the cycling.

Symbolic interaction

As we outlined in chapter 1, symbolic interactionists focus on meaning in and through interaction. Leisure and consumption practices all 'mean' something to those who participate in them (and, of course, those who choose not to). Indeed, many leisure activities are not goal-oriented as such, and so a lot of the sense we can derive from them is from the meaning people attribute to them. Going for a jog, lazing about on the beach or going to see a musical performance all mean something to those who choose to do these things, as they do for those who choose not to (reading a book may be pleasurable or boring, a crowded beach of sun-baked bodies may be a mecca or a scene of sun-drenched stultification, and jogging may be an invigorating experience or exhausting chore). Leisure is often a matter of meaningful choice then, and by definition, meaningful identities. As we have seen in chapter 1, we gain our very sense of self through 'leisurely' activity, in the form of play (Mead 1934).

Leisure as 'action'

Goffman (1967) conceptualizes leisure as 'where the action is'. Indeed, Goffman makes the point that 'action' as a notion has fed its way into contemporary vernacular, as phrases such as 'looking for some . . .', 'there isn't much . . .', or 'getting involved in . . .', etc., preface the notion in everyday talk.

There is a myriad of leisure activities and pursuits that can be conceptualized as involving 'action', from flirting at a party to involvement in the types of 'serious leisure' we will discuss shortly. In contemporary society, leisure as action is often commercialized and a range of places exist that have been designed for and are organized around particular leisurely activities. The casino with its ever-spinning roulette wheels, the amusement park with its vertigo-inducing white-knuckle rides, and the sports stadium with the adrenalin-inducing clash between two rival teams are recognizable examples. There are also more sedate commercialized settings, such as shopping arcades, that allow for what Goffman terms 'the action of consumption' – the sort of contemporary practice that we discussed at the start of this chapter. What might be loosely described as games are also a good example of leisure as action. Such activities, from tossing a coin and betting on the outcome to gambling in casinos, can all be conceptualized as action activities. These involve and require a close focus (with others involved in the game) on both the activity itself and the wider social situation in which it is taking place – what Goffman refers to as 'fields of action'.

There is always an element of risk and uncertainty in engaging in leisure as action – indeed, this is often part of the attraction. Participants let go of their hold over the outcome of events and make some commitment to the uncertainty of outcome associated with this. There is often also a degree of consequentiality to participation in leisure as action. In the above examples, this may mean losing the coin toss (and whatever bet was riding on it) or being relieved of significant sums of money. The results may be even more severe. For example, taking drugs may mean chancing psychic welfare; participating in such leisure activities as boxing, martial arts or having a night out on the town in certain milieux (see, e.g., Miller 1958) carries with it the risk of bodily injury; and involvement in activities such as motor racing, base jumping or mountain climbing carries the risk of death. Nevertheless, persons routinely and regularly (sometimes even religiously) expose themselves out of choice to such activities as part of their leisure practices and leisure biography.

The consequences of participation in leisure as action may be more symbolic in nature however. When involved in many leisure-as-action activities, persons are expected to display 'character'. This term covers such things as showing courage, gameness and integrity, maintaining composure, dignity and, in some activities, displaying what Goffman referred to as 'stage confidence'. Such character traits, as evident in action situations, can have an 'essentializing' quality to them – that is, single expressions can be read as defining the competences, character and morality of the whole of the person. Consequently, in the immediacy of such action situations, character can be sometimes easily – and dramatically – acquired or lost (for example, revealing oneself to be a 'good sport', or, conversely, showing oneself to be 'not playing by the rules'). Thus, in participating in leisure as action, one's 'face', reputation and, ultimately, social and personal identity are always at risk; there is as much a symbolic investment and commitment as there are materialistic and physical ones.

Rules and roles

In our chapter on conversation analysis (see chapter 3), we looked at Goffman's work on the Interaction Order and below we shall consider more aspects of this particular interactionist approach in relation to the social reality of leisure more generally. However, a nice – and rather sideways – way of looking at leisure and identity was provided in a classic examination of what Goffman (1961b) called 'role-distance'. Although not a study of leisure per se, Goffman used a beguiling and highly instructive metaphor of the merry-go-round to show how persons behave in various ways vis-à-vis the leisure activity they are engaged in, which might throw light on the way persons expressively align themselves with wider leisure encounters. Goffman described how, when riding a merry-go-round, persons of different ages engage in the activity with varying degrees of involvement with or distance from the activity. The forms of behaviour exhibited powerful symbolic cues for the identity claimed by various categories of persons. For example, very small children may find the task of staying on the horse as it moves along an immensely challenging one. They may require securing to their steed (selected by a parent) in some way, along with ongoing parental re-assurance. As children get older and the task in itself becomes less of a challenge, they may violate the 'norms' of the ride by, for example, riding backwards, or choosing an animal that is somewhat more difficult to ride (e.g. a slippery frog). The animal might also be 'whipped' in an attempt to move along faster. Such 'distancing' from the activity as a serious, 'rule-governed' one continues to adulthood, at which point persons may return to a parodied form of early childhood, by strapping themselves tightly in and feigning the fear and apprehension that infants genuinely experience. This very particular set of observations (like most of Goffman's work) illustrates the playful relationship to roles that is a feature of many leisure pursuits. It illustrates also a playful relationship not only to roles, but also to rules (indeed, in this example, one can image the ride operator at some point interjecting to stop the 'messing about'). This example also points to identity concerns, and the way in which behaviour in relation to roles and rules can often be modified to present a particular image of self in the eyes of observing and co-present others. Something as simple as riding a merry-go-round carries with it then varying meanings and a range of relationships to rules and identity concerns. These techniques of role distance often permeate a host of other leisure activities we engage in. Turning our collars up on soccer shirts, putting our feet up on the back of the seat in front of us at the cinema, or wearing jeans to the opera are ways in which we can distance ourselves from the leisure activities we are involved in and the rules or roles it would otherwise prescribe for us.

Affiliative identities

In the above example, the social situation of the merry-go-round consisted of (we can assume) acquainted and unacquainted persons – the (acquainted) child and parent, who maintain fleeting contact as the child rotates into view, the adult playing to a range of anonymous others who may happen to be observing the ride, etc. Leisure activities can range from solo and individualist pursuits (from reading a book to sailing single-handed around the world), through quite focused and intimate ones (from a game of chess to love-making) to ones involving large collectives (team games to spectator sports). Often, leisure practices involve 'similar' others and may foster a collective 'we' identity (albeit fleeting and transient) – indeed, being a recognizable member of some wider leisure collective is a key part of how leisure may inform our identity. Take the simple T-shirt, for example. As we have noted above, what we choose to wear can act as a powerful metaphor for identity. A quick glance round any high street on a Saturday afternoon will reveal a range of leisure 'advertisements' that persons choose to display about themselves and their leisure activities. 'Manchester United', 'The Smiths', 'Salford 10K', 'Solar Eclipse 2006' are, for example, just a selection of T-shirts that one of us writing this text has available for such advertisements. Anderson and Taylor (2010) provide a nice example of this, citing a skydivers' T-shirt that read 'It's Not a Real Sport unless You Can Die from Massive Internal Injuries' (2010: 42). Each of these will not only attract a certain meaning, but will also serve to affiliate the wearer with some larger, 'like-minded', like-tasted, etc., collective, to express some 'leisure ethnicity' (Kelly 1983: 101). In this sense, leisure and recreational activities mark not only individual identity but also group identity. A nice example of leisure affiliative identity from a symbolic interactionist perspective is provided by Allen-Collinson and Hockey (2007) who examine how runners struggle to maintain an 'athletic identity' following an injury that prevents them from going about their normal running activities. In such circumstances, runners engage in identity work in order to try to sustain, preserve and present to others a 'running self'. Various strategies are employed by runners. One strategy – 'materialistic identification' – involved injured runners doing things like using the same routes they had previously used for their running, but now briskly walking along them. In addition to treading the same route as their past running self, this allowed runners also to maintain low body fat and still 'look like' runners. Next, 'associative identifications' involved runners identifying themselves in some way with other runners. Clothing – the same running clothes they had worn pre-injury (technical shoes, running tights, etc.) – was a way to achieve this. Finally, 'vocabularic identification' involved maintaining what was in effect runners' talk, whilst in the presence of or coming across other runners (including such things as greeting, ritual exchanges and employing banter with fellow runners whilst out exercising, etc.). This work allowed injured runners to negotiate their potentially athletically 'spoiled identity' (Goffman 1963b) and maintain affiliation with the wider running community. Aside from the notion of leisure identity, what the problems encountered by injured runners further point to is strong feelings of subcultural affiliation. These identity concerns and sub-cultural affiliations were not treated by runners as trivial things, but, rather, as quite serious ones.

Seriousness and authenticity

When considering leisure as a basis for identity construction, the ideas of meaningful choice and chosen affiliation point to the notion of 'authenticity'. Indeed, what might easily be argued to be a general aversion to being perceived as 'fake' makes the notion of authenticity central to understanding many leisure practices and identity concerns. We mentioned earlier that persons express their 'taste'. This often involves the ability to make distinctions between, for example, what is 'cool' or 'naff', 'precious' or 'profane', 'authentic' or 'fake'. Drawing on Bourdieu's notion of cultural capital, Thornton (1995) examined how collectives of youths participating in dance and rave culture expressed and displayed these features in and through what she termed 'subcultural capital'. Subcultural affiliation and iden-tity are of course particularly important for 'youth' subcultures. Indeed, they often lie at the core of youth identity (a nice example of this occurs in the film *Quadrophenia* (1979), where the central character argues at one point that if he wasn't a 'Mod' he would be 'nobody'). Widdicombe and Wooffitt (1995) showed how, for example, members of youth subcultures not only affiliated themselves with larger subcultural collectives, but presented themselves as 'always' having been that way and claimed that being, for example, a punk was part of their deep-rooted, intrinsic identity. The discovery of a subculture was thus a discovery of 'kindred others'. Likewise, such individuals drew on various aspects of identity to categorize 'inauthentic' punks, the contrast in itself further adding to claims to authenticity. This lifelong affiliation to wider leisure collectives was also examined by Davis (2006), who examined the phenomenon of 'aging Punks'.

The notion of authenticity, commitment to leisure practices, and the idea of subcultural affiliation beyond the discussion of youth points us towards the concept of what has been termed 'serious leisure', that is: 'the systematic pursuit of an amateur, a hobbyist, or a volunteer activity sufficiently substantial and interesting for the participant to find a career there in the acquisition and expression of a combination of its special skills, knowledge, and experience' (Stebbins 1997, cited in Gillespie et al. 2010: 286). The notion can cover a wide range of leisure pursuits, hobbies and interests, including dog-breeding (Gillespie et al. 2010), skydiving and gun collecting (Anderson and Taylor 2010), long-distance running (Allen-Collinson and Hockey 2007) and belly-dancing (Kraus 2010). What is key is that leisure is not treated as some fanciful, 'meaningless' pursuit, but as an activity that, alongside commitment, requires knowledge, skill, competence and – perhaps ironically – often 'work'.

As is apparent with injured runners, treating some activity as serious leisure often has identity implications as participants become, in effect, particular types of persons (to themselves and others). Drawing on Goffman's (1967) comments on voluntary risk taking as being part of leisure as 'action', Hardie-Bick (2005) examined the identity changes that take place for persons who take up skydiving. Understandably, this particular form of serious leisure requires a substantial amount of training (from how to use equipment to how to orient one's body) and discipline (including appreciating and following procedure) which 'neophytes' must endure before they are allowed to participate in the activity. However, this study also showed that, as they move through this process, and go on to gain experience in this potentially risky leisure pursuit, skydivers also move through a moral career (Goffman 1961a) – that is, not only learn the necessary techniques, develop the required competences and follow the necessary precautions, but take on a particular attitude towards the activity, take on a skydiver's identity, and ultimately come to share a 'communitas' with fellow skydivers.

As with youth subcultures, participation in some serious leisure practices may on occasion result in conflict with wider society. Gillespie et al. (2010), for example, looked at the serious leisure pursuit of dog sports. There is, among dog sport enthusiasts, what they referred to as a 'culture of commitment'. This not only places great demands on those engaging in the activity, with, for example, significant amounts of time and money devoted to it, but also at times results in conflict between the world of dog sports and the 'real' world (e.g. family and work). As most of the participants in this particular study were female, this often had its own gender-specific set of commitments that participants had to manage and negotiate (the responsibilities of the wife, the mother, etc.).

Leisure and deviance

The consequences for identity from participating in serious leisure can sometimes be quite significant, with participants being perceived by wider society as in some way 'deviant'. We mentioned at the outset of this chapter the notion of leisure including various 'sins', and those involved in serious leisure and its associated subculture can sometimes run the risk of being conceptualized as 'sinners'. The idea of 'subcultural leisure' has for many years been synonymous with, to varying degrees, deviant, subversive or rebellious actions and activities. As we discussed in more detail in chapter 7, classic studies of labelling have paid particular focus to youth subcultures. Youth subcultures can be seen to be of particular interest to symbolic interactionists as they focus heavily on the symbolic aspects of identity and interaction and (at least in British studies of youth groups) much of what subcultures do has been regarded as symbolic and ritualistic (see Hall and Jefferson 1976). However, a range of other leisure activities, and leisure identities, can be ascribed with negative meaning by wider society and participants sometimes express the belief that members of the wider society may perceive them (largely because of their degree of commitment) as in some way deviant. This perception of deviance was a problem cited in the study of dog sport enthusiasts above, largely as a result of the levels of commitment involved (and perhaps amplified by the fact that participants showed some propensity to anthropomorphize the dogs, and the nature of their relationship with them, referring to them in some cases as their 'kids' or 'grand-dogs', or referring to persons who owned genetically related dogs as 'dog-in-laws').

Anderson and Taylor (2010) examined two – markedly male-

dominated – forms of serious leisure: those of skydiving and gun collecting. Participants in these activities similarly ran the risk of being
perceived as in some way deviant by wider society. For example,
skydivers could be regarded as irresponsible and reckless risk-takers,
whilst gun collectors ran the risk of being perceived as in some way
creepy, weird or suspect. In order to deal with this, participants in
these activities employed a range of 'aligning actions' (Stokes and
Hewitt 1976) to negotiate the meaning of their activities and manage
potentially deviant identities. Skydivers, for example, used a range of
'disclaimers' (Hewitt and Stokes 1975), telling non-skydivers such
things as "I'm not really a risk-taker" or explaining how they took
steps to minimize risk when skydiving. Gun collectors employed
strategies including 'techniques of neutralization' (Sykes and Matza
1957), such as denial of injury (citing gun owning as an activity in
which people were rarely injured). Members of these communities
also operated collectively to try to align their activities with wider
society. For example, gun owners often participated in public events,
at which they could emphasize the safety of their activities and act out
role plays as part of what Anderson and Taylor (2010) referred to as
'dramaturgical stereotype busting'.

The stigma of belly-dancing, another serious leisure pursuit, was
examined by Krauss (2010). There can be a tendency for members
of wider society to associate belly-dancing with something that those
who participate in it think it is certainly not, including such things
as eroticism, stripping, sexual display or even prostitution. Those
engaging in belly-dancing as a leisure pursuit can often be on the
receiving end of dirty looks, rude comments or snubs. In order to
deal with these perceptions and responses, belly-dancers employ a
range of stigma management strategies (Goffman 1963b). Thus,
for example, secrecy about participation in belly-dancing, avoiding
contact with actual erotic dancers and strippers, refraining from
teaching belly-dancing techniques to such persons, educating others
as to the true nature of belly-dancing, and what was referred to as
'semantic manipulation' (referring to themselves as 'Middle-Eastern
dancers') were used.

Such perceived deviance can then lead to negative social sanction
from wider society. This needen't be directed solely to obscure or
morally questionable behaviour, nor take on a spectacular or dramatic form. For example, Smith (1997) showed how the norms of
'civil inattention' (Goffman 1963a) normally accorded to persons
in public space could be suspended for runners. Persons choosing to pursue running or jogging as a leisure pursuit will not be

unaccustomed to comments along the lines of "knees up" or "get yer kit off", or perhaps more insulting or aggressive comments, calls which would be unlikely to be directed to many other leisure pursuits, even when practised in public space.

Phenomenology and ethnomethodology

Like any other aspect of the social world, leisure is experience (Kelly 1983: 167). As we noted above, the experience can be an individual one, e.g. listening to music with headphones on or reading a book, or may involve interaction (be it 'focused' or 'unfocused') with others, from generally unfocused interaction seen at sporting events, rock concerts or on large public beaches to more focused collections of persons (e.g. a group of friends enjoying a sociable evening together or a family on a day trip). Often we can refer to particular leisure activities as being a 'wonderful experience', or as some activity as being the 'experience of a lifetime'. The experience of leisure provides exemplary data for phenomenological and ethnomethodological research aimed at discovering the 'just-thisness' of experience.

Escaping the everyday

As we noted above, for many of us in contemporary society, when we think of leisure we think of something that is, in essence, different from, or even antithetical to, work. Rather than being restricted by formal rules, roles and relationships, leisure allows us to be free – indeed, may allow us to delve into the exotic and fantastic. In this sense leisure may be regarded as the opposite of 'everyday' life itself (which we have suggested elsewhere in this book is often characterized by the routine, monotonous, unspectacular, predictable), and the various leisure practices we engage in, or are offered, can be conceptualized as what Cohen and Taylor (1992) referred to as 'escape attempts' (from the 'everyday').

There are many ways in which we might escape the everyday. A stroll down any High Street or a glance at the TV commercial break will display offers to whisk us away into various leisure realities. Over the course of the twentieth century a traditional way to do this was via holidays and tourism. Holidays are undeniably different experiences to the rest of our everyday lives. For many (in the UK context), the fortnight 'abroad' is a clearly delineated experience, and the phenomenology of the 'tourist' experience (Cohen 1979) is a very real one.

Often the reality of the holiday involves not only 'foreign' experiences, but also 'exotic' and even 'magical' ones. A nice example of such an experience was examined by Curtin (2006). Curtin examined what she referred to as the 'swim-with-dolphins' experience that certain tourists participate in as part of their holiday. Tourists come to engage in this increasingly sought-after activity with a host of expectations, and leave with a range of recollections. The activity itself though is regarded by many as a memorable and very particular one – as a magical or 'peak' experience, quite different from everyday life. Aside from the general experience of being close to dolphins, one interesting feature of this experience is the feeling participants can have of 'connecting with' dolphins, through, for example, touch or eye contact. Curtin suggests that this interaction with dolphins leads tourists to anthropomorphize the animals. Moreover, what this study suggests is that this interaction with and attitude to the dolphins can lead to tourists perceiving a certain degree of reciprocity of perspectives or intersubjectivity (see chapter 2), as dolphins can be perceived to have 'smiles' on their 'faces', or to be equally 'enjoying' the experience themselves.

More routine activities that we all might have engaged in at some point have also been subject to phenomenological analysis, such as sporting activity. There is a certain bodily reality to most sporting activities – a 'corporeal consciousness' (Allen-Collinson and Hockey 2007). For example, sporting activities often involve some aural-respiratory experience. The rhythm and audibility of one's respiration might be an example of this, as might the sound of the feet hitting the floor for runners, for example. Another part of the sporting experience is the visual aspect, for example such things as being able to see the extent of the soccer pitch, the ball movement in racquet games, the trajectory of a boxing glove (see Wacquant (2004) for a nice study of embodied leisure). In addition, there is often an olfactory dimension to sporting reality, sometimes emitted from co-present sporting bodies, sometimes a feature of the reality of the setting (e.g. the smell of chlorine in swimming pools). These features of sporting reality are powerful cues that alert us to the sporting experience, and bring to the fore the place of the sporting body in that experience.

The body as lying at the centre of the phenomenological reality of leisure practice and experience was examined, albeit in quite a different domain, by Newmahr (2010). In her examination of sado-masochism (SM), Newmahr explored how participants in the SM scene work with others to construct, on the one hand, a performed piece of interaction (adopting, for example, particular roles or mimicking certain relationships), whilst also creating a very 'real' experience. Physical pain – its infliction and sensations on the body – lay at the heart of much of this reality construction. Whereas with, for example, sporting pursuits, pain is routinely ignored, hidden or avoided, in the context of SM interaction it is often sought, not for its own sake as such, but as an important ingredient in the social construction of SM experience.

Leisure rules and normative order

Although the preceding discussion has noted, to some extent, potential deviant readings of leisure activity, one aspect of shared experience and reciprocity of perspectives central to many leisure pursuits and activities points to a normative attitude and behaviour. We have returned frequently to the notion of 'rules' in contemporary society. We also suggested that, although much of leisure is characterized by breaking away from rules, there is often a strong normative dimension to leisure. This often finds its form in rules. Rules underpin many forms of leisure activity, particularly 'games'. The use of rules as a constitutive part of games was illustrated nicely by Garfinkel ([1967] 1984) in his breaching of the rules of the simple game of 'Tic tac toe' (a.k.a. 'Noughts and crosses'). This simple experiment illustrated how even basic leisure pursuits require close adherence, recognition and reflexive invocation of rules. Garfinkel instructed students playing this simple game to breach the underlying rules by doing such things as erasing 'noughts' or 'crosses' written by opponents, and replacing them with their own (in direct contravention of the rules of the game). This – as is the character and aim of such breaching experiments – caused some consternation among other players. The use of and demonstrative adherence to rules in and through one's actions are features of all games and many collaboratively organized leisure pursuits. Indeed, as the ability to display one's competence in using rules associated with natural language marks one out as a cultural 'member' (see chapter 3), displaying one's knowledge and practical application of rules may also feature in leisurely involvement in games.

Leisure as practical accomplishments

The idea that leisure may have some normative dimension and even formal rules points to the idea of leisure experiences as being practical accomplishments. As might have been suggested above, leisure involves not simply 'participation in', but often some 'practical accomplishment of'. This can be evident in the practical application of formal (game) rules. However (and of particular interest for ethnomethodologists), this may also be evident in more informal and mundane leisure practices. Brown and Laurier (2005), for example, examined the quite mundane activity of map reading as part of the in situ organization of a 'nice day out' – how maps in such contexts are 'naturally' read – to reveal the ethnomethodological properties of this routine aspect of this particular leisure pursuit. Making sense of the map and making sense of the journey were shown to be intimately and reflexively related. For example, the map only made sense in the context of the journey (as those on the trip made sense of where they had come from, where they were at that point, and what they needed to do to go to the next place). Additionally, reading the map, in effect, re-contextualized the journey (allowing the participants to decide what they would do on the journey, as the journey unfolded, as the map was made sense of). Moreover, this was shown to be a collective activity. In one sense the work involved and methods employed in reading the map were distributed between the occupants of the car (with each often adopting particular roles vis-à-vis the map – main reader, co-reader, holder, non-reader). Perhaps more importantly, this collective activity allowed the participants to achieve a reciprocity of perspectives. Finally, there was an element of accountability (see chapter 2) in carrying out this work, in and through reading out loud what sense was being made of the map and how the problem of navigating the journey was being resolved. Other studies have revealed how, when 'on scene' at particular locales, tourists continue sightseeing as a practical activity and accomplishment. MacCannell (1999), for example, pointed to how such things as the indentification and recognition, and appreciation and evaluation, of whatever sight one has encountered, establishing the truth about and authenticity of it, and making it memorable were all part of the ethnomethodology of sightseeing – of the sightseeing 'act'.

Conversation analysis and the Interaction Order

Conversational sociability

Few leisure activities demand *absolute* silence across their course. As we have seen above, activities from running in public to map reading in private cars can involve verbalization as part of their doing. Even the non-lexical features of talk we noted in chapter 3 can play an important part in many leisure activities, and can often be quite highly co-ordinated (e.g. 'laughing' at stand-up comics, 'booing' at panto-mime villains, 'screaming' at scary films). One endemic, indeed uni-versal, leisure activity is 'sociable interaction', that is, persons coming together for no other reason than to enjoy each others' company (see Simmel [1911] 1949, 1964). Conversation plays an important role in sociable interaction, and does much to allow persons to make claims of sociable affiliation with each other. Several studies of sociability have revealed ways in which naturally occurring conversation is col-laboratively done to, in effect, talk sociability into being (see, e.g., Eggins and Slade 1997; Riesman and Watson 1964; Watson 1958; Watson and Potter 1962). In Anglo-American society, for example, participants in sociable encounters might work to avoid serious topics and potential confrontation in favour of the relaying of narratives of telling or stories (see Tannen 1984). The type of 'facework', 'sup-portive interchanges' and dramatic 'replayings' discussed earlier (see chapter 3) are characteristic of such encounters. It should be noted of course that conversation in such encounters is subject to cultural variation. For example, potentially face-threatening actions (like teasing) are not only salient features of sociable conversation in some cultures but actually requisite to get sociability recognizably done (see e.g. Schiffrin's 1984 study of sociable argumentation, Katriel's (1986) and Tannen's (1986) study of Jewish 'straight talk', and work done on German conversational style by Byrnes 1986 and Watts 1989). Having said that, one should not think that Anglo-Amercian sociable conversation is void of conflict. We spoke earlier about what Goffman (1967) referred to as 'character'. In his discussion of action, Goffman also developed the notion of 'character contests'. In the context of leisure pursuits, often, persons have an interest in estab-lishing evidence of a strong character. As part of certain pursuits, when persons come together with similarly interested others, contests can occur. Maintaining one's poise in a poker game (or, even 'out-poising' one's opponent) is an obvious example, as is keeping one's cool in a game of 'chicken'. However, in the context of informal con-versation, character contests can occur via a range of conversational moves (see chapter 3), such as banter, slights, conflicting accounts, moral claims, threats and 'run-ins' (see Malone 1997).

Leisure expression and performance

Many leisure activities have performance at their core. This can often be professional. The stand-up comic, Shakespearian actor, or heavy metal guitarist will all have a performance role to play and performance job to do in order to satisfy the leisure demands of their performance-demanding audiences. More generally though, many of the expressive features of these and a range of other performances are reflected in everyday settings and contexts. In line with his dramaturgical model for understanding everyday life, Goffman (1969) noted that, when in interaction with others, persons 'exude expressions'. Leisure activities often have expressive dimensions to them, ones which not only convey something about persons, but form a key part of their 'leisure-specific' identities. Leisure expressiveness may range from the seemingly unconstrained (e.g. yelping gleefully when whitewater rafting or riding a roller-coaster) to the highly controlled or even 'absence of' any expression at all (e.g. in adopting a 'poker face', or when taking a last-minute soccer penalty, etc. – of course, the 'before' and 'after' expressiveness of the poker player or penalty taker can often reveal these two polar ends of the expressive continuum, the nature of the latter being dependent on the outcome of the hand / penalty kick). Expressiveness is not only deemed appropriate or relevant, but may be expected or demanded. For example, persons might be expected to take some leisure activities 'seriously' (e.g. a game of chess, or even tic tac toe – see our discussion above of ethnomethodology and game rules). Conversely, persons may be required not take them too seriously (e.g. not 'freaking out' when losing a parlour game or being bowled out by a child in a family game of cricket) (see Goffman 1961b). We discussed earlier the expressive act of laughter, in terms of its sequential organization (see chapter 3). Laughter is undoubtedly an expressive act. However, even when participating in leisure activities there may be a normative order at play, along with expectations and requirements made of participants. In this sense, as with a range of other actions, one might also consider the 'expressive propriety' of laughter. That is, even in leisure activities, there may be times when laughter is expressively relevant, so to speak, or, conversely, expressively inappropriate. For example, guffawing at a stand-up routine may be not only relevant and expressively proper, but expected (indeed, to save the comic situation and setting, and the identities of those involved, polite laughter may be employed). The same expressive display in response to Hamlet dropping the skull of Yorick on his foot may not (indeed, lack of expressive control is one reason why children and the mentally retarded always bring with them the threat of expressive violation (see Goffman 1972) to leisure frames such as plays, classical concerts and the like). Of course, persons may also employ leisure 'symbols' in some expressive manner, to signify in some way some leisure-based identity claim. Status symbols and the like allow persons to do this. We noted earlier that leisure activity often includes some affiliation with like others – some leisure 'ethnicity'. Again, status symbols allow persons to make such claims (see Goffman 1951). Finally, as Goffman noted in his (1979) discussion of gender, expressive displays allow persons not only to claim particular identities, but also to convey their alignment to the current situation. This, in turn, allows others in the situation to interpret and make sense of those persons and the identities they are claiming, and make assumptions and expectations about the interaction that might follow.

Game frames

As we saw in respect of phenomenological approaches, leisure activities are experienced realities for those persons participating in them. In focusing on games, Goffman (1961b) examined how persons co-ordinate their activities to establish the reality of the game. Games place frames (see Goffman 1974 and chapter 3) around events, that is, provide an interpretive framework that persons draw upon to make sense of the actions and behaviour of others, and that allows others to make sense of theirs. This allows person to reach a shared definition of the situation. As we saw in our discussion of deviant identities (see chapter 7), the demands of 'aliveness' also apply to leisure activities, and games in particular. Indeed, this is perhaps more so, as persons are expected to immerse and engross themselves in leisure activities, and often demonstrate this in and through their expressive actions. In addition to expectations around 'sharing' definitions of game frames, and of expressing engrossment in them, Goffman also pointed to what might be regarded as game-specific identities. The poker-faced card player we noted above is a classic example, as is the cool-headed penalty taker. Not only are certain identities made relevant, but often others are made irrelevant. For example, we mentioned above the nature of sociable interaction, and that identities that might be relevant in the 'outside world' are often suspended or regarded as irrelevant, for the purposes of 'doing' sociability (as when we might invite the boss round for dinner and treat him/her as 'any other person'). In this sense, sociable interaction allows persons to interact as equals. The same rules of irrelevance often apply to involvement in games (e.g., at a soccer match, a winning goal may see the multi-millionaire businessman hugging the unemployed manual worker, only by virtue of the fact that they occupy adjacent seats and share

– at that moment – affiliated leisure-based identities of 'supporter').
As we noted in chapter 3, frames are subject to transformations. In
this sense, game frames can be 'broken' – that is, events can occur,
or identities come into play, that have no place in the reality of the
current game. Thus, a poker-player may throw the table in the air
(or in the Wild West, shoot his opponent), a soccer player may jump
into the crowd and attack a fan (as once infamously happened in the
UK), or some third party may enter the frame to break it temporarily (e.g. a 'streaker' running onto the pitch during a cricket match).
In all cases, normally excluded identities result in frame disruptions
and breaks. The definitional power of frames (in defining the current
situation) and their transformative power (again, see chapter 3) allow
us to move away from the idea that leisure and play are somehow
restricted to *particular* times, *particular* places or *particular* participants. For example, although we contrasted leisure from work above,
we can find that much of what we do *at* work, *in* the work setting,
with colleagues is leisure. For example, we may spend a certain part
of our work-day participating in sociable conversation, chatting or
gossiping. Indeed, we must have all experienced being reproached for
this at some times in our careers (see our discussion of role distance
above). Such leisure framings can become almost routinized in essentially non-leisure contexts. Thus, a joke can be enjoyed at the start of
a work meeting, colleagues may enjoy a drink together at lunchtime,
etc. Even daydreaming at a work meeting may be a (albeit rather
individualized) way of overlaying some leisure reality on some more
serious framed activity. Thus, leisure identities and interaction need
not be regarded as necessarily separate in time and place – leisure can
be 'done' as 'framed activity' anywhere.

Conclusion

Introduction

Throughout this book we have demonstrated the ways in which the three main forms of interactionist sociology – symbolic interactionism, ethnomethodology and conversation analysis – can be brought to bear on a range of 'core' sociological issues. We have also treated these approaches as having sufficient features in common to justify our assessing them 'as a piece'. From the point of view of other sociologists, this is very much the case: all three approaches differ from mainstream sociological analysis in quite similar ways. These include such matters as treating the social world as exclusively and entirely produced by those people (members, interlocutors) who make it up; treating social facts as the outcomes of interactional work; and treating the temporal dimension of social activities as being as important – if not more so – than their 'spatial' dimension. Each of these can be dealt with in turn.

From the point of view of many mainstream sociologists, the social world is an environment in which social actors conduct their affairs. Interactions take place in institutional contexts, and these contexts shape and determine the nature of appropriate interactions. Thus, for example, there are approved and positively sanctioned ways of behaving in a religious building – a church, mosque, synagogue, etc. – and, equally, disapproved and negatively sanctioned forms of behaviour. It is proper behaviour, for instance, to remove one's shoes before entering a mosque, and a failure to do so would be a legitimate cause for complaint by other users of the space. Equally, some participants have abilities that others lack. While anyone *could* perform a Christian wedding ceremony in a Christian church, only a legitimate church official can perform a 'real' one; a couple who were 'married' by someone not authorized to perform such a ceremony would be legitimately entitled to have the ceremony undertaken again by a proper official – the first one would not 'count'. Interactionist sociologists would not claim that such rules, norms and standards 'do not exist' or are 'merely socially constructed' – indeed, they acknowledge their external and constraining nature just as much as any other sociologists. What the former would insist on, however, is that those rules are enforced solely by other participants in the institution in question. The prohibition on wearing shoes in a mosque or the expectation that someone performing a wedding ceremony is warranted to do so by a formal body are enforced *by other participants in the institution*, and have no independent existence separate to this enforcement. As Wieder's analysis of the convict code in chapter 2 demonstrates, rules 'mean' what they are understood to mean by those who use them, and apply only in those circumstances in which they can be enforced. Institutions such as churches, schools, hospitals, police forces, political parties and so on are not independent 'things' that people can join, but the products of their members' interpretation and enforcement of particular codes of conduct.

More broadly, social facts in a Durkheimian sense are also the products of interactional work. As we saw in chapter 1, although social norms can change over time, they cannot *on their own* determine individuals' actions: people will, for example, commit suicide only if they can interpret their situation in such a way as to make suicide seem to be a thing that makes some sense. Broader changes in society – which, again, from an interactionist perspective are always the result of complex interactional work – might make it more likely that more people will interpret their situation in such a way as to make suicide seem to be a solution to particular problems, a legitimate way out, a means of gaining revenge, etc., etc., but in each and every case that interpretation has to take place. Suicide *rates*, then, are not in themselves direct measures of overarching social facts – such as increasing anomie at a structural level – but are always the complex products of individuals' interpretations of their situations. Furthermore, decisions as to whether a particular death can be determined to be the result of suicide or some other cause – the decisions coroners make – are also the products of routine interactional work. Both Garfinkel ([1967] 1984) and later Atkinson (1978) point out that these decisions are themselves regulated by experts' orientation to what would count as a normal suicide rate: the competence of a pathologist or coroner depends, at least in part, on he or she finding broadly the same kinds of things as his or her peers. Scandals or public mistakes may render such professionals more sensitive to the possibilities of particular cases being suicides, while their absence may mean the 'normal' ratio of suicides to other forms of death will remain unchallenged.

Finally, the tendency of mainstream sociologists to take 'snapshots' of the social world is incommensurable with interactionist analyses. Many sociologists, for instance, compare different rates of things – unemployment, suicide, crime, etc. – across different periods of time to determine what 'trends' or 'patterns' there might be. A finding that the crime rate is increasing year-on-year might be used to argue against particular kinds of social and government policies, or to seek correlations with other quantitatively measured social trends. As well as questioning the utility of such aggregations of data – see above – interactionists would also question the sense of seeking one mono-lithic 'explanation' for what must reasonably be a host of different motivating circumstances. The *temporal* nature of the social world is made clearest in symbolic interactionist and conversation analytic studies. In the former, a cause-and-effect relationship between cir-cumstances and action is explicitly argued against, in favour of the more interpretative and meaningful analyses advocated by Blumer and others. To take this further, conversation analysis offers perhaps the most radical form of temporally-aware sociology in existence. The context for any one action is the action that preceded it – in this case, the context for a turn at talk is the *preceding* turn at talk – and, unless that preceding action cannot be shown to account for what follows it, it is the *only* necessary context for the latter's understanding. An interlocutor's action in producing a turn-at-talk immediately furnishes the following speaker with the structure in which they must operate.

Criticisms of interactionism

Where mainstream sociologists have considered the contributions of interactionist sociology, however, they have tended to misunder-stand or misrepresent its premises and the conduct of its practition-ers. Many commentators, attempting to be charitable, recognize that interactionist sociology provides useful information, but seek to restrict the purview of that information to a subset of sociologi-cal problems (see, for instance, Macionis and Plummer 1997: 537; Bilton et al. 2002: 362). Thus, for instance, Giddens (1997: 565) argues that (symbolic) interactionists 'have always found difficulty in dealing with more large-scale structures and processes'.

Such criticisms are premised on the notion that there are two 'levels' of sociological understanding: the structural and the individual. These two levels must be approached in different ways. 'Structural' features of society such as class composition, ideology, economic and industrial change, and so on, are understood to operate both independently of individuals' actions and 'behind their backs'. These features provide the context in which activities take place, but are not capable of being examined as the products of interaction: they are far too complex, too 'big', for any such analyses to ever reach the massive scale required. Some analysts (e.g. Althusser 1969) have gone as far as arguing that these structural features of society are the *only* real ones, and that both individuals and the interactions they engage in are the ways structural features of the world manifest themselves in reality.

'Individual' analyses – analyses of 'agency' – examine the motivation for, and organization and effects of individuals' actions in these contexts. Thus, for example, economists posit that individuals will behave in a personally rational manner, other things remaining equal. If they believe the value of their assets is likely to fall, they will sell those assets – and, by doing so, are likely to generate a drop in those asset prices themselves. If, however, they believe the value of their assets is likely to rise, they will hang on to them, or attempt to acquire more, thus generating a rise in those prices. The perpetual overheating and crashing of the housing market over the last twenty or thirty years can be understood using such models. Sociologically, some analysts (e.g. Elster 1982) have argued that it is possible to understand the entire complexity of the social world by treating actors as rational game-players. The 'properties, goals, and beliefs' (Elster 1982: 453) of individuals determine how they behave, and their behaviour generates the social world.

Mainstream sociologists like Giddens, Bourdieu, Habermas and Beck understand the job of sociology as being to 'reconcile' these two levels of analysis. 'Structure' and 'agency' have to be brought together, as neither alone can adequately account for the complexity of social life. Typically, the ways this 'reconciliation' are undertaken involve 'agency' being subsumed under the auspices of structure.

Less charitable analysts simply write off interactionist approaches as being individualistic, subjective and 'psychological'. Da Silva (2007), for example, argues forcibly that Blumer's conception of symbolic interactionism denies the existence of social structure and social orderliness altogether, claiming that Mead's work on the social is ignored by those interactionists working in his tradition. This is an odd position to take, particularly given Blumer's own argument that the social order *exists* *as* the product of joint social action, and that this position cannot entail a denial of 'the existence of structure in human society. Such a position would be ridiculous' (Blumer 1969: 75). Instead of representing a perspective in sociology which requires reconciling with other perspectives, such critics simply write interactionism off as not being sociology at all!

The most venomous attacks of this sort have been reserved for ethnomethodology and conversation analysis, which – particularly when studies in both perspectives started to appear in volume in the late 1960s and early 1970s – were treated as being of a piece. Alvin W. Gouldner, in his *The Coming Crisis of Western Sociology* (1971), criticized Goffman for overemphasizing 'episodic' aspects of the social world – just those aspects Goffman explicitly sought to examine and understand! – and Garfinkel for focusing unduly on dishonesty and conflict in his methods (thereby misunderstanding the point and importance of the latter's breaching procedures). Most uncharitable of all was Ernest Gellner (1975) who, despite his repeated assurances that he could not understand Garfinkel's prose, nonetheless claimed that ethnomethodology and CA gave unwarranted centrality to the 'subjective' and were nothing less than a naïve 're-enchantment industry', a product of a louche Californian youth movement.

Despite their similarities – when viewed from the perspectives of more conventional sociologies – and independently of these more mainstream criticisms, there are a number of ways in which the three perspectives we have considered in this book differ from one another, and have been subject to mutual and internal criticism. We will consider some of these differences and criticisms to conclude.

Criticisms of symbolic interactionism

Symbolic interactionism has often been criticized by other interactionists for its apparent theoretical and methodological looseness. Bittner ([1973] 2003) makes the clearest argument against the perspective. Mainstream sociology, he argues, oscillates between 'objective' and 'realist' poles. The former is exemplified by 'scientific' approaches, including those of, for example, Durkheim, controlled by two 'norms': '(a) the operational definition of meaning, and (b) strict formalization of rules of inference' (Bittner [1973] 2003: 95). The former refers to clarity of concepts: something like 'class', which can have a wide range of vernacular meanings (cultural, educational, economic, to name just three) cannot be used unproblematically by sociologists because these different meanings make the concept *slippery*. In order to use such concepts, therefore, they must be given clear and unambiguous definitions, which do not change over the course of an enquiry, and which are maintained between enquiries. This is similar to the requirements of other 'hard' sciences: the concept of weight in some branches of physics, for example, is *operationalized* to mean an object's mass multiplied by the effect of gravitational acceleration on it. This allows weight to be referred to consistently over the course of an investigation, and to be applied in the same way between investigations. The latter norm refers to the importance of consistent methodology: agreed standards for investigation, and standardized methods of drawing conclusions from evidence, allow other investigators to audit studies, and also allow studies to be corrected or falsified by undertaking other studies. Typically this means undertaking quantitative analyses.

The problem, Bittner argues, with such approaches is that they cannot be consistently applied in sociology. As Garfinkel (see chapter 2) demonstrates, in every sociological investigation without exception the standards of objectivity have to be relaxed but the investigation is still 'counted' as adequate. In real-world social investigations, objectivity is an impossible ambition. As a consequence, much sociology abandons 'objectivity' as a criterion for success and instead uses 'realism' – in particular, Bittner argues, the kinds of urban ethnographies pursued by the Chicago School and the later symbolic interactionists. The problem with such an approach, however, is that 'the arguments of the attack were often invoked as the aegis for studies of a loose, impressionistic, and personal nature' (Bittner [1973] 2003: 100). In short, academic standards dropped. There is certainly some evidence that symbolic interactionism can legitimately be accused of these criticisms: as we argued in chapter 1, Blumer's methodological tenets are difficult if not impossible to follow in practice, which has meant that a wide range of methods and theoretical frameworks have been utilized under the banner of 'SI'. The failure to work carefully through the reconciliation of Everett C. Hughes' institutional analysis and Herbert Blumer's concern with meaning has not done the perspective any favours in this sense.

Some, however, have seen this apparent vagueness as a strength. Fine (1993), for instance, argues that the suppleness of symbolic interactionist methods and theory has allowed it to move from being an 'oppositional' sociology to being central to many contemporary trends in the discipline – albeit without being acknowledged as such. Qualitative and ethnographic sociological approaches are far more widespread than in the past, and there is much wider suspicion of naive scientism, the unreflective use of quantitative materials, and the notion that social activities can be described with reference to a cause–effect model of behaviour. The fact that the approach's boundaries were always somewhat indistinct means it has been far more able to integrate with other forms of sociology than its other interactionist counterparts.

Criticisms of ethnomethodology

Ethnomethodology has proved far less digestible by the mainstream. Its insistence on studying the specifics of particular situations and settings, and its rejection of theory and explanation in favour of description, means it is difficult to use its studies and study policies as conventional sociological resources. Furthermore, Garfinkel's own analyses of 'professional' sociology – in particular his criticisms of the latter's capacity to stick to rigorous methodological tenets (Garfinkel [1967] 1984: ch. 1) and of its inability to operationalize such simple concepts as 'in' and 'out' in quantitative analysis (Garfinkel [1967] 1984: ch. 7) – has made the perspective indigestible more generally. While Garfinkel claimed that ethnomethodology was not meant to be a criticism of, or attempt to correct, conventional, 'constructive' sociology, it is difficult to see how his analyses can fail to be read in such a way. Thus:

> there can be nothing to quarrel with or to correct about practical socio-logical reasoning, and so, because professional sociological inquiries are practical through and through, except that quarrels between those doing professional inquiries and ethnomethodology may be of interest as phenomena for ethnomethodological studies, these quarrels need not be taken seriously (Garfinkel [1967] 1984: viii);

and, concerning the results of sociologists' coding clinic results:

> if the work of *ad hocing* is required to make such claims [about the clinic] intelligible, it can always be argued – and so far I do not see a defensible reply – that the coded results consist of a persuasive version of the socially organized character of the clinic's operations, regardless of what the actual order is, perhaps independently of what the actual order is, and even without the investigator having detected the actual order. Instead of our study of patients' clinic careers (as well as the multitude of studies of various social arrangements that have been carried out in similarly conventional ways) having described the order of the clinic's operations, the account may be argued to consist of a

socially invented, persuasive, and proper way of talking about the clinic
as an orderly enterprise, since 'after all' the account was produced by
'scientific procedures'. (Garfinkel [1967] 1984: 23)

Although some have criticized ethnomethodology for not engaging
more with the concerns of mainstream sociology (e.g. Pollner 1991),
they are very much in the minority. A case can be made, however,
for arguing that ethnomethodology's 'purity' may also have been its
downfall. Studies such as Livingston's (2008) often appear wilfully
obscure, describing in detail the mundane logic of, for example,
playing checkers (draughts). More problematically, such studies
sometimes appear to be the only ways in which one can *rigorously*
follow Garfinkel's study policies: the indexicality and reflexivity
of the reasoning process are found in cases such as playing checkers, drawing and reading maps, and so on, but they appear to have
the character of being found 'one more time', 'again', 'in another
context'. Rather than generating new studies of different social settings, much contemporary ethnomethodology sometimes appears to
be simply a re-demonstration of those aspects of practical reasoning
first identified by Garfinkel in the 1960s.

Where such criticisms cannot be made – as, for instance, in
ethnomethodological studies of work (e.g. Anderson et al. 1987;
Lynch 1982) – it is precisely because such studies often conduct ethnomethodological enquiries *specifically to* criticize their constructive
sociological counterparts. Thus, Anderson et al. examine the ways in
which a routine managerial decision is reached in a soft-drink supply
company in order to demonstrate, among other things, that such
decisions are overwhelmingly mundane and ordinary in their organization. Claims that business decision making, management, entre-
preneurialism and risk-taking are somehow distinct or special forms
of activity are *thereby* criticized. Equally, Lynch goes to some length
to show how microscopy slides of rat brains are selected for analysis
or rejected as 'not good enough', emphasizing the ad hoc nature of
the expertise required to make such distinctions. He conducts this
analysis partly to demonstrate that 'critical' studies of science – which
claim to show that such situated practices are somehow improper –
miss the point that there is no other way ordinary laboratory science
could be carried out: mundane knowledge and skills are the root of all
other forms of knowledge and skill, and to take them out of ordinary
settings would not make those settings 'more scientific' but would
render work in those settings impossible. The rise of 'ethnomethod-
ologically-informed ethnography' as a means of conducting studies

of work has proved immensely fruitful in its commercial application – especially in the field of interface design (e.g. Suchman 1987) – and influential in sociology more broadly (e.g. Bittner 1967a, b), but it often sits uncomfortably with the 'pure' ethnomethodological analyses of Garfinkel as his thought developed.

Criticisms of conversation analysis

Similar internal frictions have occurred within conversation analysis, although these have generally been more open and explicit than those in the previous two perspectives. The most divisive disputes have concerned the use of 'conventional' sociological concepts and categories as explanatory resources for mundane talk. Thus, for instance, Heritage and Greatbatch (1986) describe how particular ways of designing utterances in political speeches 'elicit' applause as a response. By treating 'political speeches' as a distinct category of talk – rather than using analyses of talk in a range of different settings to examine *whether* such speeches *can be shown to be* distinct – they are able to generate a set of guidelines for turn construction that seem more likely to elicit applause than others. The problem here is that these turn types are far more ubiquitous than this: the three-part list, for instance, can be used in a wide range of settings to elicit a wide range of responses. The fact that in one particular setting it elicits applause does not therefore mean that it is *designed to* elicit applause or that it is *specific to* that setting. By considering talk in a particular setting, therefore, conversation analysis is not 'applied' so much as 'shown to work again', albeit with the unexamined assumption that the responses particular turn-designs elicit are *therefore* the responses those turns *were designed to elicit*. Drew and Heritage's (1992) 'talk at work' programme subsequently built on just these kinds of analysis.

More seriously, interlocutors' sociological characteristics are sometimes used as explanatory features of the kinds of talk they produce. Thus, for example, Fishman (1978) argues that women tend to ask more questions, interrupt less frequently, fill more silences and use more 'attention-getting' beginnings than their male interlocutors. West and Zimmerman (1983) make similar claims using a quantitative analysis of conversational excerpts between unacquainted male and female speakers. Such analyses are problematic from a conversation analytic perspective insofar as they do not adequately demonstrate that these differences are the result of the genders of the interlocutors in question. To be sure, a larger sample could be considered, grounds for generalization laid out and so on, but such measures would look a lot more like the practices of quantitative survey analysis than of any interactionist method. Ultimately, 'what is going on' in the conversation becomes something the analyst determines and argues about: the primacy of the data is lost. Such analyses reach their nadir in Kitzinger's 'feminist conversation analysis' (Kitzinger 2000). In this, Kitzinger interprets specific utterances not on the basis of what precedes and follows them but using conventional sociological categories: thus, for instance, Kitzinger argues that a speaker revealing her status as a lesbian 'actively uses the turn-taking organization of conversation to extend her turn beyond her coming out moment to decrease the likelihood of anyone offering an assessment of, or any other response to, it' (Kitzinger 2000: 186). It is unclear how such an assessment can be made without privileged knowledge of the speaker's motivation, and – given no response is made – it is equally unclear whether the speaker's interlocutors are appalled, outraged or simply disinterested. The mechanics of turn-taking analysis are simply used here to allow for a very conventional sociological analysis (Wowk 2007).

Apart from Goffman's analyses of conversation analysis (see chapter 3), there have been three main ethnomethodological attacks on the perspective, which take very similar lines. Schwartz (1976) implicitly compares conversation analysis to forms of psychodynamic counselling insofar as it tends to treat what people say not in terms of the content of their turn at talk but in terms of the interactional effect their turn has. Thus, for example, a question–answer insertion sequence may be treated as a technical matter (Q1–Q2–Q3–A3–A2–A1) but the actual content of the questions and answers is largely ignored. This, Schwartz argues, is similar to the ways counsellors and therapists may 'interpret' clients' utterances as 'evasion', 'attempts to change the subject', 'resistance', etc., rather than responding to them in terms of their content – which, in ordinary conversation, would be an appropriate and positively sanctioned thing to do.

Sharrock and Anderson (1984) take a similar line, questioning the legitimacy of Schegloff's analyses of disparate conversational phenomena. They argue that his bringing together of a wide range of disparate fragments of talk under particular analytic rubrics such as 'pre-self identifications' depends on Schegloff systematically overlooking the specific differences between those fragments, and the ways in which those rubrics have to act as generalizing glosses to do their work. Such rubrics generate a complex analytical framework, but the means by which the data Schegloff is examining are transformed to allow for such analyses are *themselves* interesting ethnomethodological phenomena: they are analytic work, just as any other form of constructive sociology might be. Lynch (1994) further argues that such constructivism was apparent from Sacks' very early work, in his desire to develop a vernacular set of understandings of ordinary talk into a scientific discipline.

Conclusion

The tensions and mutual criticisms that operate within and between our perspectives reveal dynamic and vibrant communities, eager to move beyond their roots and to develop their understandings of the social world in new and increasingly rigorous ways. As we have seen, however, common to all three are tensions between 'purity' (adhering to a set of methodological and theoretical precepts) and 'application' (seeking either to engage with broader sociological concerns or to adapt or relax these precepts in particular cases). We cannot adjudicate on these tensions, but would agree with Becker (on Blumer) that it is very difficult to conduct studies that rigidly adhere to abstract principles and with Wowk (on Kitzinger) that simply bashing interactionist practice and conventional sociological terms of reference together rarely improves either. It is likely that these tensions will remain with us, but – if the study rather than any particular theory is the basis of any interactionist sociology – these things can be worked out better or worse, more or less successfully, in the practice of interactionist research. It is to this that we hand you over.

Notes

1 Pragmatism and Symbolic Interactionism

1 This is not quite accurate. A correlation between variables such as unemployment and crime does not demonstrate a causal link. Either one could cause the other, or both could be caused by something else entirely. Nevertheless, there is a tendency to extrapolate causal relationships from relationships of this sort throughout the social sciences.

2 Phenomenology and Ethnomethodology

1 A less direct influence on Garfinkel was the later philosophy of Ludwig Wittgenstein, especially his thinking about language games and his admonition that, to resolve many philosophical puzzles, we need to *'look and see . . . don't think, but look!'* (Wittgenstein [1958] 1968: §66). There are clear affinities and complementarity between Garfinkel's project and the later Wittgenstein. See Garfinkel and Sacks (1970: 169), and chapter 3 of this book.

2 Garfinkel ([1967] 1984: 67–8) distinguishes two kinds of judgemental dope: the 'cultural dope' and the 'psychological dope'. The cultural dope is 'the man-in-the-sociologist's-society who produces the stable features of the society by acting in compliance with pre-established and legitimate alternatives of action that the common culture provides'. The psychological dope is an equivalent type constructed out of the psychologist's theories of biography, conditioning and mental functioning. Both dopes are antithetical to the practical actor as conceived by Garfinkel.

4 Status and Power

1 Some members of the ruling class may be motivated by more humanitarian or paternalistic concerns. Competition between enterprises, however, will mean that any such employer who fails to increase productivity or

reduce wage costs is likely to suffer in the marketplace compared to competitors who are able to effect such changes.

2 Such institutional statuses do not necessarily ensure that an incumbent of any of these groups will necessarily be treated one way or another in different situations: as in the preceding discussion, how someone is *actually* treated is interactionally determined.

References

Abbott, Andrew. 1999. *Department and Discipline: Chicago Sociology at One Hundred*. Chicago: University of Chicago Press.

Allen-Collinson, Jacquelyn and Hockey, John. 2007. Working out identity: distance runners and the management of disrupted identity. *Leisure Studies* 26(4): 381–98.

Althusser, Louis. 1969. *For Marx*. London: Verso.

Anderson, Leon and Taylor, Jimmy D. 2010. Standing out while fitting in: serious leisure identities and aligning actions among skydivers and gun collectors. *Journal of Contemporary Ethnography* 39: 34–59.

Anderson, Nels. 1923. *The Hobo: The Sociology of the Homeless Man*. Chicago: University of Chicago Press.

Anderson, R. J. and Sharrock, W. W. 1984. Analytic work: aspects of the organization of conversational data. *Journal for the Theory of Social Behaviour* 14(1): 103–24.

Anderson, R. J., Hughes, J. A. and Sharrock, W. W. 1987. Executive problem finding: some material and initial observations. *Social Psychology Quarterly* 50(2: June): 143–59.

Atkinson, J. Maxwell. 1978. *Discovering Suicide: Studies in the Social Organization of Sudden Death*. London: Macmillan.

Atkinson, J. Maxwell. 1992. Displaying neutrality: formal aspects of informal court proceedings. In Paul Drew and John Heritage (eds.), *Talk at Work: Interaction in Institutional Settings*, Cambridge: Cambridge University Press, 199–211.

Atkinson, J. Maxwell and Drew, Paul. 1979. *Order in Court: The Organization of Verbal Interaction in Judicial Settings*. London: Macmillan Press.

Atkinson, J. Maxwell and Heritage, John. 1984. *Structures of Social Action: Studies in Conversation Analysis*. Cambridge: Cambridge University Press.

Austin, John Langshaw. 1962. *How to Do Things with Words*. Oxford: Oxford University Press.

Baker, Carolyn D. 1997. Ticketing rules: categorization and moral ordering in a school staff meeting. In Stephen Hester and Peter Eglin (eds.) *Culture in Action: Studies in Membership Categorization Analysis*, Washington: International Institute for Ethnomethodology and Conversation Analysis / University Press of America, 77–98.

Bauman, Zygmunt. 2007. *Consuming Life*. Cambridge: Polity Press.

Becker, Howard S. 1952a. The career of the Chicago public schoolteacher. *American Journal of Sociology* 57(5): 470–7.

Becker, Howard S. 1952b. Social-class variations in the teacher–pupil relationship. *Journal of Educational Sociology* 25(8): 451–65.

Becker, Howard S. 1953. Becoming a marihuana user. *American Journal of Sociology* 59(3: November): 235–42.

Becker, Howard S. 1963. *Outsiders: Studies in the Sociology of Deviance*. New York: The Free Press.

Becker, Howard S. 1967. Whose side are we on? *Social Problems* 14(3): 239–47.

Becker, Howard S. 1982. *Art Worlds*. Berkeley, CA: University of California Press.

Becker, Howard S. 1993. How I learned what a crock was. *Journal of Contemporary Ethnography* 22(1): 28–35.

Becker, Howard S. 1998. *Tricks of the Trade: How to Think About Your Research While You're Doing It*. Chicago: University of Chicago Press.

Becker, Howard S. 1999. The Chicago School, so-called. *Qualitative Sociology* 22(1): 3–12.

Becker, Howard S. 2006. The lay referral system: the problem of professional power. *Knowledge, Work and Society* 4: 65–76.

Becker, Howard S. and Carper, James W. 1956. The elements of identification with an occupation. *American Sociological Review* 21(3): 341–8.

Becker, Howard S. and Geer, Blanche. 1958. The fate of idealism in medical school. *American Sociological Review* 23(1): 50–56.

Berger, Peter and Luckmann, Thomas. 1966. *The Social Construction of Reality*. New York: Doubleday.

Beynon, Huw. 1973. *Working for Ford*. London: Allen Lane.

Bilton, Tony, Bonnett, Kevin, Jones, Pip, et al. 2002. *Introductory Sociology*. 4th edition. Basingstoke: Palgrave Macmillan.

Bittner, Egon. [1965] 1974. The concept of organization. In Roy Turner (ed.) *Ethnomethodology: Selected Readings*, Harmondsworth: Penguin, 69–81.

Bittner, Egon. 1967a. Police discretion in emergency apprehension of mentally ill persons. *Social Problems* 14(3): 278–92.

Bittner, Egon. 1967b. The police on skid-row: a study of peace keeping. *American Sociological Review* 32(5): 699–715.

Bittner, Egon. [1973] 2003. Objectivity and realism in sociology. In Michael Lynch and Wes Sharrock (eds.) *Harold Garfinkel*. Vol. III. London: Sage, 93–107.

Blumer, Herbert. 1937. Social psychology. In Emerson Peter Schmidt (ed.)

Man and Society: A Substantive Introduction to the Social Sciences, New York: Prentice-Hall, 144–98.

Blumer, Herbert. [1956] 1969. Sociological analysis and the 'variable'. In *Symbolic Interactionism: Perspective and Method*, Englewood Cliffs, NJ: Prentice-Hall, 127–39.

Blumer, Herbert. [1963] 1969. Society as symbolic interaction. In *Symbolic Interactionism: Perspective and Method*, Englewood Cliffs, NJ: Prentice-Hall, 78–89.

Blumer, Herbert. 1969. *Symbolic Interactionism: Perspective and Method*. Englewood Cliffs, NJ: Prentice-Hall.

Bourdieu, Pierre. 1984. *Distinction: A Social Critique of the Judgement of Taste*. London: Routledge.

Brake, Mike. 1980. *The Sociology of Youth Culture and Youth Subcultures: Sex and Drugs and Rock 'n' Roll?* London: Routledge and Kegan Paul.

Braverman, Harry. 1976. *Labor and Monopoly Capital: The Degradation of Work in the Twentieth Century*. New York: Monthly Review Press.

Brown, Barry and Laurier, Eric (2005) Maps & car journeys: an ethnomethodological approach. *Cartographica*, 4(3): 17–33.

Brown, Penelope and Levinson, Stephen. 1987. *Politeness: Some Universals in Language Usage*. Cambridge: Cambridge University Press.

Bulmer, Martin. 1984. *The Chicago School of Sociology: Institutionalization, Diversity and the Rise of Sociological Research*. Chicago: University of Chicago Press.

Bury, Michael. 1982. Chronic illness as biographical disruption. *Sociology of Health and Illness* 4: 167–82.

Bury, Michael. 1988. Meanings at risk: the experience of arthritis. In Robert Anderson and Michael Bury (eds.) *Living with Chronic Illness: The Experience of Patients and their Families*. London: Unwin Hyman, 89–116.

Button, Graham and Casey, Neil. 1984. Generating topic: the use of topic initial elicitors. In J. Maxwell Atkinson and John Heritage (eds.) *Structures of Social Action: Studies in Conversation Analysis*. Cambridge: Cambridge University Press, 167–90.

Button, Graham and Casey, Neil. 1985. Topic nomination and topic pursuit. *Human Studies* 8(1): 3–55.

Byrnes, Heidi. 1986. Interactional style in German and American conversations. *Text* 6(2): 189–206.

Charmaz, Kathy. 1983. Loss of self: a fundamental form of suffering of the chronically ill. *Sociology of Health and Illness* 5: 168–95.

Charmaz, Kathy. 1991. *Good Days, Bad Days: The Self in Chronic Illness and Time*. New Brunswick, NJ: Rutgers University Press.

Cicourel, Aaron V. 1964. *Method and Measurement in Sociology*. New York: The Free Press.

Cicourel, Aaron V. [1968] 1976. *The Social Organization of Juvenile Justice*. London: Heinemann Education.

Cicourel, Aaron V. 1973. *Cognitive Sociology*. Harmondsworth: Penguin.

Cleaver, Harry. 2000. *Reading* Capital *Politically*. 2nd edition. Leeds: Anti/ Thesis.

Cloward, Richard A. and Ohlin, Lloyd E. 1961. *Delinquency and Opportunity: A Theory of Delinquent Gangs*. London: Routledge and Kegan Paul.

Cohen, Albert. 1955. *Delinquent Boys: The Culture of the Gang*. Glenco, IL: The Free Press.

Cohen, Erik. 1979. A phenomenology of tourist experiences. *Sociology* 13(2): 179–201.

Cohen, Stanley. 1972. *Folk Devils and Moral Panics: The Creation of the Mods and Rockers*. London: MacGibbon and Kee.

Cohen, Stanley and Taylor, Laurie. 1992. *Escape Attempts*. London: Routledge.

Corbin, Juliet and Strauss, Anselm 1985. Managing chronic illness at home: three lines of work. *Qualitative Sociology* 8: 224–47.

Coulter, Jeff. 1975. Perceptual accounts and interpretive asymmetries. *Sociology* 9(3: September): 385–96.

Cressey, Paul G. 1932. *The Taxi-dance Hall: A Sociological Study in Commercialized Recreation and City Life*. Chicago: University of Chicago Press.

Cuff, E.C. 1993. *Problems of Versions in Everyday Situations*. Washington, DC: International Institute for Ethnomethodology and Conversation Analysis / University Press of America.

Curtin, Susanna. 2006. Swimming with dolphins: a phenomenological exploration of tourist recollections. *International Journal of Tourism Research* 8: 301–15.

Da Silva, Filipe Carreira. 2007. *G. H. Mead: A Critical Introduction*. Cambridge: Polity Press.

Davidson, Judy A. 1984. Subsequent versions of invitations, offers, requests and proposals dealing with potential or actual rejection. In J. Maxwell Atkinson and John Heritage (eds.) *Structures of Social Action: Studies in Conversation Analysis*, Cambridge: Cambridge University Press, 102–28.

Davis, Fred. 1961. Deviance disavowal: the management of strained interaction by the visibly handicapped. *Social Problems* 9(2): 120–32.

Davis, Fred. 1992. *Fashion, Culture, and Identity*. Chicago: University of Chicago Press.

Davis, Joanna R. 2006. Growing up punk: negotiating aging identity in a local music scene. *Symbolic Interaction* 29(1): 63–9.

Deleuze, Gilles and Guattari, Félix. 1994. *What is Philosophy?* London: Verso.

Dewey, John. [1896] 1981. The reflex arc concept in psychology. In John J. McDermott (ed.) *The Philosophy of John Dewey*, Chicago: University of Chicago Press, 136–48.

Doubt, Keith. 1989. Garfinkel before ethnomethodology. *The American Sociologist* 20(3): 252–62.

Drew, Paul. 1984. Speakers' reportings in invitation sequences. In

J. Maxwell Atkinson and John Heritage (eds.) *Structures of Social Action: Studies in Conversation Analysis*. Cambridge: Cambridge University Press, 129–51.

Drew, Paul. 1987. Po-faced receipts of teases. *Linguistics* 25(1): 219–53.

Drew, Paul and Heritage, John, eds. 1992. *Talk at work: interaction in institutional settings*. Cambridge: Cambridge University Press.

Duneier, Mitchell. 2000. *Sidewalk*. New York: Farrar, Strauss and Giroux.

Durkheim, Émile. [1897] 2006. *On Suicide*. Harmondsworth: Penguin.

Durkheim, Émile. 1915. *The Elementary Forms of the Religious Life: A Study in Religious Sociology* (translated from the French by Joseph Ward Swain). London: G. Allen & Unwin.

Eggins, Suzanne and Slade, Diana. 1997. *Analysing Casual Conversation*. London: Cassell.

Eglin, Trent. 1986. Introduction to a hermeneutics of the occult: alchemy. In Harold Garfinkel (ed.) *Ethnomethodological Studies of Work*, London: Routledge, 121–56.

Elster, Jon. 1982. Marxism, functionalism and game theory: the case for methodological individualism. *Theory and Society* 11(4: July): 453–82.

Emerson, Joan P. 1970. Behavior in private places: sustaining definitions of reality in the gynaecological examination. In Hans P. Dreitzel (ed.) *Recent Sociology No. 2: Patterns of Communicative Behavior*, New York: Macmillan, 74–96.

Filmer, Paul, Philipson, Michael, Silverman, David and Walsh, David. 1972. *New Directions in Sociological Theory*. London: Collier-Macmillan.

Fine, Gary Alan. 1993. The sad demise, mysterious disappearance, and glorious triumph of symbolic interactionism. *Annual Review of Sociology* 19: 61–87.

Fine, Gary Alan, ed. 1995. *A Second Chicago School? The Development of a Postwar American Sociology*. Chicago: University of Chicago Press.

Fish, Stanley. 1980. *Is There a Text in this Class? The Authority of Interpretive Communities*. Cambridge, MA: Harvard University Press.

Fishman, Pamela M. 1978. Interaction: the work women do. *Social Problems* 25(4: April): 397–406.

Frank, Arthur W. 1991. *At the Will of the Body*. Boston: Houghton Mifflin.

Freidson, Eliot. 1970. *Profession of Medicine*. New York: Dodd, Mead and Company.

Garfinkel, Harold. 1949. Research note on inter- and intra-racial homicides. *Social Forces* 27(4: May): 369–81.

Garfinkel, Harold 1952. The perception of the other: a study in social order. Unpublished Ph.D. dissertation, Department of Social Relations, Harvard University.

Garfinkel, Harold. 1956. Conditions of successful degradation ceremonies. *American Journal of Sociology* 61(5): 420–4.

Garfinkel, Harold. [1967] 1984. *Studies in Ethnomethodology*. Cambridge: Polity Press.

Garfinkel, Harold. 1974. The origins of the term 'ethnomethodology'. In Roy Turner (ed.) *Ethnomethodology: Selected Readings*, Harmondsworth: Penguin, 15–18.

Garfinkel, Harold, ed. 1986. *Ethnomethodological Studies of Work*. London: Routledge & Kegan Paul.

Garfinkel, Harold. 1988. Evidence for locally produced, naturally account-able phenomena of order*, logic, reason, meaning, method, etc. in and as of the essential quiddity of immortal ordinary society (I of IV): an announcement of studies. *Sociological Theory* 6(1): 103–9.

Garfinkel, Harold. 2002. *Ethnomethodology's Program: Working Out Durkheim's Aphorism*. Edited and introduced by A.W. Rawls. Lanham, MD: Rowman and Littlefield.

Garfinkel, Harold, Lynch, Michael and Livingston, Eric. 1981. The work of a discovering science construed with materials from the optically discov-ered pulsar. *Philosophy of the Social Sciences* 11: 131–58.

Garfinkel, Harold and Sacks, Harvey. 1970. On the formal structures of practical actions. In John C. McKinney and Edward A. Tiryakian (eds.) *Theoretical Sociology*, New York: Apple Century Crofts, 338–66.

Gellner, Ernest. 1975. Ethnomethodology: the re-enchantment industry or the Californian way of subjectivity. *Philosophy of the Social Sciences* 5(3): 431–50.

Giddens, Anthony. 1979. *Central Problems in Social Theory: Action, Structure and Contradiction in Social Analysis*. London: Macmillan.

Giddens, Anthony. 1997. *Sociology*. 3rd edition. Cambridge: Polity Press.

Gillespie, Dair L., Leffler, Ann and Lerner, Elinor 2010. If it weren't for my hobby, I'd have a life: dog sports, serious leisure, and boundary negotia-tions. *Leisure Studies* 21: 285–304.

Girton, George D. 1986. Kung Fu: toward a praxiological hermeneutic of the martial arts. In Harold Garfinkel (ed.) *Ethnomethodological Studies of Work*, London: Routledge, 59–88.

Glaser, Barney G. and Strauss, Anselm L. 1964. Awareness contexts and social interaction. *American Sociological Review* 29: 669–79.

Glaser, Barney G. and Strauss, Anselm L. 1965. *Awareness of Dying*. Chicago: Aldine.

Glaser, Barney G. and Strauss, Anselm L. 1967. *The Discovery of Grounded Theory: Strategies for Qualitative Research*. New York: Aldine de Gruyter.

Goffman, Erving. 1951. Symbols of class status. *British Journal of Sociology* 2(4): 294–304.

Goffman, Erving. 1952. On cooling the mark out: some aspects of adaption to failure. *Psychiatry: Journal of Interpersonal Relations* 15: 451–63.

Goffman, Erving. 1959. *The Presentation of Self in Everyday Life*. New York: Doubleday.

Goffman, Erving. 1961a. *Asylums: Essays on the Social Situation of Mental Patients and Other Inmates*. New York Doubleday.

Goffman, Erving. 1961b. *Encounters*. Indianapolis: Bobbs-Merill.

Goffman, Erving. 1963a. *Behavior in Public Places: Notes on the Social Organization of Gatherings*. New York: The Free Press.

Goffman, Erving. 1963b. *Stigma: Notes on the Management of Spoiled Identity*. Englewood Cliffs, NJ: Prentice-Hall.

Goffman, Erving. 1967. *Interaction Ritual: Essays on Face-to-Face Behavior*. Chicago: Aldine.

Goffman, Erving. 1969. *Strategic Interaction*. Philadelphia: University of Pennsylvania Press.

Goffman, Erving. 1972. *Relations in Public: Microstudies of the Public Order*. Harmondsworth: Penguin.

Goffman, Erving. 1974. *Frame Analysis: An Essay on the Organization of Experience*. New York: Harper and Row.

Goffman, Erving. 1979. *Gender Advertisements*. London: Macmillan.

Goffman, Erving. 1981. *Forms of Talk*. Oxford: Basil Blackwell.

Goffman, Erving. 1983a. Felicity's condition: *American Journal of Sociology* 89(1): 1–53.

Goffman, Erving. 1983b. The interaction order. *American Sociological Review* 48: 1–17.

Gold, Ray. 1952. Janitors versus tenants: a status–income dilemma. *American Journal of Sociology* 57(5: March): 486–93.

Goodwin, Charles. 1994. Professional vision. *American Anthropologist* 96(3): 606–33.

Gouldner, Alvin W. 1971. *The Coming Crisis of Western Sociology*. London: Heinemann.

Grice, H. Paul. 1975. Logic and conversation. In Peter Cole and Jerry L Morgan (eds.) *Syntax and Semantics 3: Speech Acts*, New York: Academic Press, 41–58.

Habenstein, Robert W. 1962. Sociology of occupations: the case of the American funeral director. In Arnold M. Rose (ed.) *Human Behavior and Social Processes: An Interactionist Approach*, New York: Houghton Mifflin, 225–46.

Hall, Stuart and Jefferson, Tony, eds. 1976. *Resistance through Rituals: Youth Subcultures in Post-war Britain*. London: Hutchinson in association with the Centre for Contemporary Cultural Studies, University of Birmingham.

Hammersley, Martin and Atkinson, Paul 2007. *Ethnography: Principles in Practice*. 3rd edition. London: Routledge.

Hardie-Bick, James. 2005. Dropping out and diving in: an ethnography of skydiving. Unpublished Ph.D. thesis. University of Durham.

Hebdige, Dick. 1979. *Subculture: The Meaning of Style*. London: Methuen.

Helm, David. 1982. Talk's form: comments on Goffman's *Forms of Talk*. *Human Studies* 5(1): 147–57.

Henslin, James M. and Biggs, Mae A. 1971. Dramaturgical desexualization: the sociology of the vaginal examination. In J. M. Henslin (ed.) *Studies in the Sociology of Sex*, New York: Appleton-Century-Crofts, 141–70.

Heritage, John. 1984. *Garfinkel and Ethnomethodology*. Cambridge: Polity Press.

Heritage, John and Clayman, Steven. 2010. *Talk in Action: Interactions, Identities, and Institutions*. Chichester: Wiley-Blackwell.

Heritage, John and Greatbatch, David. 1986. Generating applause: a study of rhetoric and response at party political conferences. *American Journal of Sociology* 92(1: July): 110–57.

Hester, Stephen. 1998. Describing 'deviance' in school: recognizably educational psychological problems. In Charles Antaki and Sue Widdicombe (eds.) *Identities in Talk*, London: Sage, 133–50.

Hester, Stephen and Eglin, Peter, eds. 1997. *Culture in Action: Studies in Membership Categorization Analysis*. Washington, DC: International Institute for Ethnomethodology and Conversation Analysis / University Press of America.

Hewitt, John P. and Stokes, Randall. 1975. Disclaimers. *American Sociological Review* 40: 1–11.

Hockey, John and Allen-Collinson, Jacquelyn. 2007. Grasping the phenomenology of sporting bodies. *International Review for the Sociology of Sport* 42(2): 115–31.

Hughes, David 1977. Everyday and medical knowledge in categorizing patients. In Robert Dingwall, Christian Heath, Margaret Reid and Margaret Stacey (eds.) *Health Care and Health Knowledge*, London: Croom Helm, 128–40.

Hughes, David 1982. Control in the medical consultation: organizing talk in a situation where co-participants have differential competence. *Sociology* 16: 359–76.

Hughes, Everett C. [1945] 1971. Dilemmas and contradictions of status. In *The Sociological Eye: Selected Papers*, Chicago: Aldine-Atherton, 141–50.

Hughes, Everett C. [1948] 1971. The study of ethnic relations. In *The Sociological Eye: Selected Papers*, Chicago: Aldine-Atherton, 153–8.

Hughes, Everett C. [1949] 1971. Queries concerning industry and society growing out of study of ethnic relations in industry. In *The Sociological Eye: Selected Papers*, Chicago: Aldine-Atherton, 73–86.

Hughes, Everett C. [1951] 1971. Mistakes at work. In *The Sociological Eye: Selected Papers*, Chicago: Aldine-Atherton, 316–25.

Hughes, Everett C. [1952] 1971. Cycles, turning points, and careers. In *The Sociological Eye: Selected Papers*, Chicago: Aldine-Atherton, 124–31.

Hughes, Everett C. [1957] 1971. Going concerns: the study of American institutions. In *The Sociological Eye: Selected Papers*, Chicago: Aldine-Atherton, 52–64.

Hughes, Everett C. [1962] 1971. Good people and dirty work. In *The Sociological Eye: Selected Papers*, Chicago: Aldine-Atherton, 87–97.

Hutchby, Ian. 1992. The pursuit of controversy: routine skepticism in talk on 'Talk radio'. *Sociology* 26(4): 673–94.

Hutchby, Ian and Wooffitt, Robin. 2008. *Conversation Analysis*. 2nd edition. Cambridge: Polity Press.

Hutson, David. J. 2010. Standing OUT / fitting IN: identity, appearance, and authenticity in gay and lesbian communities. *Symbolic Interaction* 33(2): 213–33.

James, William. 1890. *The Principles of Psychology*. New York: Henry Holt.

James, William. [1892] 1977. Habit. In John J. McDermott (ed.) *The Writings of William James: A Comprehensive Edition*, New York: Random House, 9–21.

James, William. [1907] 1977. What pragmatism means. In John J. McDermott (ed.) *The Writings of William James: A Comprehensive Edition*, New York: Random House, 376–90.

James, William. [1909] 1977. Radical empiricism. In John J. McDermott (ed.) *The Writings of William James: A Comprehensive Edition*, New York: Random House, 136.

Jefferson, Gail. 1978. Sequential aspects of storytelling in conversation. In J. Schenkein (ed.) *Studies in the Organization of Conversational Interaction*. New York: Academic Press, 219–48.

Jefferson, Gail. 1979. A technique for inviting laughter and its subsequent acceptance/declination. In George Psathas (ed.) *Everyday Language*, New York: Irvington Press, 79–96.

Jefferson, Gail. 1984a. Notes on the systematic deployment of the acknowledgement tokens 'yeah' and 'hm mm'. *Papers in Linguistics* 1(7): 197–206.

Jefferson, Gail. 1984b. On the organization of laughter in talk about troubles. In J. Maxwell Atkinson and John Heritage (eds.) *Structures of Social Action*, Cambridge: Cambridge University Press, 346–69.

Jefferson, Gail. 1986. Notes on latency in overlap onset. *Human Studies* 9: 153–83.

Katriel, Tamar. 1986. *Talking Straight: Dugri Speech in Israeli Sabra Culture*. Cambridge: Cambridge University Press.

Kelly, John R. 1983. *Leisure Identities and Interactions*. London: George Allen and Unwin.

Kitzinger, Celia. 2000. Doing feminist conversation analysis. *Feminism and Psychology* 10(2): 163–93.

Knopp, Timothy B. and Tyger, John D. 1973. A study of conflict in recreation land use: snowmobiling vs ski touring. *Journal of Leisure Research* 5(3): 6–17.

Knorr-Cetina, Karin and Cicourel, Aaron V., eds. 1981. *Advances in Social Theory and Methodology: Towards an Integration of Micro- and Macro-Sociologies*. London: Routledge & Kegan Paul.

Kraus, Rachel. 2010. "We are not strippers": how belly dancers manage a (soft) stigmatized serious leisure activity. *Symbolic Interaction* 33(3): 435–55.

Kurtz, Lester R. 1984. *Evaluating Chicago Sociology: A Guide to the Literature, with an Annotated Bibliography*. Chicago: University of Chicago Press.

Lee, John R. E. 1984. Innocent victims and evil-doers. *Women's Studies International Forum* 7(1: Jan–Feb): 69–73.

Lemert, Edwin M. 1958. The behavior of the systematic check forger. *Social Problems* 6: 141–9.

Lemert, Edwin M. 1967. *Human Deviance, Social Problems, and Social Control.* Englewood Cliffs, NJ: Prentice-Hall.

Livingston, Eric. 2008. Context and detail in studies of the witnessable social order: puzzles, maps, checkers, and geometry. *Journal of Pragmatics* 40(5: May): 840–62.

Lorber, Judith 1967. Deviance as performance: the case of illness. *Social Problems* 14(3): 302–10.

Lynch, Michael E. 1982. Technical work and critical inquiry: investigations in a scientific laboratory. *Social Studies of Science* 12(4: November): 499–533.

Lynch, Michael. 1991. Method: measurement – ordinary and scientific measurement as ethnomethodological phenomena. In Graham Button (ed.) *Ethnomethodology and the Human Sciences*, Cambridge: Cambridge University Press, 77–108.

Lynch, Michael. 1993. *Scientific Practice and Ordinary Action: Ethnomethodology and Social Studies of Science.* Cambridge: Cambridge University Press.

Lynch, Michael. 2011. Harold Garfinkel obituary: sociologist who delved into the minutiae of daily life. *The Guardian* 13 July. www.guardian.co.uk/education/2011/jul/13/harold-garfinkel-obituary. Last accessed 28 March 2013.

Lynch, Michael and Bogen, David. 1997. Lies, recollections and categorical judgements in testimony. In Stephen Hester and Peter Eglin (eds.) *Culture in Action: Studies in Membership Categorization Analysis*, Washington, DC: International Institute for Ethnomethodology and Conversation Analysis / University Press of America, 99–121.

Macbeth, Douglas H. 1990. Classroom order as practical action: the making and un-making of a quiet reproach. *British Journal of Sociology of Education* 11(2): 189–214.

MacCannell, Dean. 1999. The ethnomethodology of sightseers. In *The Tourist: A New Theory of the Leisure Class*, Berkeley and Los Angeles: University of California Press, 135–44.

Macionis, John J. and Plummer, Ken. 1997. *Sociology: A Global Introduction.* London: Prentice-Hall Europe.

Malone, Martin. 1997. *Worlds of Talk: The Presentation of Self in Everyday Conversation.* Cambridge: Polity Press.

Manning, Phil. 1989. Ritual talk. *Sociology* 23(3): 365–85.

Marx, Karl. [1845] 1975. Theses on Feuerbach. In Lucio Colletti (ed.) *Karl Marx: Early Writings*, Harmondsworth: Penguin, 421–3.

Maynard, Douglas W. 1989. Perspective-display sequences in conversation. *Western Journal of Speech Communication,* 53: 91–113.

Maynard, Douglas W. 1992. On clinicians co-implicating recipients' perspective in the delivery of diagnostic news. In Paul Drew and John Heritage (eds.) *Talk at Work: Interaction in Institutional Settings,* Cambridge: Cambridge University Press, 331–58.

Mead, George Herbert. 1934. *Mind, Self and Society: From the Standpoint of a Social Behaviorist.* Chicago: University of Chicago Press.

Menand, Louis. 2001. *The Metaphysical Club: A Story of Ideas in America.* New York: Farrar, Strauss and Giroux.

Miller, Walter D. 1958. Lower class culture as a generating milieu of gang delinquency. *Journal of Social Issues* 15: 5–19.

Newmahr, Staci. 2010. Power struggles: pain and authenticity in SM play. *Symbolic Interaction* 33(3): 389–411.

Park, Robert E. 1925. *The City.* Chicago: University of Chicago Press.

Parsons, Talcott. 1937. *The Structure of Social Action.* New York: Free Press.

Parsons, Talcott. [1951] 1991. *The Social System.* New edition. London: Routledge.

Parsons, Talcott. 1975. The sick role and the role of the physician reconsidered. *The Millbank Memorial Fund Quarterly. Health and Society* 53(3): 257–78.

Peirce, Charles S. [1878] 1992. How to make our ideas clear. In Nathan Houser and Christian Kloesel (eds.) *The Essential Peirce: Selected Philosophical Writings.* Vol. I, Bloomington: Indiana University Press, 124–41.

Peirce, Charles S. [1905] 1998. What pragmatism is. In The Peirce Edition Project (eds.) *The Essential Peirce: Selected Philosophical Writings.* Vol. II, Bloomington: Indiana University Press, 331–46.

Pollner, Melvin. 1975. The very coinage of your brain: the anatomy of reality disjunctures. *Philosophy of the Social Sciences* 5(3): 411–30.

Pollner, Melvin. 1991. Left of ethnomethodology: the rise and decline of radical reflexivity. *American Sociological Review* 56(3): 370–80.

Pomerantz, Anita. 1978. Compliment responses: notes on the cooperation of multiple constraints. In Jim Schenkein (ed.) *Studies in the Organization of Conversational Interaction,* New York: Academic Press, 79–112.

Pomerantz, Anita. 1984. Agreeing and disagreeing with assessments: some features of preferred/dispreferred turn shapes. In J. Maxwell Atkinson and John Heritage (eds.) *Structures of Social Action: Studies in Conversation Analysis,* Cambridge: Cambridge University Press, 57–101.

Pomerantz, Anita. 1986. Extreme case formulations: a way of legitimizing claims. *Human Studies* 9(2–3): 219–29.

Rawls, Anne. 1987. The interaction order sui generis: Goffman's contribution to social theory. *Sociological Theory* 5(2): 136–49.

Rawls, Anne. 1990. Emergent sociality: a dialectic of commitment and order. *Symbolic Interaction* 13(1): 63–82.

Riesman, David and Watson, Jeanne. 1964. The sociability project: a chronicle of frustration and achievement. In Phillip E. Hammond (ed.)

Sociologists at Work: Essays on the Craft of Social Research, New York: Basic Books, 235–321.

Robillard, Albert B. 1996. Anger in-the-social-order. *Body and Society* 2: 17–30.

Rokeach, Milton. 1964. *The Three Christs of Ypsilanti*. New York: Alfred A. Knopf.

Rorty, Richard. 1979. *Philosophy and the Mirror of Nature*. Princeton, NJ: Princeton University Press.

Rosenhan, David L. 1973. On being sane in insane places. *Science* 179: 250–8.

Rouncefield, Mark and Tolmie, Peter, eds. 2011. *Ethnomethodology at Work*. Aldershot: Ashgate.

Roy, Donald F. 1952. Quota restriction and goldbricking in a machine shop. *American Journal of Sociology* 57(5: March): 427–42.

Sacks, Harvey. 1972a. Notes on police assessment of moral character. In David Sudnow (ed.) *Studies in Social Interaction*, New York: Free Press, 280–93.

Sacks, Harvey. 1972b. On the analyzability of stories by children. In John J. Gumperz and Dell Hymes (eds.) *Directions in Sociolinguistics: The Ethnography of Communication*, New York: Rinehart & Winston, 325–45.

Sacks, Harvey. 1975. Everyone has to lie. In B. Blount and M. Sanchez (eds.) *Sociocultural Dimensions of Language Use*, New York: Academic Press, 57–80.

Sacks, Harvey. 1984a. Notes on methodology. In J. Maxwell Atkinson and John Heritage (eds.) *Structures of Social Action: Studies in Conversation Analysis*, Cambridge: Cambridge University Press, 21–7.

Sacks, Harvey. 1984b. On doing 'being ordinary'. In J. Maxwell Atkinson and John Heritage (eds.) *Structures of Social Action: Studies in Conversation Analysis*, Cambridge: Cambridge University Press, 413–29.

Sacks, Harvey. 1987. On the preferences for agreement and contiguity in sequences in conversation. In Graham Button and John R. E. Lee (eds.) *Talk and Social Organization*, Clevedon: Multilingual Matters, 54–69.

Sacks, Harvey. 1992a. *Lectures on Conversation*, Vol. 1, Oxford: Blackwell.

Sacks, Harvey. 1992b. *Lectures on Conversation*, Vol. 2, Oxford: Blackwell.

Sacks, Harvey, Schegloff, Emanuel and Jefferson, Gail. 1974. A simplest systematics for the organization of turn-taking in conversation. *Language* 50(4: Dec.): 696–735.

Scheff, Thomas J. 1966 *Being Mentally Ill: A Sociological Theory*. Chicago: Aldine.

Schegloff, Emanuel A. 1968. Sequencing in conversational openings. *American Anthropologist* 70: 1075–95.

Schegloff, Emanuel A. 1972. Notes on a conversational practice: formulating place. In David Sudnow (ed.) *Studies in Social Interaction*, New York: Free Press, 75–119.

Schegloff, Emanuel A. 1982. Discourse as an interactional achievement: some uses of 'uh huh' and other things that come between sentences. In Deborah Tannen (ed.) *Analysing Discourse: Text and Talk*, Washington DC: Georgetown University Press, 71–93.

Schegloff, Emanuel A. 1988. Goffman and the analysis of conversation. In Paul Drew and Anthony Wootton (eds.) *Erving Goffman: Exploring the Interaction Order*. Cambridge: Polity Press 89–135.

Schegloff, Emanuel A. 1992. Repair after next turn: the last structurally provided defense of intersubjectivity in conversation. *American Journal of Sociology* 97: 1295–345.

Schegloff, Emanuel A. 1992. On talk and its institutional occasions. In Paul Drew and John Heritage (eds.) *Talk at Work: Interaction in Institutional Settings*, Cambridge: Cambridge University Press, 101–34.

Schegloff, Emanuel A. 2000. Overlapping talk and the organization of turn-taking for conversation. *Language in Society* 29: 1–63.

Schegloff, Emanuel A. and Sacks, Harvey 1974. Opening up closings. In Roy Turner (ed.) *Ethnomethodology*, Harmondsworth: Penguin, 233–64.

Schegloff, Emanuel A, Jefferson, Gail and Sacks, Harvey. 1977. The preference for self-correction in the organization of repair in conversation. *Language* 53: 361–82.

Schiffrin, Deborah. 1984. Jewish argument as sociability. *Language in Society* 13: 311–35.

Schutz, Alfred. 1953. Common-sense and scientific interpretation of human action. *Philosophy and Phenomenological Research*. 14: 1–38.

Schutz, Alfred. 1962. *Collected Papers*, Vol. I. The Hague: Martinus Nijhoff.

Schutz, Alfred. 1964. *Collected* Papers, Vol. II. The Hague: Martinus Nijhoff.

Schutz, Alfred. 1972. *The Phenomenology of the Social World*. Evanston, IL: Northwestern University Press.

Schwartz, Howard. 1976. On recognizing mistakes: a case of practical reasoning in psychotherapy. *Philosophy of the Social Sciences* 6(1): 55–73.

Scott, Marvin B. and Lyman, Stanford M. 1968. Accounts. *American Sociological Review* 32: 46–62.

Searle, John. 1969. *Speech Acts*. Cambridge: Cambridge University Press.

Sharrock, W. W. 1979. Portraying the professional relationship. In Digby C. Anderson (ed.) *Health Education in Practice*. London: Croom Helm.

Shaw, Clifford R. and McKay, Henry D. 1942. *Juvenile Delinquency in Urban Areas*. Chicago: University of Chicago Press.

Silverman, David. 1998. *Harvey Sacks: Social Science and Conversation Analysis*. New York: Oxford University Press.

Silverman, David. 2009. *Doing Qualitative Research: A Practical Handbook*. London: Sage.

Silverman, David. 2011. *Interpreting Qualitative Data*. 4th edition. London: Sage.

Simmel, Georg. [1911] 1949. The sociology of sociability. *American Journal of Sociology* 55(3): 254–61.

Simmel, Georg. 1964. Sociability: an example of pure, or formal sociology. In Kurt H. Wolff (ed.) *The Sociology of Georg Simmel*, New York: The Free, 40–57..

Slater, Don. 2005. The sociology of consumption and lifestyle. In Craig Calhoun, Chris Rojek and Bryan S. Turner (eds.) *The SAGE Handbook of Sociology*. London: Sage, 174–187.

Smith, Dorothy. 1978. 'K is mentally ill': the anatomy of a factual account. *Sociology* 12(1): 23–53.

Smith, Greg. 1997. Incivil attention and everyday tolerance: vicissitudes of exercising in public places. *Perspectives on Social Problems* 9: 59–79.

Smith, Robin James. 2011. Goffman's interaction order at the margins: stigma, role, and normalization in the outreach encounter. *Symbolic Interaction*. 34(3): 357–76.

Stivers, Tanya. 2002. Participating in decisions about treatment: overt parent pressure for antibiotic treatment in pediatric encounters. *Social Science & Medicine* 54: 1111–30.

Stokes, Randall and Hewitt, John P. 1976. Aligning actions. *American Sociological Review* 41: 838–49.

Strauss, Anselm L., Fagerhaugh, Shizuko, Suczek, Barbara and Wiener, Carolyn. 1982. 'Sentimental work in the technologized hospital'. *Sociology of Health and Illness* 4: 254–78.

Strauss, Anselm L., Schatzman, Leonard, Bucher, Rue, Ehrlich, Danuta and Sabshin, Melvin. 1964. *Psychiatric Ideologies and Institutions*. New York: Free Press.

Strong, Philip M. 1979. *The Ceremonial Order of the Clinic*. London: Routledge and Kegan Paul.

Suchman, Lucy. 1987. *Plans and Situated Actions: The Problem of Human–Machine Communication*. Cambridge: Cambridge University Press.

Sudnow, David. 1967. *Passing On: The Social Organization of Dying*. Englewood Cliffs, NJ: Prentice-Hall.

Sudnow, David. [1978] 1993. *Ways of the Hand: The Organization of Improvised Conduct*. New edition. Cambridge, MA: MIT Press.

Sutherland, Edwin. 1947. *Principles of Criminology*. 4th edition. Philadelphia: J. B. Lippincott.

Sykes, Gresham M. and Matza, David. 1957. Techniques of neutralization: a theory of delinquency. *American Sociological Review* 22: 664–70.

Tannen, Deborah. 1984. *Conversational Style: Analyzing Talk Between Friends*. Oxford: Oxford University Press.

Tannen, Deborah. 1986. *That's Not What I Meant: How Conversational Style Makes or Breaks your Relations with Others*. New York: Ballantine Books.

Tannenbaum, Frank. 1938. *Crime and the Community*. New York: Columbia University Press.

ten Have, Paul. 2007. *Doing Conversation Analysis: A Practical Guide*. 2nd edition. London: Sage.

Terasaki, Alene K. 1976. *Pre-announcement Sequences in Conversation*. Social Science Working Paper 99. School of Social Sciences, University of California, Irvine.

Thomas, William I. and Thomas, Dorothy Swaine. 1928. *The Child in America: Behavior, Problems and Programs*. New York: Knopf.

Thornton, Sarah. 1995. *Club Cultures: Music, Media and Subcultural Capital*. Cambridge: Polity Press.

Travers, Max. 2001. *Qualitative Research through Case Studies*. London: Sage.

Veblen, Thorsten. 1925. *The Theory of the Leisure Class: An Economic Study of Institutions*. London: Allen and Unwin.

Wacquant, Loïc J. D. 2004. *Body and Soul: Ethnographic Notebooks of an Apprentice Boxer*. Oxford: Oxford University Press.

Wadsworth, Michael. 1976. The physician and the management of childhood epilepsy. In Michael Wadsworth and David Robinson (eds.) *Studies in Everyday Medical Life*, London: Martin Robertson, 13–31.

Watson, Jeanne. 1958. A formal analysis of sociable interaction. *Sociometry* 21: 269–80.

Watson, Jeanne and Potter, Robert. 1962. An analytic unit for the study of interaction. *Human Relations* 15: 245–63.

Watson, Rod. 1997. The presentation of motive and victim in discourse: the case of murder interrogations. In Max Travers and John F. Manzo (eds.) *Law in Action: Ethnomethodological and Conversation Analytic Approaches to Law*, Aldershot: Ashgate, 77–98.

Watts, Richard. 1989. Relevance and relational work: linguistic politeness as politic behaviour. *Multilingua* 8(2/3): 131–66.

Weber, Max. 1968. *Economy and Society*. Berkeley, CA: University of California Press.

West, Candace. 1984. *Routine Complications: Troubles with Talk between Doctors and Patients*. Bloomington, IN: Indiana University Press.

West, Candace. 1990. Not just 'doctors' orders': directive–response sequences in patients' visits to women and men physicians. *Discourse and Society* 1: 85–113.

West, Candace and Zimmerman, Don H. 1983. Small insults: a study of interruptions in conversations between unacquainted persons. In Barrie Thorne, Cheris Kramarae and Nancy Henley (eds.) *Language, Gender and Society*, Rowley, MA: Newbury House, 102–17.

Widdicombe, Sue and Wooffitt, Robin. 1995. *The Language of Youth Subcultures*. New York: Harvester Wheatsheaf.

Wieder, D. Lawrence. 1974. *Language and Social Reality: The Case of Telling the Convict Code*. The Hague: Mouton.

Wilson, Thomas P. 1991. Social structure and the sequential organization. In Deirdre Boden and Don H. Zimmerman (eds.) *Talk and Social Structure: Studies in Ethnomethodology and Conversation Analysis*, Cambridge: Polity Press, 22–43.

Wittgenstein, Ludwig. [1958] 1968. *Philosophical Investigations*. Oxford: Blackwell.

Witzel, Andreas and Mey, Gunter 2004. Aaron V. Cicourel: I am not opposed to quantification or formalization or modeling, but I do not want to pursue quantitative methods that are not commensurate with the research phenomena addressed. *Forum: Qualitative Sozialforschung / Forum: Qualitative Social Research* (North America) 5(Sept). www.qualitative-research.net/index.php/fqs/article/view/549>. Date last accessed 16 April 2012.

Wowk, Maria T. 2007. Kitzinger's feminist conversation analysis: critical observations. *Human Studies* 30 2: June): 131–55.

Young, Jock. 1971. *The Drugtakers: The Social Meaning of Drug Use*. London: MacGibbon and Kee.

Zimmerman, Don H. and Pollner, Melvin. 1970. The everyday world as a phenomenon. In Jack D. Douglas, *Understanding Everyday Life: Toward the Reconstruction of Sociological Knowledge*, London: Routledge and Kegan Paul, 80–103.

Zimmerman, Don H. and West, Candace. 1975. Sex roles, interruptions and silences in conversation. In Barrie Thorne and Nancy Henley (eds.) *Language and Sex: Difference and Dominance*, Rowley, MA: Newbury House, 105–29.

Zola, Irving K. 1973. Pathways to the doctor: from person to patient. *Social Science and Medicine* 7: 677–89.

Index

access rituals 73, 92–3
accounts, accountability 52, 64, 65,
    80, 81, 92, 170, 181, 185, 203
action 12, 37, 39, 41
    completed act 41
    consequentiality 193
    'glossed' 60, 65
    in progress 41
    indexicality 51–2, 65, 87, 179, 215
    leisure as 192–4
    members' methods 51, 55
    moral character of 57
    motives 41
    preferred and dispreferred actions
        76, 182
    reflexivity 65
    see also accounts, accountability
activities
    category-bound activities 5, 82,
        84
    corporeal consciousness 201
    ethnomethodological description of
        153–4
    meaningful 14
    rational 149
    retrospective–prospective sense of
        150–1
    spatial distribution 144–5
    temporal distribution 145
actor's point of view 36, 38, 39, 40, 41
ad hoc considerations 47, 48
adjacency pairs 73–4, 78, 80, 84
    doctor–patient transcripts 131

first-pair parts 74
    second-pair parts 74, 76, 182
affiliation 100, 102, 173–4, 191,
    195–7, 206, 207
agency–structure debate 61, 211
agreement and contiguity, preference
    for 76, 117–18
Allen-Collinson, Jacquelyn 195
alternate sociologies 2
Althusser, Louis 211
Anderson, Leon 198–9
Anderson, Nels 23
Anderson, R. J. 215, 217
anger 138–9
animal gestural action 15
animal–human distinction 15, 23,
    121–2
anomie 20, 31, 163
apartment block janitors 105
applause 157, 216
archaeological fieldwork 59
archaeologists 58, 59
assessments 76, 77, 118
association
    deviance and 163, 165
    see also affiliation; group
        membership
associative identifications 196
athletic identity 195–6
Atkinson, J. Maxwell 156, 175–6, 177,
    209
audio-vocalic system 122
authenticity 7, 196–7

authority
  bureaucratic 101
  charismatic 101
  doctor–patient interactions 5,
    129–35
  traditional 101
  see also power
'automatic pilot' 26
awareness context 139–40

back-channelling 91
bad news, delivering 17–18
Baker, Carolyn D. 158, 184
Bauman, Zygmunt 189
Beck, Ulrich 211
Becker, Howard S. 8, 9, 21, 32–3, 33,
    107, 120, 146, 147, 148, 153,
    164, 172, 174, 218
belly-dancing 199
Berger, Peter 44
binocular vision 121–2
bipedalism 122
Bittner, Egon 33, 152, 212, 213
Blumer, Herbert 1, 8, 11–12, 18, 21,
    22, 31, 33, 166, 211–12, 213
  see also symbolic interactionism
body
  naturalness of 121
  social significance of 121, 124
  see also death and dying; doctor–
    patient encounters; illness
Bourdieu, Pierre 190, 196, 211
brain function
  central activities 13, 14
  peripheral activities 13, 14
breaching 49–50, 65, 69, 152, 167,
    202
Brown, Barry 203
Brown, Penelope 93
bureaucratic authority 101
bureaucratic rationality 102
Bury, Mike 136–7

Campaign for Nuclear Disarmament
    100
capitalism 99–100, 143
careers 30, 145–6, 151
  deviant careers 172–3
  moral careers 173, 197
  progression 47, 173

turning points 30, 145, 146, 151,
    173
Carper, James W. 147
caste system 109
category-bound activities 5, 82, 84
causal models 18–19, 214
character contests 204
charismatic authority 101
Charmaz, Kathy 137–8
Chicago School
  centrality of meaning 11–12
  deviance studies 163
  fieldwork 9–10, 32–3, 213
  first 9–10, 32
  Second Chicago School 8–9, 33
children
  classroom interactions 84, 107,
    158, 161, 184
  conversational competences 80
  delinquency 175, 184
  play 23–4
  school careers 145–6
  socialization 39, 146
chronic illness and disability 135–9
  anger 138–9
  biographical work 136–7
  ethnomethodological approach
    138–9
  everyday work 136
  illness work 136
  loss of self 137–8
Church of Scientology 101–2
Cicourel, Aaron V. 44, 45–6, 48
civil inattention 164, 170, 199
class affiliations 100, 102
classroom interactions 84, 107, 161
classroom punishments and reward
    systems 158, 184
Clayman, Steven E. 85
clothing as metaphor for identity 195,
    196
co-operation 24, 38, 164
coding practices 47–8, 214–15
cognitive sociology 46
Cohen, Stanley 191, 200
commitment, culture of 197, 198
commodity fetishization 102
common-sense knowledge 42, 43, 44,
    46, 48
  moral character of 50

common-sense reasoning 44, 61, 129,
    175, 176–7, 178, 179
communication 63–4
    animal 15
    see also conversation; language; talk
comparative analysis 31–2
competence 64, 69, 80, 81, 94,
    111–12, 149, 180–1, 190, 197,
    202
    cultural 178
    differential 130
compliments 77–8
con artists 17
conflict theory 102
consciousness 40
Conservative Party (UK) 100
conspicuous consumption 191
consumption practices 7, 188–9, 191,
    192, 193
    see also leisure
continuers 70, 71, 79
contrast structures 54–5
conversation
    accountability and 80, 81, 181
    agreement and contiguity,
        preference for 76, 117–18
    collaborative doing 64, 78, 80, 87,
        88, 91, 94
    competences 64, 69, 80, 81, 94
    context-dependent nature of 154–5
    context-free 155, 157
    continuers 70, 71, 79
    conversational line 93
    disorderliness 64, 67, 70
    dramaturgical metaphor 89–91,
        96, 97
    embedding 90
    expectations from co-
        conversationalists 64, 181, 186
    footings 87–8
    and identity 64, 80–5, 90, 186
    intersubjectivity and 66–7
    laughter 79, 81, 181, 183, 205
    machinery of 68–85, 154, 155
    non-lexical utterances 70, 71, 181,
        203–4
    openings and terminal exchanges
        78, 80–1, 92–3
    orderliness 64, 65–6, 68–9, 70, 71,
        73, 75, 80

orientation to common topics 78
overlap 70, 89
participation frameworks 87–91,
    179–80, 190, 193–4, 206–7
participation status 87, 88
perturbations 64, 74, 75–6, 80–1,
    158, 181, 183, 186, 187
power of talk to dominate 118–19
preferred and dispreferred actions
    76, 182
remedial interchanges 91–2, 187
repair 64, 74, 75–6, 80, 183, 186,
    187
replaying of experience 89, 90, 91,
    204
as ritual interaction 91-5, 183, 185
self-correction, preference for 76
sequential organization 73–9, 80,
    86, 91, 181, 182, 183
serial interrupters 69
sociability 204
storytelling 78–9
supportive interchanges 92–3,
    204
topic talk 78
'tries for the floor' 70, 119–20
    see also face and facework; turns
        and turn-taking
conversation analysis (CA) 1–2, 4, 61,
    63–97, 210
    criticisms of 212, 216–18
    gendered analysis 119–20, 130–1,
        216–17
    methodology 95–6
    notation systems 59
    origins 63–5
    post-Sacksian 114, 119–20
    temporal awareness 210
convict code 56–8, 110–11
cooling the mark out 17–18, 171
Copernican revolution 10–11
coroners 112, 150, 176–7, 209–10
corporeal consciousness 201
Coulter, Jeff 113
courtroom interactions 36, 48, 155–6,
    159, 176, 177–9, 181
Cressey, Paul 9–10
criminality 106, 107, 109–10, 152,
    167, 172, 174
    see also halfway house programmes

criticisms of interactionism 210–18
Cuff, E. C. 113, 180
cultural capital 196
cultural dopes 39, 58, 219
culture, sociology of 153
Curtin, Susanna 201

Da Silva, Filipe Carreira 211–12
Davis, Fred 8, 169, 188, 197
death and dying as social process 5,
    139–41
degradation ceremonies 173
Deleuze, Gilles 10
delinquency 175, 184
deviance 6, 162–87
    affiliation–disaffiliation 173–4
    association and 164
    behaviours 167–8
    biographical aspects 167–8
    breach of social contract 162
    civil inattention 164, 170, 199
    classical perspective 162–3
    conversation analysis' approach
        180–7
    deviant careers 172–3
    deviant groups 173–4
    deviant identity 164–5
    embodied indicators 166–7
    ethnomethodological approach
        175–80
    institutional intervention 171–3
    leisure and 198–200
    mental illness as 53–5
    moral dimension 164, 167, 173,
        177–8
    neutralization 170–1, 199
    non-ordinary-ness 164, 166
    normalization 171, 185
    primary 172
    recognizing, defining and theorizing
        175–7
    secondary 163–4, 172
    sick role as 125–6
    societal responses to 163, 164, 165,
        172, 199–200
    subcultures 163, 182–3, 184–5,
        191, 196–7, 198
    symbolic interactionist approach
        166–74
    versions 175, 179–80

deviant identities
    attribution 170, 173, 174, 176, 181,
        182, 183, 184, 185, 186–7, 191
    contestation of 116, 165, 173,
        181–2, 184
    management and negotiation of 6,
        165, 168–71, 182–3, 184, 199
    self-ascription 184
    sources of 164–5, 166, 191
Dewey, John 10, 12, 13, 14, 31, 34
differential association 163, 173–4
disclaimers 170, 199
discretion 152
disruption experiments 50–1
division of labour 143
doctor–patient encounters 5, 103–4,
    125, 127–9, 157
    bureaucratic format 128
    control 129–35
    conversation analysis perspective
        130–5
    directives 132
    ethnomethodological perspective
        128–9
    gender and 127–8, 131–2
    going to see the doctor 126–7
    gynaecological examinations 127–8
    interruptions 131–2
    paediatric consultations 128
    patient categorization 128–9
    patient pressure 133–5
    power imbalance 129
    race-based status dilemmas 103–4
    see also psychiatric patients
doctors 5
    gatekeepers 144
    membership status 98, 112
    student doctors 147
documentary methods of
    interpretation 65–6, 87
dog sports 198
'doing being ordinary' 154, 155, 159,
    164, 181, 185
Drew, Paul 155, 177, 216
Durkheim, Émile 19–20, 31, 62, 65,
    91, 142, 143, 144, 163, 212

Elster, Jon 211
embedding 90
embodied leisure 201–2

embodiment, sociology of *see* death
and dying; doctor–patient
encounters; illness
emergency service calls 85
Emerson, Joan P. 127
empirical sciences 19
engineers 147
ethnomethodology (EM) 1, 2, 35–62
anthropological analogue 36
characteristic features 37
criticisms of 61, 212, 214–16
critique of standard research
methods 45–9
ethnomethodological indifference
61–2
impact on conversation analysis
65–6
origins 35–7
phenomenology as a resource for
35, 37, 40–4, 61
'proto-ethnomethodology' 46
as reflexive ethnography 55–8
as sociological approach 35
speech ethnomethodology *see*
conversation analysis (CA)
experience
centrality of 41–2, 190
'just this-ness' 154, 200
particularity of 40–1
politics of experience 113
shared experience *see*
intersubjectivity
expressive capacities 122, 205
expressive control and violation
205

fabrications 90, 180
face and facework 17, 68, 72, 78,
93–5, 170, 182, 204
aggressive facework 94
corrective facework 94
leisure action and 193–4
preventative facework 94
face-to-face interactions 1, 43, 63, 83,
94, 163, 187
factory workforce interactions 108,
148
faux pas 167, 170, 185
feudal society 142–3
fieldwork 9–10, 32–4, 213

Fine, Gary Alan 213
Fish, Stanley 10
Fishman, Pamela M. 216
footings 87–8, 89, 187
forgery 174
frameworks *see* participation
frameworks
free will 162
Freidson, Eliot 126–7
fresh talk 7, 87
funeral directors 144–5

gaffes 167, 170, 185
Galileo Galilei 11
games 24, 193, 202
language games 67–8
games theory 51
Garfinkel, Harold 1, 4, 36, 38, 39–40,
44, 46, 47–8, 49–52, 52, 55, 58,
62, 65, 80, 111, 150, 151, 153,
178, 181, 202, 209, 212, 213,
214–15, 219
see also ethnomethodology
gatekeepers 144
Geer, Blanche 32–3, 147
gender identity, performing 50–1
gendered talk 120, 130–1, 132,
216–17
generalized other, orienting to 24–5,
27
gestures 15
Giddens, Anthony 188, 210–11
Gillespie, D. L. 198
Glaser, Barney 139
glossing practices 60, 65, 111,
112
go-betweens 108
Goffman, Erving 2, 4, 8, 9, 17, 32,
52, 63, 64–5, 86, 87, 88, 89, 90,
91, 92, 93, 94, 95, 96–7, 104,
122–3, 124, 145, 164, 166, 167,
168, 169, 170, 171, 172, 185–7,
192, 193, 194, 197, 204, 205,
206, 212
Gold, Ray 8, 105
Goodwin, Charles 58–9, 60
Gouldner, Alvin W. 212
Greatbatch, David 157, 216
greetings 73, 92–3
grooming talk 93

group membership 98, 111–12
  competence and 111–12, 181
  group identification 148
  group loyalty 147, 148
  mastery of natural language 111,
    112, 149, 180, 181, 202
  professionals 112
  see also membership categorization
gun collecting 199
Gurwitsch, Aron 40
gynaecological examinations 127–8

Habermas, Jürgen 211
habit 28
haecceity 154
halfway house programmes 55–8,
    109–11, 152
Hardie-Bick, James 197
Hebdige, Dick 191
Heritage, John 66, 78, 85, 155, 157,
    216
Hester, Stephen 184
Hewitt, John 171, 199
Hobbes, Thomas 38
Hockey, John 195
holidays 200–1
Homo sapiens 121–2
Hughes, Everett C. 1, 8, 9, 27, 30, 32,
    33, 103, 104, 105–6, 107, 108,
    128, 130–1, 145, 147–8, 213
  see also symbolic interactionism
human–computer interaction 160
Husserl, Edmund 3, 40, 41
  see also phenomenology
Hutchby, Ian 70, 182

identity
  actual and virtual 168
  affiliative identities 195–6
  authenticity 7, 196–7
  consumption practices and 188,
    189
  conversation and 64, 80–5, 90, 186
  deviant *see* deviant identities
  'doing being ordinary' 154, 155,
    159, 164, 181, 185
  fluidity and instability of 189
  institutional identities 85
  labelling 164, 172, 175, 198
  leisure-based 189, 191–200

management 148
  performance 64
  stigmatic 104
  subcultural 191, 196–7
  typification and categorization 64
  work-based 189
  youth 196
  see also membership categorization
illness
  chronic illness and disability 135–9
  'crocks' 148
  death and dying as social process 5,
    139–41
  deviant aspects of 125–6
  illness trajectories 5, 135–6
  lay referral structures 126–7, 129
  sick role 5, 124–6
  social construction of 124, 125,
    126–7
  temporal dimension 5, 135–6
  see also doctor–patient encounters
impression management 51
in- and out-groups 106–7, 108, 109,
    110, 111
indexicality 51–2, 65, 71, 87, 179,
    215
individual sociological understanding
    211
inequality *see* social inequality
inference, inferentiality 36, 49, 64, 66,
    74, 81, 82, 83, 84, 85, 129, 176,
    177, 178, 181, 191, 212
insertion sequences 73–4, 183
institutional identities 85
institutionalized interactions 5, 85
  see also specific types, e.g. courtroom
    interactions
intentionality 40
inter-group communication 108
Interaction Order 4, 63, 86, 96–7,
    180, 185, 186, 187, 194
interactional achievement 105
interpretation
  asymmetries 138
  documentary methods of 65–6, 87
  of meaning 16, 17, 18–21
interpretive sociology 4, 41, 42, 44
interruption 69, 81, 131–2, 136, 186,
    216
  illness as 136

intersubjectivity 42, 44, 64, 65, 66–7, 180, 201
in and through conversation 66–7, 69, 73, 74
interviews 25–6, 33, 45
invitations 74, 76, 77, 182
perspective-display invitations 133
Iowa School of symbolic interactionism 32
Islam 22

James, William 10, 12, 28, 34
Jefferson, Gail 63
jogging and running 199–200
joking 90, 117, 183
judgemental dopes 39, 219
jury deliberations 36, 178–9

'K is mentally ill' 52–5, 116
Kelly, John R. 195
keying 89, 180
King, Rodney 59–60
Kitzinger, Celia 120, 217
knowledge
asymmetry 129, 131
common-sense knowledge 42, 43, 44, 46, 48, 50
social distribution of 42–3
specialist knowledge 42, 58
working knowledge 58–60
Krauss, Rachel 199

labelling 164, 172, 175, 198
Labour Party (UK) 100
labour-power 99
laminations 89, 180
language 23, 63–4
always social 23
indeterminacy 68
linguistic turn 68
mastery of natural language 111, 112, 149, 180, 181, 202
see also conversation; talk
language games 67–8
laughter 79, 81, 181, 183, 205
Laurier, Eric 203
lawyers 58, 59–60
learner drivers 111–12
Lebenswelt (life-world) pairs 150, 153–4

Lee, John R. E. 115
leisure 7, 188–207
as action 192–4
affiliation 195–6, 206, 207
antithetical relationship to work 189–90, 191, 200
character traits and 193–4, 204
collective activities 195, 196, 197, 203
competence requirement 190, 197, 202
conversation analysis' approach 203–7
and deviance 198–200
emancipatory quality 189–90, 200–2
embodied leisure 201–2
expressive dimension 205–6
focused/unfocused interaction with others 190
game frames 206–7
identity concerns 189, 191–200
meaningful choices 192
normative dimension 191, 202, 205
performative dimension 191, 204–5
phenomenological and ethnomethodological approach 200–3
as practical accomplishments 202–3
rules and roles 194–5, 202, 205
serious leisure 197–8, 199, 205
sociable interaction 204, 206
subcultural practices 191
symbolic interactionist approach 192–200
synonymous with experience 190, 200
Lemert, Edwin M. 172, 174
Levinson, Stephen 93
linguistic turn 68
Livingston, Eric 150, 215
Lloyd Warner, William 8, 9
Lorber, Judith 125–6
Luckmann, Thomas 44
Lyman, Stanford 170
Lynch, Michael 46, 150, 158, 215, 218

Macbeth, Douglas H. 159, 160, 181
MacCannell, Dean 203

map reading 203
marijuana users 21, 174
Marx, Karl 35, 98–9, 102, 143, 144
materialistic identification 196
Maynard, Douglas 132–3
Mead, George Herbert 10, 15, 23–4,
    25, 26, 34, 121, 212
meaning
    causal explanations 19–29
    centrality of 11–12
    as consequence 137
    finite provinces of 43
    interpretation 16, 17, 18–21
    of objects 12
    shared understandings 15
    as significance 137
    social interaction and 15–17
    structural explanations 19–21, 22
    symbolic 15–16, 18
measurement, problems of 44, 45–6,
    114–15
mechanical solidarity 142–3
medical students 147
members' methods 51, 55
membership categorization 5, 6, 81–5,
    90, 95–6, 123, 183–4
    category-bound activities 5, 82, 84
    contextualized use of categories
        84–5
    inferential 84
    'natural' categories 84
    patients 128–9
    standard relational pairs (SRP) 82
    work and 157–60
mental illness 52–5, 112–14, 179,
    181
    see also psychiatric patients
merry-go-round 194–5
Merton, Robert 163
methodological individualism 21–3,
    27
microsociology 27, 37
modifiers, status 116
moral careers 173, 197
moral categorizing 158, 184
    see also deviance
moral inference 177–8
moral status 115–16
Mugabe, Robert 101
multiple realities 43

Munsell colour charts 59
murder interrogations 184

negotiation 6, 15–16, 29–30, 129–30,
    149, 165, 170–1
nervous system 13–14
neutralization 170–1, 199
Newmahr, Staci 201–2
news delivery 17–18
non-normality 164
    see also deviance
normalization 171, 185

objectivity 213
objects, meaning of 12
openings 73, 78, 80, 92–3, 182
orderliness 1, 37, 39, 151, 180, 212
    conversational 64, 65–6, 68–9, 70,
        71, 73, 75, 80
    negotiated order 29–30
    production of 37, 64, 154
    in work 154
organic solidarity 142
orienting to generalized others 24–5,
    27
overlapping talk 70, 89
    see also interruption; turn-taking

paramount reality 1, 43
Park, Robert 9, 32
Parks, Rosa 38
Parsons, Talcott 4, 38, 39, 124–6,
    144
participant observation see fieldwork
participation frameworks 87–91,
    179–80, 190, 193–4, 206–7
    definitional power of 207
    frame disruptions 207
    frame transformations 89–90,
        179–80, 207
    framing strategies 89–90
    participation status 87, 88
particularity of experiences 40–1
party affiliations 100
passing 50–1, 123, 169
Peirce, Charles Sanders 10, 11, 34
perspective-display series 133
phenomenology 3–4, 35
    as resource for ethnomethodology
        35, 37, 40–4, 61

social phenomenology 37
study of consciousness 40
physiologists 147
play 23–4
  see also games
poker-players 204, 205, 206, 207
police 59–60, 98, 152, 172, 175, 184
politeness theory 68
politics of experience 113
Pollner, Melvin 113, 120, 156, 180
Pomerantz, Anita 118, 185
postulate of adequacy 44, 45
power 4, 5, 61
  contrastive category 115, 116
  conversation analysis' approach
      114–20, 130, 131–4
  directional term 115
  ethnomethodological approach
      109–14, 130
  imbalanced relationships 102, 111,
      129
  and inequality 98–9, 100
  institutionalized 60, 130
  interactional achievement 111
  invocation of rules 109–11
  labour-power 99
  professional dominance 60, 129–35
  symbolic interactionist approach
      129–30
  use of talk to dominate 118–19
  see also authority; status
practical reasoning 36, 52
  moral character of 50
practicality 10–11, 51
pragmatism 3, 10–11, 30, 34
production line workers 148
productivity 149
professional power 60, 129–35
professional vision 58, 59–60
psychiatric patients 29–30, 47–8,
      112–14, 145, 149, 173, 180
  see also mental illness
psychodynamic counselling 217
psychological dopes 219
pulsars 150–1
punk identity 182–3, 184–5, 197

qualitative methodology 32–3
quantitative methodology 32, 45
question–answer exchanges 117, 217

questionnaires 45, 46
Quixote, Don 180

race-based status dilemmas 103–4
radical empiricism 30
radio phone-in shows 113, 182
rationality
  bureaucratic 102
  professional/lay 46
  scientific 43
  see also common-sense reasoning
reality
  disjunctures 113, 180
  multiple realities 43
  paramount reality 1, 43
  social construction of 44
reassurance displays 93
recipient design 71, 74, 86–7
reflex arc concept in psychology 12,
      13, 31, 34
reflexivity 52, 58, 65, 109, 110, 156,
      203, 215
religious groups 106–7
remedial interchanges 91–2, 187
Republican Party (US) 100
rhetorical devices 157
ritual accountability 92
ritual aliveness 186, 187, 206
ritual equilibrium 94
ritual interaction 91–5
  remedial interchanges 91–2
  ritual trouble 92, 94, 183, 185
  supportive interchanges 92–3
  see also face and facework
Robillard, Albert 138–9
roles
  alignment 25
  playful relationship to 194–5
  role-distance 194, 195
  role-taking 25–6, 29, 103
Rorty, Richard 10
Rosenhan, David 179
Roth, Julius 8
Roy, Donald F. 148
rules
  breaching 49–50, 65, 69, 152, 167,
      202
  corroborative reference 152
  ethnomethodological notions about
      56, 58

rules (*cont.*)
   gambit of compliance 152
   orienting to 69, 151–2, 180, 202,
      205, 208–9
   stylistic unity 152

Sacks, Harvey 2, 62, 63, 64–5, 68–9,
      80, 81, 95, 114, 115, 116, 117,
      118, 154, 155, 164, 181, 182,
      183, 218
   see also conversation analysis (CA)
sado-masochism (SM) 201–2
sarcasm 52, 90
Schegloff, Emanuel A. 63, 74, 75, 96,
      156, 217
schizophrenia 113
school careers 145–6
Schutz, Alfred 1, 3, 4, 37, 40, 41, 42,
      43–4, 45, 65, 66
Schwartz, Howard 118, 119, 217
Scott, Marvin 170
self
   'I' and 'me' 26
   loss of self 137–8
   and other 24–5
   and society 27
self-correction 26, 76
self-criticism 26
self-deprecations 76, 77, 118
self-identification 147
self-labelling 125, 126
self-monitoring 26
self-perceptions 147
semantic manipulation 199
sense-making practices 51, 176
   see also common-sense reasoning;
      rationality
sensory-motor coordination 14
sequential organization of
      conversation 73–9, 80, 86, 91,
      181, 182, 183
   adjacency pairs 73–4, 78, 80, 84
   insertion sequence 73–4, 183
   move formulation 86–7
   see also turns and turn-taking
Sharrock, W. W. 130, 217
Shibutani, Tamotsu 8
shopping 28, 189, 193
sick role 5, 124–6
sightseeing 203

Simmel, Georg 37, 204
situated conduct 51, 52, 60, 61
situation-defining 25–6
skydiving 197, 199
Slater, Don 188
Smith, Dorothy 52–5, 179
Smith, Greg 199
sociability 204, 206
social action *see* action
social contract 162
social death 140, 141
social facts 209–10
social identity *see* identity
social inequality
   and conflict theory 102
   in health care 140–1
   Marxist analysis 98–9, 102
   Weberian analysis 4, 99–102
social order
   Interaction Order 4, 63, 86, 96–7,
      180, 185, 186, 187, 194
   problem of 38–40, 98
   see also orderliness
social phenomenology 37
social stability 26, 27, 28–9, 30
   under threat 30
social stratification 43, 98, 100
   see also social inequality
social structures 22–3, 27, 61, 211
social world 208–10, 211
socialization 39, 146
Speech Act theory 68
speech ethnomethodology *see*
      conversation analysis (CA)
speech exchange systems 155
   see also conversation
sporting activities 24–5, 195–6, 201,
      202
stage confidence 193
standard relational pairs (SRP) 82
startle reflex 15
status 4, 5, 100–1, 102
   categorical status attributions
      114–16
   contrastive category 115, 116
   conversation analysis' approach
      114–20
   degradation 106
   differentials 6, 107, 108
   dilemmas 103–5, 108, 131–2, 172

ethnomethodological approach
109–14
group membership and 100–1,
106–7, 108
handling status though talk 117–18
in- and out-groups 106–7, 108,
109, 110, 111
inequality and separation,
legitimation of 104, 107
institutionalized 105–8, 220
interactional achievement 105,
107–8, 111
invocation of rules 109–11
low-status classifications 116
master statuses 104, 132, 191
modifiers 116
moral status 115–16
multiple statuses 105
occupational 105, 106, 108, 146,
147
positive/negative/neutral statuses
104–5
symbolic interactionist approach
103–9
symbols 206
see also power
stigma 104, 109, 122–3, 191
biographical 122–3
the discreditable 123, 169
the discredited 123, 137, 169
illness and 137
leisure and 199
management 6, 123
observability 123
physical 122, 123, 166
tribal 123
stimulus–response 12–13, 14
Stivers, Tanya 133–4
Stokes, Randall 171, 199
Stone, Gregory 8
Stonewall 100
storytelling 78–9
Strauss, Anselm L. 8, 135–6, 139,
148
straw-bosses 108
Strong, Philip M. 128
structural determinism 19–21, 22
structural-functionalism 144, 149
structural sociological understanding
211

subcultures 163, 182–3, 184–5, 191,
196–7, 198
Suchman, Lucy 160
Sudnow, David 139, 140–1, 153
suicide 19–20, 31–2, 150, 175–7,
209–10
suicide prevention centres 182, 183
supermarkets 28, 29
supportive interchanges 92–3, 204
Sutherland, Edwin 163, 173
swim-with-the-dolphins experience
201
symbolic communication 15–16
symbolic interactionism (SI) 1, 2
centrality of meaning 11–12
criticisms of 27, 33–4, 212–14
definitions 11
methodology 30–3
origins 8–9, 60–1
pragmatist remit 9, 10–11, 30, 31
premises 11–12
theoretical position 11–30
symbols 15, 23, 205–6

T-shirts 195
taken-for-granted assumptions 49
talk
competitive and conflictual system
114
indexicality 51–2, 65, 179
talk at work 155–7
see also conversation
Tannenbaum, Frank 172
taste, notion of 190, 196
tax system 21
Taylor, Jimmy 198–9
Taylor, Laurie 200
teasing 185, 204
temporal nature of the social world
210
terminal exchanges 78, 80, 93
Thomas, Dorothy 165
Thomas, William I. 9, 26, 165
Thornton, Sarah 196
'tic tac toe' 202
'tinkering trades' 172, 173
tool-use 122
topic talk 78
total institutions 172
transcription 95

transition-relevance places 69, 70
Travers, Max 184
turning points, career 30, 145, 146,
    151, 173
turns and turn-taking 5, 68–9, 70,
    155, 156, 210
  agreement/disagreement turns 76–7
  assessments, responses to 76, 77
  breaching 69, 81
  dispreferred turns 77
  indexical nature of 71
  interruptions 69, 81, 131–2, 136,
    186, 216
  invitations, responses to 74, 76, 77,
    182
  monitoring turns 72, 73, 74
  preference organization 74–8,
    181–2
  projectability 72, 73, 74, 77
  recipient-designed turns 71, 73, 74,
    86–7
  requests, responses to 77
  retrospective dimension of turns 72
  self-deprecations, responses to 77
  transition-relevance places 69, 70,
    75, 79
  trouble source turns 75–6, 80
  turn allocation 69
  turn construction 71, 73, 77, 157,
    181, 182, 216
  turn distribution 69
  turn-transition points 120
  see also sequential organization of
    conversation

understanding 64
  as a methodological problem 41–2
  mobilization of sense-making
    methods 50
  as a philosophical problem 41
  Weber's account of 41
  see also interpretation; interpretive
    sociology
unique adequacy requirement 58, 139
urban ethnographies 9–10, 32–4, 213

variable analysis 31, 132
violence, legitimate, state monopoly
    of 102
vocabularic identification 196

Wadsworth, Michael 130
Watson, Jeanne 184
Weber, Max 3–4, 22, 27, 41, 99–100,
    101, 102, 103
West, Candace 131–2, 216
Widdicombe, Sue 182, 184, 196–7
Wieder, D. Lawrence 55–8, 109–10
Wilson, Thomas P. 156
Wirth, Louis 8
Wittgenstein, Ludwig 4, 37, 61, 65,
    67–8, 86, 219
Wooffitt, Robin 70, 182, 184, 196–7
work 5–6, 142–61
  careers 145–6
  client-based work 148
  collective enterprise 153
  computer-supported co-operative
    work 160
  conversation analysis' perspective
    154–60, 161
  definitions of 142
  'dirty work' 105–6, 107, 145,
    171
  Durkheimian view of 142, 143,
    144
  ethnomethodological perspective
    149–54, 160–1
  formal features of 147–8
  identification with 146–7
  labour-power 99
  leisure framings 197, 207
  Marxist view of 99, 143–4, 144
  membership categorization and
    157–60
  negotiation and disagreement at
    148–9
  orienting to rules 151–2, 189–90
  symbolic interactionist perspective
    144–9, 153, 160
  talk at work 155–7
  temporal dimension 145
working knowledge 58–60
Wowk, Maria 120, 218

youth identity 196
youth subcultures 182–3, 191, 196–7,
    198

zero-sum phenomena 115, 116
Zimmerman, Don H. 156, 216